TRAIL

of

CRUMBS

TRAIL

of

CRUMBS

Hunger, Love,

and the Search

for Home

A MEMOIR

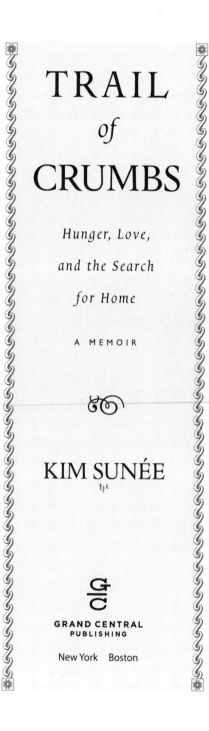

KIM SUNÉE

GRAND CENTRAL
PUBLISHING

New York   Boston

B
Sunee K

The names of certain persons have been changed.

Grand Central Publishing
Hachette Book Group USA
237 Park Avenue
New York, NY 10017

Visit our Web site at www.HachetteBookGroupUSA.com.
Printed in the United States of America
First Edition: January 2008
10 9 8 7 6 5 4 3 2 1

Grand Central Publishing is a division of Hachette Book Group USA, Inc. The Grand Central Publishing name and logo is a trademark of Hachette Book Group USA, Inc.

Library of Congress Cataloging-in-Publication Data
Sunée, Kim.
    Trail of crumbs : hunger, love, and the search for home / Kim Sunée.
        p. cm.
ISBN-13: 978-0-446-57976-6
ISBN-10: 0-446-57976-9
    1. Sunée, Kim. 2. Women cooks—Biography. 3. Cookery, International. I. Title.
TX649.S86A3 2007
641.5092—dc22
[B]
                                                                            2006027624

Text design by Meryl Sussman Levavi

For my family

ACKNOWLEDGMENTS

THIS BOOK WOULD NEVER HAVE BECOME WHAT IT IS TODAY without the love and encouragement of so many people. I want to thank David Black for responding quickly to a late-night message one December evening and for introducing me to Joy Tutela, a woman of many talents. Thank you, Joy, for your enthusiasm and fierce loyalty. You continue to amaze me every day.

To my editor, Amy Einhorn: thank you for your wisdom and patience, and for generating so much enthusiasm for this book. Thank you for making my first author-editor experience unforgettably delicious.

No book comes into the world without a hardworking group of passionate and intelligent people. At Grand Central Publishing, thanks to the brilliant team of Emily Griffin and Les Pockell for taking me over the finish line. For fully supporting this book from the beginning, I'd like to thank Jamie Raab, Karen Torres, Martha Otis, and Jennifer Romanello. I'd also like to thank Erica Gelbard and Bill Tierney, who love to eat and cook as much as I do. And thanks to Judy Rosenblatt, Susan Richman, and Jill Lichtenstadter for their support and enthusiasm. In production and copy, thanks to the very patient Tareth Mitch, Tom Whatley, Allene Shimomura, and Sona Vogel.

Thanks to the delightful Anne Twomey for her wise and intuitive art direction, to Louise Fili for her gorgeous cover design, and to Mark Yankus for the back cover photo.

To those who read early drafts of this manuscript at James Nolan's writing workshop in New Orleans, many hurricanes ago, especially James Nolan and Melissa Phipps Gray.

A special thank-you to Frances Mayes for her generosity and suggesting more comfort food. *Grazie mille.*

To Rachel Beardsley and Charles Walton for astute and enthusiastic recipe testing and tasting. And for honoring my grandfather's crawfish bisque one spring afternoon (yes, we really did stuff three hundred heads) and helping to get it oh so close, thanks to Donna, Rachel, Erin, Robbie, Catie, Lolis, and Charles.

I want to thank my first set of parents, wherever they may be, who loved me enough to let me go, and Mom and Dad, who loved me enough to not leave me behind. And I want to thank my family: the Hoppes, Keims, Tuckers, Cieutats, Baylisses, Suzy, and Josh, for sharing the stories and recipes; Grammy and Poppy, for their love and always having something good for us to eat.

Mes remerciements à Olivier Baussan et Laure Baussan.

Thanks to Jan, for the very special gift of her friendship, and for always making me laugh. And to Florent, for teaming up with the most amazing woman to create an even more amazing gift to the world—little Olivia. To Brigitte et Hervé, who were there for me, even in the loneliest of times. To Charlotte, a woman of many cities and words and silences.

A Olivier Grignon, mes hommages les plus sincères. Vous êtes, entre autres, la poésie et vous m'avez fait comprendre que je ne peux pas *tout* dire, pas cette fois-ci en tout cas.

Thanks to my extended family at *Cottage Living,* and at Southern Progress Corporation, for allowing me to do what I love every day. To my personal cheerleaders, Martha Johnston and Jake Reiss of Alabama Booksmith, and James Schwartz.

To Val, for gently guiding me through the Amazon and helping me on my way home again.

To Dorie and Michael Greenspan, for always allowing me a little bit of paradise—a room (and kitchen) of my own—when I need it most. Jean Anderson, for her guidance and sound advice on the quirky ways of food science and the even quirkier ways of the food world.

And last, but never least, thanks to Charles for so much more than I can ever thank him, including his patience, enthusiasm, and intuition, and for not saying anything when I was in the final drafts and drinking way too much Lillet Blanc, and for always caring and styling the food, even a plate of pickles and barbecue.

AUTHOR'S NOTE

Trail of Crumbs is a memoir. I have changed some names and the timeline of several events to protect certain individuals' privacy, not in an attempt to make light of the truth, but to enlighten it.

In the end, this story is as much mine as it is theirs.

*Where you come from is gone, where you thought
you were going to never was there, and where you are
is no good unless you can get away from it. In yourself
right now is all the place you've got.*

—FLANNERY O'CONNOR

*Here before me now… my map, of a place and therefore
of myself, and much that can never be said adds to its
reality… just as much of its reality is based on my own
shadows, my own inventions.*

*Over the years I have taught myself, and have been
taught, to be a stranger. A stranger usually has the
normal five senses, perhaps especially so, ready to
protect and nourish him.*

—M. F. K. FISHER, *Map of Another Town*

WHERE I AM

❧

*L*ET ME START BY SAYING WHERE I AM. I'VE ALWAYS THOUGHT that knowing this much may help me understand where I was and, if I'm lucky, to better know where it is I'm going. Luck. I know something about it—it got me out of an orphanage in Asia and across the waters, through various port cities, to right here, in France, where I am.

Looking out onto the foothills of the High Alps, in a damp Missoni bathing suit, I'm sitting on a cane-seat chair that once belonged to the father of the man I love. The father is long dead, of cancer, too much alcohol, and not enough tenderness. He's buried in a monastery high in the hills of Ganagobie, just a few kilometers from here. Olivier, my companion of nearly three years, is somewhere on the property. I hear his voice every now and then as he goes from room to room discussing colors with Ariane, the artisan from Carcassonne he has hired to repaint the walls of the entire house before the end of summer.

"*Ici, un bleu chaud, pas clair . . . là, du vert foncé . . . à la main . . . Tout.*" He wants warm, chalky blues, strong greens, and everything rubbed in with bare hands—the reason Ariane charges so much money. Ariane lights a cigarette and, after taking a long, dramatic puff, stops to nod at the appropriate moments.

Tout, I repeat to myself, trying to say it like Olivier, but the *o* and *u* together is a sound I still have trouble pronouncing. *Tout, not tu.* Everything, not you.

After he has finished instructing Ariane, Olivier will busy himself with various tasks: opening bottles of red Bordeaux, negotiating tickets for a performance of *La Bohème* at La Scala, and tasting the mint sauce for a fresh fava bean salad I have chilling in the refrigerator. He'll do this and more while waiting for me.

I have just finished swimming forty laps and am trying to catch my breath before the long evening ahead. It is midsummer, the longest day of the year, perhaps one of the longest years of my life, and I'm barely twenty-five years old. It's almost dusk, the first starlight splinters through the slender leaves of the linden trees. If I open the upstairs window wide enough, I can catch glimpses of Olivier's daughter, Laure, and her best friend, Lulu, the caretakers' daughter, as they chase each other barefoot through the orchards. They have eaten so many wild berries and plums that their small round mouths will be stained for days.

Maybe because they are French children, or because I want them to be like me, I think they enjoy being at the table. But today the girls have so thoroughly stuffed themselves they will not be hungry for dinner. It seems we are always finishing one meal and preparing for the next. This is the way it's been every day, every season, for the last three years together with Olivier. But tonight's meal seems different somehow. I have taken extra care to tend to all the details.

Sophie, the caretaker's wife, and I were first at the market this morning, choosing small, ripe melons only from Cavaillon, the fattest white asparagus, and long, fragrant branches of fresh lemon verbena. The best salt-cured ham from Bayonne, fresh pork livers, and juniper berries for a terrine still warm from the oven. Our friend Flora gathered poppy leaves and wild mushrooms to bake with yard eggs and flowering thyme to accompany the lamb. Olivier always roasts the meat and chooses the wines. Laure and Lulu helped shell garden peas, the bright green juice spreading across the prints of their tiny fingers. And they played with pastry, smearing rich butter into the dough and cutting out hearts and stars before helping me to wrap it gently around wild peaches. Zorah, the Moroccan housekeeper, has been baking large golden moons of semolina bread all day.

All this for Olivier's family and our friends who have come from both small surrounding towns and as far away as Marseille and Paris. Some will stay through August and maybe into September. They watch as I begin to cook and then ask me questions about where I'm from. Olivier's friends from deep Provence still think it exotic—an Asian face telling stories in French about *la Nouvelle-Orléans, le jazz, la cuisine Créole.* Olivier, who loves to be in the kitchen, feels that I am better suited for it—he thinks it is here that I am happiest. And because I'm young, or haven't yet mastered the language of opposition, because I don't quite know what it is that makes me happy, I oblige as they gather for the spectacle: Midas and his Golden Girl.

Later, with full stomachs and slipping, slightly tipsy, between crisp, heavy linen sheets, the visitors will ask one another: What more could she possibly want? If they looked a bit closer, would they notice that despite Olivier's insistence on making me the mistress of the house, I still don't have a clue as to what is expected of me? And that Laure is both fascinated by how different I am and envious of the love her father bestows on me? Her mother, Dominique, a French woman whose beauty has been pinched with bitterness, sends letters filled with threats due to the pending divorce and malicious remarks in reference to the *chinoise* Olivier has taken up with.

But they do not see any of this, because in the face of gastronomic pursuits, I appear fearless and without age. I am filled with courage as I take on two ovens, three refrigerators, one neglected caretaker's wife, a few sleepy housekeepers who turn about like broken clockwork, and a soon-to-be-official stepdaughter who loves me instinctively but hasn't quite figured out why I am sometimes distant, melancholy.

As always, at some point toward the end of the meal, Olivier will propose a toast, pleased that I can make a *daube* or *soupe d'épeautre* like the best of the locals. Laure will lean into me, her small ear pressed just at the level of my stomach, and she'll whisper to me that it's grumbling, that I must still be hungry. Then her giggle will turn into a deep, rich laughter, like a drunken sailor's. This always makes me smile. Olivier, who's always searching for a sign, will see this and think that I am almost happy. And sometimes I think so, too, believe that I have buried my constant need for departure. I always remind him, though, that this is really not my home, that I am just a small part that completes his world and not the whole of it. Nonsense, he declares.

After years spent expanding his company while ignoring the yearnings of the heart, Olivier tells his friends and family that meeting me has proven that love—despite its elusive market value—is also an enterprise worth investing in. And sometimes I believe him, because being loved by him makes me feel whole, makes me forget sometimes that life was not always like this.

With Olivier, I am the least lonely, and I love the family he has tried to give me, love this country that will never be mine but whose language and markets and produce, flavors and secret recipes, I have come to know and desire as well as any native.

Later, when I tuck the children into bed, Laure, cranky and still smelling of suntan lotion, complains of a bellyache. She holds up her tiny hand to mine, marveling at how close they are in size. *Tu t'es coupée.* You cut yourself, she remarks. And then she shows me her green fingertips, stained from shelling the spring peas, before she and Lulu giggle themselves into a half sleep.

Sometimes, late at night, Laure asks to hear the story about how I met her father, in a cold country, how he rescued me from winter and brought me to be her American *belle-mère.* Then she hugs me with all the love of a ten-year-old stepchild, as she has been doing ever since we met.

Before I turn out the lights, she makes me promise to take her and Lulu along wherever it is I may be going tomorrow. *Mais il faut revenir avant qu'il fasse nuit.* She wants to be back before nightfall. She has been having nightmares lately that she is lost in a forest, and just before dark her father comes to save her. *Mais parfois, j'ai peur. Je ne sais pas quand il reviendra.* Sometimes she's afraid; she never knows when he'll return. *Et toi?* And you? she asks. I hug her one last time, amazed and surprised at how a little human being can already sense so much.

I wait a few minutes more until I hear Laure's breathing slow down, until she finally lets go of my fingers. If I move too quickly, though, she grasps my hand again. *Tu te rappelles la première fois où l'on s'est rencontrés?* Do you remember when we first met? she mumbles. Yes, I nod.

IT WAS SUMMER 1993; she would soon turn eight. Olivier and I picked her up at her mother's in Forcalquier, the nearby village, just about a kilometer from the house here in Pierrerue. I was still expecting boxes to arrive from Stockholm, where I had been living when Olivier and I first met. While waiting for Dominique to move the rest of her stuff from the house, Olivier had rented a huge apartment in Aix-en-Provence for us, but we spent most of the time in the Pierrerue house anyway. He and Dominique had been separated almost a year when we met. She lived part-time with Laure in Forcalquier and the rest of the time in an apartment in Paris. Olivier was paying for both and more, all because this was what Dominique demanded, knowing he would do nothing to jeopardize custody of his daughter.

When Laure and I met, she greeted me with the customary kiss on both cheeks. I remember thinking how much more radiant she was than in the photos Olivier had shown me. A Venetian blonde with violet blue eyes, resembling, she claimed rather proudly, neither her mother nor her father. She ran her tiny hand along my smooth skin before turning to her father to say that she wished her limbs were brown and freckleless like mine.

"My name ees Laure, what ees your name?"

I told her slowly in English, but then she responded in French that she was learning my language in her school this year. Muscular and animated, breathless with questions, she seemed to understand I was the new woman in her father's life. She had never met anyone named *Keem.* She wanted to know how old I was, where I was from, but twenty-three and New Orleans meant nothing to her.

"*Je te montre le jardin?*" When we got to the house, she took my hand and showed me through the gardens and the fruit orchard. "*Voilà mes arbres.*" These are my trees. She stood firmly on the ground. Like her father, she knows and loves where she is from. *"Cerises. Figues. Mirabelles."* She waited, like a patient schoolteacher, for me to repeat after her as she pointed to the cherries, figs, and tiny yellow plums. *"Et des pêches de vigne."*

Together we stooped to pick up fallen wild peaches. Blood peaches. It was the first time I had ever seen a wild peach. I held one up to the light, broke it in two to study the scarlet veins running through the flesh.

"Do you sleep with Papa?" Laure asked, picking distractedly at a scab above her knee. Her question seemed so natural, so French, but I was still torn between nervous laughter and scolding.

"Yes," I answered firmly, biting into my first *pêche sauvage* ever. I had never tasted anything so delicious and forbidden. I almost wanted to cry, not from joy, but from some distant awareness that we would pay dearly one day for such sweetness.

I KISS LAURE's ear good night and wish her sweet dreams, and she whispers it back to me. *Sweet dreams.* It is one of her favorite phrases she has learned in English.

As I walk back downstairs to the remnants of the dinner party, I think of what I will teach her tomorrow and the next day, because soon, in a month, two, a year from now, I may be on a high-speed train back to Paris. On the TGV, men will look at me and see a foreign woman in an expensive dress and sandals, carrying a soft leather bag, and one of them may ask me to spend a moment telling him something it looks as though I should know.

Staring out the train window, though, I'll think of all the things I have yet to learn, and I might catch a fractured glimpse of this same woman and see her for who she really is: a lonesome voyager, with uneven tan lines, knife cuts on her hands, and a heart speeding fast toward the season of fall.

⌒◡⌒◡⌒◡⌒◡⌒◡⌒◡⌒◡⌒◡⌒◡⌒◡⌒

WILD PEACHES POACHED
IN LILLET BLANC
AND LEMON VERBENA

We picked *pêches de vigne** direct from our trees in Provence. If you don't have access to wild peaches, use ripe yet slightly firm and blemish-free white or yellow peaches. Substitute aromatic Pineau des Charentes Blanc, Monbazillac, or your favorite white wine for the Lillet Blanc. I've experimented cooking these in red wine, and the peaches, although delicious, are not as pretty.

> *6 medium-size ripe wild peaches**
> *1 (750-ml) bottle Lillet Blanc*
> *⅓ cup sugar*
> *2 to 3 tablespoons honey*
> *1 (3-inch) piece orange rind*
> *Squeeze of fresh orange juice (from 1 quarter)*
> *4 to 5 fresh lemon verbena sprigs, plus leaves for garnish*

Cut an X in blossom end of each peach. Plunge in boiling water, about 30 seconds. Remove and peel peaches. Place peeled peaches in a large, wide, heavy-bottomed pot. Pour Lillet Blanc over. Add sugar, honey, orange rind, and juice. Gently crush lemon verbena leaves with hands to release fragrance and add sprigs to pot. Bring to a boil, reduce heat to medium, and poach, occasionally turning peaches gently for even cooking, 20 to

30 minutes (depending on ripeness) or until peaches are tender when pierced gently with tip of knife. Carefully remove peaches and place in a large serving bowl. Turn heat to high and cook poaching liquid 6 to 8 minutes or until thick and syrupy. Pour over peaches. Let cool and chill in refrigerator at least 4 hours or overnight. Garnish with more lemon verbena leaves. This is also delicious with a swirl of crème fraîche or soft vanilla ice cream and grated Amaretti di Saronno cookies. *Serves 6.*

I

STAR OF THE SEA

✺

NOVEMBER 1973 WAS WHEN I FIRST GOT LUCKY. I WAS A scrawny three-year-old sitting on a bench in a South Korean marketplace waiting for *Omma* to come back and take me home. My *omma*, my mother, had left me a tiny fist-ful of food that had crumbled in the three days and nights of waiting—endless hours of darkness with huge shadows and no promise of return.

When local policemen finally brought me into the station, I shook my clenched fist at them. As they proceeded with abandonment papers, I scrambled to the ground to gather the crumbs, insisting: *She told me not to leave. She promised she'd be back.*

Of course, I don't remember everything. The policemen, for example—shady contributors to my first days as an orphan— are figures I am told existed, like in any ordinary fairy tale. But I wonder how they could have left a child alone for three days and nights. I imagine it was a time of survival for most. It was the early seventies, in a country still searching for an identity after decades of war and division. There were lots of us, aban-doned or lost, and perhaps many, like myself, still questioning where it is we're really from.

Although memories are distorted, there are true sensations one doesn't forget, like fear and hunger, deep rumblings echoing in a cavernous heart and belly. I still see rat-colored streets, try to focus in on market vendors, the swift movements of street cooks; I am forever trying to decipher a familiar face. I want warmth and a mouthful of hot fermented cabbage, a bowl of plain rice.

My adoptive mother keeps changing the story every time I ask her. I don't think she does it on purpose, but she has repeated the circumstances of my adoption many times over the years and always with discrepancies. Sometimes she insists I was never in an orphanage and stayed with an American serviceman and his Korean wife. But according to certain documents, I was also at the Star of the Sea orphanage.

I'm sure I was there because there are photos—I'm wearing an oversize polka-dot dress, sitting on a tattered sofa, squeezed between an Asian boy my age and a little girl much younger. There's another picture of me with other children who look as hollow as I do. Lined up like rows of fruit for sale, we're looking not at the camera, but beyond, as if expecting someone, anyone, to come and press on our skins to test for ripeness and cart us home.

The few papers I do have—documents from this period—state "Dap Dong, Inchon City, Republic of Korea, Special City of Seoul," the address of an old woman who is "Superior of the Star of the Sea." Not much else is really decipherable.

Nightmares sometimes help discern what's true and false. My Korean brother, I remember as younger but taller, huddles over me as we look out over the busy streets of our village. His skin is smooth and warm and glows golden, like the color of the moon in cold months. Below, women waddle back and forth, carrying baskets of fruit on their heads all day long. We take turns standing guard, searching for our *omma* among them—we are convinced our mother is one of the fruit ladies. But it gets dark fast, and the house fills up with damp shadows before we can even sense her shape.

In a letter dated 1973 or 1974, my adoptive mother writes to her family back in New Orleans that she and my father, on leave from Okinawa, have decided to adopt an infant girl. A newborn, abandoned on a doorstep. But, she writes, there is also another child who comes every day and jumps in our laps. I am the other girl. My mother continues to explain that I was found on a bench in the marketplace, cigarette burns stamped into my arms and shoulders. When the policemen finally brought me into the station, I told them defiantly that I was three years old, that I was called Chong Ae Kim and was waiting for my mother to return. I held up a scarred fist smeared with soot and starch and shook it at them. "She's only twenty-three pounds, but perhaps she is older, because they say she speaks a strange yet beautiful Korean." The curious thing, my mother concludes, is they reported that I never cried.

Somewhere in the world is a man who sized me up, measured me, and estimated my bones—a type of carbon dating for lost children. I imagine him with pen and paper, arriving at the Star of the Sea to count heartbeats, trace circles, check teeth. Maybe he added up the number of burns and bruises on my upper arms and neck, calculated that I wasn't missing too many pounds, before deciding I was fit for adoption.

"Born between January and June," the doctor announced to my soon-to-be parents. Maybe a Pisces?

He validated me and decided my place among the stars. My birth date is a compromise, my beginnings a constellation of in-betweens and connect-the-dots. Since the approximate age of three, I've been a fish and swimming upstream ever since.

There is no room for tears. Instead, I swim holding my breath. I've learned to ration the air, so vital for when I return to the surface of the sea, when it is safe to drift near the coastline of a warm and secure body.

~~~~~~

QUICK-FIX KIMCHI

Korean cuisine—hearty, rustic, and beautiful—shines as the unsung hero of Asian cooking. A variety of vegetables, pickled, packed, and buried in the earth, is a traditional accompaniment. I could never pretend to prepare them the way Korean cooks do, but I make this express version of cabbage kimchi—sometimes adding or substituting for the cabbage sliced cucumbers, zucchini, or bean sprouts—whenever I long for a spicy hit of Korea.

1 small head Napa cabbage

¼ cup sea salt

1 (4-inch) piece fresh ginger, minced or grated

1 garlic clove, minced

3 to 4 tablespoons hot red chili paste (or Sriracha or sambal oelek)

1 teaspoon hot red pepper flakes

1 tablespoon sesame or walnut oil

⅓ cup rice wine vinegar

1 teaspoon fish sauce or 2 crushed anchovies

1 tablespoon sugar or honey

3 to 4 green onions, thinly sliced

1 small head escarole, frisée, or Romaine, torn or chopped

Remove outer leaves of cabbage, quarter lengthwise, core bottoms, and cut across into 1-inch pieces. Place in a colander in sink and sprinkle with salt. Let sit 45 minutes to 1 hour. Rinse and dry cabbage thoroughly, preferably using a salad spinner (otherwise the kimchi will be watery). Whisk together ginger and next 8 ingredients in a large bowl. Add cabbage, escarole, and toss to combine. Pack kimchi in a glass jar or bowl. Cover and refrigerate 2 hours and up to 2 weeks. Serve with steamed rice, grilled meat, on sandwiches, or stirred into soups.

II

YOUR REFRIGERATOR
SMELLS LIKE KOREA

৩৩

*M*Y PARENTS ARE YOUNG, JUST TWENTY-TWO AND TWENTY-three years old, when they decide, on a whim, to adopt two abandoned children from South Korea. With my soon-to-be baby sister, Suzy (An Sunée), my soon-to-be parents return to Okinawa, where my father is stationed in the air force, while I wait back in Seoul for papers and vaccinations. After several months, I join them on the Japanese island before we all return to the States, to my mother's native city of New Orleans. We will meet my father's family, far away in a land called Minnesota, much later. My mother, the eldest of five children, seems to blossom suddenly at the center of attention. Her whole family is there to greet her and the two orphans—aged six months and three—who will need attention, nourishment, and love.

Soon, as my parents fall into the routine of their lives, it is my grandparents who are looking after us. After school, we go to their house and wait for Mom and Dad to come home from work, always tired, never enough time to do what they want or enough money to buy back their youth. Maybe because I sense this, I am immediately drawn to my new grandparents, especially my grandfather. I can't pronounce "Grandma," "Grandpa," so I call them Grammy, Poppy. My grandmother's sister, Nani, an actress, is also there, always ready with a gift, a theatrical pronunciation of a new word in this new language I am quickly devouring.

My early memories are always related to hunger. My grandmother has told me this story many times over the years.

"Your refrigerator smells like Korea," I tell Grammy, plugging my nose. "Pee-you, it stinks."

My new grandmother laughs, sticks her head in, and pulls out a rotting pineapple from the fruit drawer. I shove my way in, too. I want to smell Korea.

"She's so little, and look how she squats, just like in the Orient," Dad remarks. "They say their muscle structure is different."

I only hear "different" and plop down butterfly style on the kitchen floor in front of the open refrigerator. If it smells like Korea, maybe there are others who squat different like me in there. It's cool inside, with lots of colors I don't have words for yet. I try the new ones my grandmother tries to teach me: hot dog, Cool Whip, Tabasco.

"What would you like, Kim Sunée?" She pronounces my name slowly, like the new words she teaches me, words from books and magazines with shiny pictures of people with big creases down the middle of the page; it tears their smiles in two.

I point to a bowl of lump crabmeat because I worked real hard to help Poppy dig it out of its shell. It smells like the sea, and lights like pearls.

"How about cookies and milk? All the American kids want cookies and milk."

But I'm not like the other kids she's talking about. In my school, some are black, most are white, but no others have hair like me. They eat brownies and red Jell-O and drink lots of white milk.

"Cookies. No milk." I watch carefully as Grammy takes out the red carton with the white smiling cow. I tilt my head as she pours

some in a glass and see the photo of the girl who looks my age. "Who's that?" I ask. I know exactly who the girl is. I know they put faces of disappeared people on the milk so in the morning when you're feeding your bones, you can grow strong to find the missing faces.

"Brown milk," I say, crossing my fingers, hoping my new grandmother knows I want the dark syrup in the squeeze bottle that swirls the white into sweet.

In my memories, sometimes Poppy sports a white apron flecked with brown gravy stains, but mostly he is opening huge packs of pork chops, picking crabs and crawfish for pan-fried cakes and chocolate-roux gumbos. A large man of German descent, Poppy is always ready with a joke or anecdote—he tells us his great-grandfather was a German shepherd—and he loves to see Suzy and me laugh so hard that our round yellow faces turn hot pink.

Poppy served in World War II, among other duties, as a cook in France. He doesn't talk much about the war, or maybe I'm not interested enough. Instead, my sister and I sit with him on weekends and watch the Cajun Justin Wilson, Julia Child, and other great chefs on PBS as they sip and sauté. Poppy and Julia have similar-shaped bodies, so sometimes he puts on my great-aunt's wig and does a little jig. He tells us how to proceed, in Julia Child falsetto, with mashing the lumps out of perfect potato purée. My sister gets so excited, she jumps up and down on her tiny feet and squeals at the top of her lungs, her two shining pigtails flapping the sides of her ears.

Everything in my new world seems shiny and palatable, especially my new favorite color. The bright red on my tennis shoes suddenly makes me run real fast. Orange red is the color of fire under the pots and peppers of all shapes and sizes. Some become a liquid called Tabasco from Avery Island, others get ground into a dark magical powder with the beautiful name of cayenne.

"Mirliton, okra, sassafras," my grandfather booms like a marching band leader. "These are the words you need to learn."

Suzy and I follow him with metal lids and spoons accompanying his orders: "Cayenne [*boom!*], crawfish [*clack!*], blue crabs [*ding!*]."

I gobble all the new words and sounds I can manage at one time, because when my new grandfather speaks, I listen. Poppy, a native New Orleanian, seems always to talk about things that are important. "The trinity," he says solemnly. "Onion, bell pepper, celery."

He hands me the crisp, ribbed stalks that I discover always hide an exquisite, tender heart. I stand for hours in the kitchen as he stirs, chops, fries. The day he announces me his official taster, I know I am the luckiest child in the world. I will myself to never again think about the dark and hollow streets I dream of at night, but I know it's impossible.

I run around the house singing, Omma, Abba, kundungi. *This makes everyone in my new family laugh, but I don't know what's so funny about Mama, Papa, bottom. I like to sleep on the hardwood floor next to Grammy's side of the bed and feel the cool air from the ceiling fan against my face. I close my eyes, though, real tight before the dark comes into the room and makes things move like famished giants. I dream a lot. Sometimes good. Sometimes bad.* Nightmare. *It's not a beautiful word like* mirliton *or* gumbo, *but it's a real word, and I need it so they can understand why I am so afraid, especially of the night.*

Nightmare about the rat and the woman who carries fruit on her head all day long. It's the chop, chop noise of Korean helicopters hovering low in the sky. Nightmare's when the dark comes home faster than Omma does and it's cold on the floor and I'm too small to shut the door all by myself. I feel lucky when I dream about my brother, because he taught me how to hold my eyes closed real tight. I know he is real. He has hair like me, squats like me, and smells like Grammy's refrigerator.

Sundays, as we head out of the Lutheran church on the corner of Port and Burgundy, Poppy or my mother invites anyone who seems lonely or the slightest bit capable of appreciating a home-cooked meal to have dinner with us. Friends stop by to order a pound of crabmeat salad, a dozen garlic-and-herb-stuffed artichokes. Poppy takes Italian bread crumbs, olive oil, dried parsley, and lots of garlic, lemon juice, and hot red pepper, pats it all with his hands until it holds together just so. Then he lovingly stuffs each steamed, tender leaf. Sometimes he chops up hearts and adds them, along with shrimp or lump crabmeat, into the stuffing.

Other friends beg for jars of his famous crawfish bisque made with Binder's French bread that he fries off in a big cast-iron skillet with garlic and spices. The crawfish heads have been pulled and cleaned at the most recent seafood boil, and the sweet tail meat gets chopped and stirred into the stuffing. To eat this fragrant stew, we ladle heaping portions over hot boiled rice and use the tips of our tongues to scoop out the stuffing from the heads. I don't know how to say it yet, but I want this heat, this unprecedented sweetness, to nourish me the rest of my life.

Everyone says Poppy should open a restaurant. But money and fame don't matter to him. He loves feeding his family and watching as Suzy and I stand in the kitchen waiting for him to finish adding a squeeze of lemon to the whole-roasted redfish, a sprinkle of hot sauce to the dirty rice. Then, just when we can't stand it anymore, he sneaks us a taste before serving steaming portions to everyone. Our grandfather sits at the head of the table, leaning back a bit in his chair, his hands folded across his round belly, a smile across his face, spreading out to the corners of his bright blue eyes.

Suzy and I are the only Oriental girls, as we are called, in our school, so the comfort of Poppy's kitchen after school every day, the promise of his home-cooked meals, are a refuge, a safe place where our grandparents nourish us—solid food to remind us that we exist, that we live in a new world where we have not been forgotten.

POPPY'S CRAWFISH BISQUE

The men in my family used to gather all the goods for a traditional seafood boil—blue crabs, crawfish, and shrimp, an enormous pot of water with liquid crab seasoning, and lots of Dixie beer. Into the pot we'd throw garlic heads, bay leaves, onions, corn, potatoes, and andouille sausage. While we devoured our mudbugs, Poppy whistled along, cleaning the crawfish heads, picking the tail meat, and setting it aside for a labor-intensive but most rewarding dish.

My aunt Amy and uncle Odie Tucker marketed this for a while as Poppy's Crawfish Bisque, which sold briefly in local restaurants and at New Orleans Airport. I urge you to stuff the heads because there's truly nothing more satisfying than scooping out the spicy crawfish stuffing with the tip of your tongue; but if you want to save time, just make the stuffing below, form into 2-inch round balls, and let simmer in the tomato sauce.

For cleaned, ready-to-use crawfish heads, the Louisiana Seafood Exchange (504-834-9393) will ship.

Note: Prep time on this with 8 friends is about 3 bottles of Prosecco, 2 ginger beers, 1 bottle of Albariño, and 2 Tecates.

CRAWFISH STUFFING

It's best to fine dice all the ingredients for the stuffing.

> *2 (12-ounce) loaves (Louisiana-style) French bread (preferably*
>   *day-old)*
> *2 tablespoons canola or olive oil*
> *2 tablespoons butter*
> *1 medium yellow or Vidalia onion, finely diced*
> *2 celery ribs with leaves, finely diced*
> *2 green onions, thinly sliced*
> *3 to 4 tablespoons fresh finely chopped parsley*
> *3 to 4 cloves fresh garlic, smashed and minced*
> *1½ tablespoons dried Italian seasoning*
> *¾ to 1 tablespoon salt*
> *1 teaspoon fresh-ground black pepper*
> *¾ to 1 teaspoon ground cayenne pepper*
> *Water or shellfish stock, as needed*
> *2 pounds cooked and peeled crawfish tails, divided*

Cube bread into small pieces and dampen with enough water just to cover (or to moisten). Heat oil and butter in a large skillet over medium high heat. Add onion, celery, and green onions and cook, stirring occasionally, about 7 minutes or until soft. Squeeze out excess liquid from bread, add to skillet, and cook, stirring occasionally, about 2 minutes. (If bread is too chunky, use side of spoon to break it up.) Add parsley and next 5 ingredients. Cook, scraping bottom of skillet as stuffing browns. Add water or shellfish stock a bit at a time if stuffing gets too dry. It should be moist but not saturated with liquid. Chop about two-thirds of crawfish tails (reserve other third for sauce). Stir in chopped tails. Taste and rectify seasoning, depending on saltiness of crawfish and amount of heat you prefer. Remove stuffing from heat and let cool enough to handle.

CRAWFISH BISQUE

*Y*ou can make a roux, but Poppy never did because he used the extra stuffing to thicken and flavor the sauce. Serve this with hot cooked rice.

> *1 teaspoon canola or olive oil*
> *½ small onion, diced*
> *1 celery rib with leaves, diced*
> *2 garlic cloves, smashed and chopped*
> *2 (28-ounce) cans good-quality tomato sauce*
> *5 to 6 cups shellfish stock or water*
> *2 bay leaves*
> *4 sprigs fresh thyme or oregano or 1 tablespoon dried Italian*
>   *seasoning*
> *Salt and fresh-ground black pepper, to taste*
> *Ground cayenne pepper, to taste*
> *1 teaspoon Creole seasoning (optional)*
> *Pinch of sugar, as needed*
> *About 1½ cups reserved crawfish stuffing*
> *50 to 60 cleaned crawfish heads (if using purchased ready-to-*
>   *use heads, place in a bowl of very hot water and let soak*
>   *about 10 minutes)*
> *Garnish: chopped green onions*

Heat oil over medium high heat in a large pot (big enough for 60 stuffed heads). Add onion and celery and cook about 5 minutes. Add garlic and cook about 1 minute. Stir in tomato sauce and stock. Add bay leaves and next 5 ingredients. Taste and add a pinch of sugar, depending on quality of tomatoes. Bring to a low boil; reduce heat and let simmer about 30 minutes.

Stuff heads with as much crawfish stuffing as possible, reserving at least 1½ cups stuffing. Gently place stuffed heads in sauce and stir reserved stuffing into sauce. Let simmer on low about 30 minutes or until heated through.

To serve: Mound hot cooked rice in large shallow bowls and divide bisque and heads evenly (this way there will be no arguments at the table). This is the best of finger foods. Be careful not to cut yourself when scooping out the delicious stuffing with the tip of your tongue. Garnish bisque with chopped green onions. Serve with lots of French bread to dip in the sauce. *Serves 8 to 10.*

WHISPERY EGGS WITH
CRABMEAT AND HERBS

*M*y grandfather used to put fresh crabmeat in everything from seafood casseroles to stuffed mirlitons. Use the freshest lump crabmeat you can find. Pick through carefully to remove any shells. Many different herbs complement crabmeat. I like fresh chervil, tarragon, thyme, parsley, chives. In Provence, Laure and Lulu used to call scrambled eggs *nuageux* (cloudy) and *chuchotants* (whispery). Whisking the eggs vigorously yields light, fluffy, "whispery" scrambles.

> *4 eggs*
> *¼ teaspoon salt*
> *Fresh-ground black pepper, to taste*
> *1 tablespoon crème fraîche*

1 tablespoon butter
1 teaspoon olive oil
1 spring onion (or green onion or shallot), chopped
1 to 2 tablespoons combination fresh chopped herbs
1 cup fresh lump crabmeat
Fresh lemon zest or hot sauce (optional)

Whisk eggs vigorously in a large bowl 1 to 2 minutes, using a handheld whisk (note: an immersion blender whips these up in a flash). Add salt, pepper, and crème fraîche and whisk 1 minute more. Set aside.

Heat butter and oil in a large (preferably nonstick) skillet over medium high heat. Cook onion and herbs about 2 minutes. Give eggs one last whisk (or whir of the immersion blender) and pour into skillet. Reduce heat to medium low and gently stir eggs about 2 minutes. Add crabmeat and cook another minute (for soft eggs). Serve warm with fresh lemon zest, more herbs, or a dash of hot sauce. *Serves 2.*

III

TRACKS OF DESIRE

ॐ

OUR PARENTS, BECAUSE THEY ARE SO YOUNG OR BECAUSE OF things they cannot begin to understand about us, don't know how to react, especially to my sister's anger, explosive even as a baby. When my mother tries to comfort her, she cries for hours—a long, lonesome howl. She's strong-willed and thick-boned and throws tantrums, knocking beer bottles to spill out onto the newly cleaned carpets. My inexperienced father, thinking this is what fathers do, whacks her on the legs, leaving handprints up and down her chubby thighs until she stops for one peaceful moment before crying some more. My father's eyes, sometimes the color of the Gulf of Mexico on a bright day, sometimes the deep green gray of hurricane season, hold no clues as to what's storming inside. I don't want to be in the path of his fury, so I tie up my new red sneakers and run as fast as I can.

My aunts play games with us and teach us new words. I don't have to really share Poppy with little Sue because she's only one and a half and too busy breaking things. We put MADE IN KOREA stickers on her forehead. Someone calls her Genghis Khan, and she cries. I don't know who Genghis Khan is, but maybe Sue does because she throws a glass bottle on the floor. It breaks like tiny stars all over her fat little legs. They start bleeding, and Grammy and Poppy whisk her off to the emergency room. Sometimes I get mad at her because she lets it all out, shows everyone how vulnerable she really is. I prefer silence, scribbling down new words, and making books from scraps of wallpaper to house stories about imaginary places.

Later, at school, though, Suzy and I are united, if only because we are the same in our differences. Her eyes are more slanted than mine, so the kids make fun of her more, knowing they can always elicit tears at the slightest taunt. Even though I want to shake some sense into her, I realize, being three years older, that I must protect her, especially when the bigger boys, pale Tommy and his dark-haired sidekick, Paul, are feeling particularly cruel.

I AM ALWAYS crossing and landing near water. We drive by the Mississippi River every day when Mom drops us off at school. Tommy and Paul, who ride the school bus back, live near our grandparents, almost the last stop. When it's only the boys and Suzy and me, I take my sister's hand and our lunchboxes and march up to the front of the bus to sit right behind Mr. Larry, the bus driver. He's got a dark spot on the back of his head that looks like a crater. He smells like soft caramel and dough and keeps a picture of his dog taped to the rearview mirror. I like him, especially when he yells at the boys. They are always calling my sister Suzy Wong or asking us if we know "the ancient Chinese secret."

Sometimes they even sing a little song and tug at their eyes until they're stretched like knife slits. "Chinese, Japanese," they taunt. "Dirty knees, look at these."

"We're not Chinese!" my little sister screams. "We don't know the ancient secret."

She's so mad that she closes her eyes and cups her ears. I wish I could fly away with her under my wing, and I get madder now because tears are starting to squirt down her puffed-up cheeks. Mr. Larry makes the boys get off the bus blocks before their stop.

"Chinks," they spit from the sidewalk. The bus door slides closed, and Mr. Larry speeds off. "Gooks," we hear them yell.

Suzy wipes her nose on my sleeve, and I close my eyes and think of new words, whisper new names for myself: Catherine. Jenifer. Alison. But I can still hear their voices. Chink. Crack. Cleft.

"What do you think Poppy's made for dinner?" I ask my sister, hoping to distract her. It's Monday, so I tell her that maybe he has made red beans. I remind her how much she likes to help him with the long wooden spoon smash some of the beans on the side of the pot to make them creamy and thick. I like the hot cooked rice, with just a pat of melted butter. I tell her we'll make her favorite dessert, and suddenly the thought of poking warm yellow cake with her fingers before sprinkling it with red Jell-O powder and slathering it with whipped cream calms her down.

She leans against me for the rest of the ride home. I remind her that Mom and Dad said we're soon going to be naturalized, and she perks up at the thought of it.

"We're going to get natural eyes?"

"Yes," I whisper, pressing my face to the cold glass window. It's almost dark out, and when it's dark, you can't tell the difference between sky and water. *Horizon.* Another beautiful word, although I can't touch or taste it.

I TRY TO imagine what life will be like when I become like all the others. But for now, the kids think I have a strange name, strange face. One of the few black kids, an older girl in the sixth grade with long stiff braids and the beautiful name of Shalane, told me the reason I'm different is that I don't have a bridge to my nose.

Sometimes the mean boys call me moonface or pignose, and now I know it's because I don't have a bridge. I look up the word in the encyclopedia during library hour and read something about connections and passageways, a bony structure, but it explains nothing more about noses. After I say my prayers at night, I rush to the mirror to see if I've changed. Sometimes if I fall asleep with my index finger pushing up the tip of my nose and suck in my cheeks real hard, I think I'll wake up with dimples and look like Pam and Kathy in my class, instead of resembling a pig.

But then I fall into a dream where the teacher makes me stand up and starts asking me a series of questions. I know the answers to all the hard ones. I can spell better than any other kid. I hunger after long vowels and multiple definitions. But when she asks the questions, all I can do is oink, and the whole class laughs.

"Spell 'subterranean.'" Mrs. Borschelt hates me. I know it. And I'm sure she thinks my face is flat, too. But she knows I know the word. I spell it perfectly in my head: *s-u-b-t* . . .

"Oink," I hear myself say. The kids are roaring in their chairs, crying with laughter, and they look like huge waves coming in from the Pacific Ocean. "Oink. Oink. Oink," I protest until the waves get louder and bigger, and soon I'm underwater.

A few years later, I write my first real poem, handwritten on a lined notebook page, about a timid baseball player, and it wins me first prize at my junior high school fair; but that evening I hear my mother whisper to my father that she wonders where I copied the poem from. I fall into a restless sleep of more waves that come storming in, a hurricane of gigantic question marks and doubts.

MY MOTHER AND father come home one day with another baby. We knew Mom was getting rounder and rounder, but no one talked about how or when or why. These are questions we do not ask in my family. My mother looks nervous, tired. Our new brother, Joshua, smells like talcum powder and cherry Benadryl—he's allergic to everything, it seems, but he has the blue eyes of our father on the brightest days. Suzy and I take turns holding him, squeezing him too much, loving him so.

My mother soon becomes the volunteer maven, spending more and more weekends tutoring junior high school kids, chauffeuring the elderly, and singing in the choir. Sometimes she takes us along with her when she is going to play games with less fortunate children. "Just remember how lucky you kiddies are," she says, buckling us up tight in the backseat of Dad's clunky old pale blue Mercedes. She gives us each extra-quick kisses on the head, which we savor. We like it here because she drives fast and sings along with the radio, old deep-throated tunes by Sarah Vaughan, Billie Holiday. When she leaves us behind, my sister waves good-bye with her favorite book, cheeks puffing out with the promise of tears and a good scream. I grab the book and start reading to her. "We don't want her charity," I mumble. I don't want to be her cause.

LATER, WHEN BOYS become interested in us, my sister and I have very different tastes. She's attracted to everything all-American, dating mostly boys in baseball caps with parents who winter in places we've never heard of. She reads *Seventeen* and wears penny loafers and openly disdains my flashdance look or the floppy hats I wear with long skirts, black kohl to highlight my eyes, and bangles around my wrists and ankles. By the age of thirteen, I am drawn to the marginal types—a young vicar who gives me books by Kerouac, Jim Harrison, Dickinson, the older skinny chess champ who takes me to see Truffaut films and after to eat crusty baguettes, funny-shaped, tiny pickles, and country pâté at Café Degas on Esplanade Avenue—always someone, anyone, with the promise of someplace other than here.

At fourteen, I audition for the creative writing program at the New Orleans Center for the Creative Arts on Perrier Street. I'm surprised to hear myself answer the director that I want to be a writer, a poet, maybe. It's the first time I've ever allowed myself to say what I want out loud. Did he know, I wonder, at fourteen what he wanted to be? I show him some poems, and after another hour of questions, I'm accepted into the program and breathe easy when Mom and Dad let me participate.

"Look around you," the principal tells us on the first day of orientation. There are fat kids, multicolored skinny kids in tattered clothes. The ones who look hungry, some with greasy hair and torn cuticles, I find out are the writing students. The music students are too cool for us. "Only half of you will be here in a week." The young dancers, with their perfect posture and thin, graceful necks, keep their distance.

Sometimes music drifts in during class, sweet, sad sounds from Ellis Marsalis and his students. Our instructors, visiting writers from Oxford, New York, Zurich—places I love the sounds of—let us write anything we need to. I like it here. I'm a high school freshman, but because I skipped a year in grade school and the first-year program here is for sophomores, I'm two years younger than the other students; but Tom Whalen, the director of the writing program, let me in anyway. He makes us read Nabokov, Cheever, Rich, watch Wenders and Godard. I have no idea what any of it means. *Une femme est une femme*—I want to be Anna Karina, batting big-eyelashed eyes, breaking eggs into a bowl, singing about being a woman. After only six days, Whalen kicks out half of our class, but I am determined to stay.

My first published poem is called "Foreigner," and my parents remain speechless as they read about a bald nameless man who visits two sisters every Thursday. He makes them spumoni. Once, when he is finally about to tell the sisters his name, their mother comes home to punish them for talking to strangers. When they try to protest, only odd-sounding words fly from their mouths.

MY FATHER'S GRANDMOTHER speaks flying English with a bobbing accent. She is visiting from International Falls, Minnesota, talking about how cold it is back home. Her name is Nora, and I have only ever known her with white hair, her thin frame wrapped in cotton floral-printed aprons. She hand-knits sweaters with elaborate patterns—Bert and Ernie for Suzy and me—that are too warm for our subtropical climate, but we wear them anyway in the air-conditioned house. For the two weeks each year she's with us, we don't go to Grammy and Poppy's; instead we come back from school to a kitchen that smells of rising yeast, scraped cinnamon, hot melted butter. Nora's a breath of fresh air—she makes my father smile, which he doesn't do often enough. Even my mother is more attentive, cheerful.

"*Ja*, this is how you do it," she sings one afternoon, smashing hot boiled potatoes into flour and butter. She is making our favorite, a Norwegian flatbread called *lefse*. Suzy and I watch carefully as Nora and Dad cook thin layers on the smoking griddle. When the golden bubbles pop out and lift up the dough, Joshua waves his magic wand to indicate that it's time to turn them over. A pile of the soft layers appears magically at the table. Nora says a prayer in Norwegian that makes Suzy and Josh giggle. Then we watch Dad and Nora show us how to spread the hot potato flatbread with butter and then sprinkle the sugar evenly. We roll it and bite into layers of sweetness that dries on our lips and fingers. Sometimes Dad gets up early before the sun and makes apple pancakes, big, fluffy biscuits, his blue eyes shining bright as we fight over the last crumbs.

"Uff-da," we mimic as Nora gets up to clear the table. We rush to her side, gladly washing and drying dishes, ready to help her with the next batch of cinnamon rolls or our new favorite casserole of cabbage and rice smothered in a white cream sauce. We don't know this secret language that she speaks, but we like the way it makes her bounce and bake and makes our father finally sit back at ease.

NOTHING'S EASY WHEN I'm fifteen. My father remarks that I'm growing. I don't look like a little girl anymore. My hips are widening—like a woman's—childbearing hips, he assures me. I don't know how I'm supposed to respond. There are awkward moments like this, more as I get older because my father sometimes tries so hard to be something that he's not—an openly warm and loving person. In my mother's family, we are always at the table, making plans, organizing events, but my father seems to be an outsider. He tries to explain to me one day about his own childhood, his own distant father who drank too much and who eventually divorced his mother. I knew this about him, but only through his whispered conversations with my mother behind closed doors. I am convinced he loves us, but the sadness in him is deep, and I am too young to know how to help him. Instead, I have learned to mimic his gestures, to resemble him the only way I can—for now, I keep my distance.

"The devil's beating his wife again," my little brother pipes up, jumping up and down and pointing at the sky. "It's raining and sunning at the same time." His blond curls bounce as he tugs my arm. We're on the outside porch watching the sky. It's hurricane season again. It has been raining for weeks now, and every day the experts try to track the eye of the storm as we listen, anxious, restless.

Some people build their houses up high, hoard batteries and water. There are also levees to protect from overflow. But I've never quite understood how it is we are to survive seven feet below the level of the sea. I don't want to board up windows or have duct-taped views of the world. I'm restless, too, and all I long for is solid shelter.

Joshua bounces up into my lap. He's six and golden and sweet. He dons a plastic nose and fake mustache, a black cape, and does more magic tricks for us. A rabbit pops out of my father's sleeve, a scarf disappears into thin air. We applaud as shiny coins appear from our mother's ear. He loves games, is always inventing new contraptions, and I like teaching him new words. Prestidigitator. Merlin the Magician. Houdini.

I'm practicing my own art of escape. One day my mother comes home and sees me getting ready to go out with my girl-friends. I see her reflection in the mirror—she picks nervously at her worn cuticles, afraid of every day that goes by, watching as my body becomes more like a woman's, my face nowhere near resembling hers. Everything about her is so tightly closed, her life so carefully portioned out. Her short brown hair frizzes in the summer heat. She watches as I rub blush into my olive skin. I smooth magnolia-rich cream into my arms and legs. I love the way the scent rises off the skin and mixes with the August heat.

"Let me look at you," my mother says, squeezing my cheeks tight between her thumb and forefinger, making my lips puff out. "You're not going out looking like *that*." She starts picking at her nails again. "I know what you're up to."

If she really knew me, she would understand that all I really want is for her to hold me, to whisper that she loves me even though I am not like her. Instead, I try to break free—I want to be like the other girls. I want to ride around with my friends—to the lake, to the bayous, to sit high on the levees, ride up and down the streetcar path with the windows rolled down and our hair spread out like wings. We make up our lips at red lights and blow sweet violet kisses to the young interns on Tulane Avenue. We stop for Coca-Colas at the corner K&B, sip them slowly as though they're bourboned mint juleps, and call one another by our nicknames—Betsy, Camille, Scarlet. We're fifteen, sixteen, and think we know everything about freedom and possibility.

My mother's lips are clamped shut, and I try not to stare at the dry skin flaking around the edges. She's standing behind me with her arms folded tight across her ample chest. I know she and my father—the only parents I really have—want to teach me good judgment and values, but I don't know the currencies of their country; I don't understand their exchange rates and can't begin to fathom the depth of my debt.

"I know you lie about where you go with boys. I know what you do with your *body*." My mother pronounces "body" as if it were a dirty rug that needed to be beaten and hung out in the fresh air. I want to wear lipstick, have feathered bangs, and kiss boys, but I am grounded all the time—even for things I have not yet done—as if grounding will keep me from wanting to fly away. I am trying as fast as I can to grow up. I want so much, but I don't have words for it all. I ask my mother what desire means, but she tells me it's like a four-letter word. For now, desire is just a wooden streetcar that used to rattle up and down the tracks of my childhood city.

UNCLE KERRY'S MONDAY
RED BEANS AND RICE

All Louisiana home cooks have a version of this classic one-pot dish. You'll find it in many New Orleans restaurants, especially on Mondays, served with fried pork chops, sausage, or, if you're really lucky, hot, crispy fried chicken. The secret to this recipe, adapted from Kerry Hoppe (my grandfather's only son), is Zatarain's Liquid Shrimp & Crab Boil. Also, my uncle doesn't soak his beans, but you can do a quick soak (boil enough water to cover beans and let soak 1 hour). For a garnish, my grandfather used to marinate sliced sweet onions in white vinegar with dried Italian seasoning. In Provence, I used shallots and *herbes de Provence* or fresh thyme picked straight from the fields during my morning run.

1½ *tablespoons butter*
1 *medium yellow onion, chopped (about 2 cups)*
1 *green bell pepper, chopped (about 1½ cups)*
4 *celery ribs, chopped (about 1½ cups)*
3 *garlic cloves, smashed*
1 *teaspoon salt*
½ *teaspoon fresh-ground black pepper*
1 *smoked ham hock (about ¾ pound) or pickled pork*
1 *(1-pound) bag dried kidney beans (soaked, if desired)*
1 *teaspoon liquid crab boil*
1 *teaspoon Creole seasoning*
2 *to 3 sprigs fresh thyme*
1 *pound smoked sausage (such as andouille or kielbasa)*
2 *tablespoons cornstarch (optional)*
Hot sauce, to taste
Garnishes: green onions, shallots in vinegar, parsley

Heat butter on medium high in a large pot or Dutch oven. Add onion, bell pepper, and celery and cook, stirring occasionally, about 7 minutes or until soft. Add garlic, salt, and pepper and cook 3 more minutes. Add smoked ham hock, beans, liquid crab boil, Creole seasoning, and thyme and stir. Add enough water (about 2 quarts) to cover beans. Stir, bring to a boil, reduce heat to medium, and let simmer, stirring occasionally, about 1½ hours. If beans get too thick, add more water, about ½ cup at a time. Add sausage to pot and let beans cook another 30 minutes or until tender. For creamy beans, I like to smash some of them on the side of the pot with a wooden spoon. Uncle Kerry mixes 2 tablespoons cornstarch with cold water and adds to sauce. Season to taste with more salt, pepper, or hot sauce. Garnish, if desired. Serve with hot boiled rice and shallots in vinegar. *Serves 6 to 8.*

Shallots in Vinegar

Combine 3 to 4 tablespoons rice or white wine vinegar, 2 thinly sliced shallots, and *herbes de Provence* or fresh thyme leaves in a bowl and stir to combine.

∽◌◞∽◌◞∽◌◞∽◌◞∽◌◞∽◌◞∽◌◞∽◌◞∽◌◞∽◌◞

CINNAMON CREAM CHEESE ROLLS

For this recipe, all-purpose flour is fine, but bread flour results in a lighter confection. You can also omit the cream cheese and sprinkle the dough with cinnamon and sugar instead.

1 (16-ounce) container sour cream
⅓ cup sugar
⅓ cup unsalted butter
1 teaspoon salt
2 (¼-ounce) envelopes active dry yeast
½ cup warm water (100 to 110 degrees)

1 tablespoon sugar
2 large eggs, lightly beaten
6 to 6½ cups bread flour
Cream cheese cinnamon filling
2 tablespoons melted butter (optional)
Citrus vanilla drizzle

Cook first 4 ingredients in a medium saucepan over low heat, stirring often, until butter melts. Set aside and let cool. Stir together yeast, warm water, and sugar in a bowl; let stand 5 minutes.

Beat sour cream mixture, yeast mixture, eggs, and 2 cups flour at medium speed with an electric mixer until smooth. Gradually add in enough remaining flour, ½ cup at a time, to make a soft dough. Turn dough out onto a lightly floured surface; knead until smooth and elastic (about 10 minutes). Place in a well-greased bowl, turning to grease top. Cover and let rise in a draft-free, warm (about 85 degrees) place 1 hour or until dough is doubled in size.

Punch dough down and divide in half. Roll each portion into a 24 by 12-inch rectangle. Spread half of cream cheese cinnamon filling (or other flavor) on each rectangle.

Roll each dough rectangle, jelly roll fashion, starting at the long side. Place each dough roll, seam side down, on a lightly greased baking sheet. Slice into 12 equal slices. Place cut rolls, cinnamon side up, on baking sheets. (You can also make ahead to this point, cover with plastic wrap or foil, and freeze. When ready to serve, unwrap and proceed with directions.) Cover and let rise in a draft-free, warm place 20 to 30 minutes or until doubled in size. Brush with melted butter, if desired.

Bake, uncovered, at 375 degrees for 15 to 17 minutes or until golden. Let cool on pans on wire rack (about 5 minutes). Top with citrus vanilla drizzle.

CREAM CHEESE CINNAMON FILLING

⅓ cup sugar
1 tablespoon ground cinnamon
2 (8-ounce) packages softened cream cheese
1 large egg

Combine all ingredients, using a hand mixer, until smooth and blended well.

CITRUS VANILLA DRIZZLE

3 cups powdered sugar
½ cup fresh orange juice
1 tablespoon butter
1 tablespoon fresh lemon juice
2 teaspoons grated lemon zest
¼ teaspoon vanilla extract

Stir together all ingredients in a small saucepan over low heat until butter is melted and all ingredients well blended.

CHESTNUT-MASCARPONE ROLLS

Whip together 1 (8-ounce) container mascarpone with ½ cup *crème de marrons* to make filling. Prepare cinnamon cream cheese rolls and substitute mascarpone filling for cream cheese cinnamon filling.

IV

CULINARY OPERA

I'M FLYING AGAIN. I GET A RUNNING START AND FLAP MY ARMS, head straight into the wind, bracing myself for liftoff. If it's a good dream, I get to glide high above the treetops—centuries-old live oaks and sycamores. Other times when someone is chasing after me, I blink and turn myself invisible.

I really started vanishing at the age of seventeen, forcing people to forget about me. I left on a creative writing scholarship to a liberal arts college in Florida to study poetry, but it felt as though I had landed in a cultural desert with another group of people who looked nothing like me or wanted anything I recognized—athletic boyfriends, fast cars, deep tans, and degrees in marine biology. I muddled through my freshman year, and what saved me during my sophomore year—I had decided to minor in French—was being able to put together an independent study program to study in France.

Strangely, Europe was the first place where I felt almost at home. It reminded me how much I always dreamed of being away, heading fast to a place that could have been the moon for all my family knew. I was eighteen when I landed in Paris for the first time. Nicole, the mother of my host family, worked from home and took me into the city for classes and excursions. She loved being the tour guide but spoke French so fast that I had no choice but to learn the language quickly.

My second day, I convinced her to let me take the train in alone, even though I had no idea how to do it and hadn't really adjusted to the time change. But I loved the idea of being in Paris by myself. I hadn't really slept, which, oddly enough, heightened my senses even more. I remember walking the boulevard Raspail toward the Montparnasse tower, toting a navy blue backpack, taking in the smells and sounds of this new city. The air smelled of coffee and rising yeast, and mixed with my excitement and lack of sleep; I felt surprisingly hopeful.

I walked into a Montparnasse café called the Cosmos. It was early, so there were mostly men at the bar drinking from tiny cups, a few blue-collar workers nursing their first beers of the workday, eating what looked like dried sausage sandwiches. I realized that I was hungry. A paunchy waiter came over to my tiny round table and stood above me like a rising tower.

"*Alors?*"

"*Parlez-vous anglais?*" I managed. The waiter shrugged and started tapping his foot. "What is the difference between *croque-monsieur* and *croque-madame, s'il vous plaît?*"

"*Croque-madame* is with egg. Of course."

"Yes, of course," I agreed. "One, *s'il vous plaît*. And a glass of *vin rouge.*"

The waiter pointed to the list of red wines: Haut-Médoc, Saint-Amour, Graves.

"Saint-Amour," I blurted out.

I ate heartily, breaking the warm yolk over the ham and creamy béchamel sauce. After, I ordered an espresso, and as I sat there looking around, I noticed a young woman across the room. She vaguely resembled someone I knew, a bit off balance, but her dark eyes were not as immediate as the expression of something between sheer exhaustion and hope. I kept trying to place her, and when I lifted the cup to my lips, I realized that the woman was me. But I was only really seeing myself for the first time, in a different sort of way. I ordered another glass of the red Amour and drank, not knowing when I would ever be able to sleep or dream again.

A man walked into the Cosmos and sat at the table next to mine. He was concentrating on his newspaper. I glanced at some of the headlines, trying not to stare at him. He must have sensed I was reading his paper because he closed it suddenly and looked straight at me.

"Excusez-moi, I'm very sorry." When I blinked, my eyes burned from lack of sleep.

He smiled and went back to his reading. I could see part of him in the mirror, the same one in which I hadn't recognized myself. He was about ten years older than me, dressed in black. Everything about him was impeccable except for his thick curls, which gave him a look of fine-tuned neglect. He seemed at ease sitting there, securely holding *Le Monde* between his hands. Watching his lips move as he read, I felt a small crush come over me.

"Mademoiselle." He was talking to me. *"Je peux vous offrir un café?"*

"Oui. Yes. *Avec plaisir."*

He gestured to the waiter, who promptly brought me another tiny cup of black coffee, and when I held it up to thank him, he was sitting at my table. He introduced himself as François, from Bordeaux. He had studied modern letters but also dabbled in the dead languages, even translating parts of the Vedas. I had no idea what he was talking about, but I listened as he spoke English with a half-British, half-French accent. He was intriguing but spoke too quickly for me to question anything.

"And you, you are new here, *non?*" he said, looking at my college backpack.

I nodded, and the movement of my head made me dizzy. I saw him looking at my watch, which read 12:30 a.m. "Eastern time," I offered.

"I see. You are still in the past. Here it is already morning, and I have already finished my work for the day." He spoke in riddles, with strange lulls in between.

When I didn't respond, he went on to explain that he was an antiquarian, that he found the most valuable objects between 3:00 a.m. and now. He stared at me, and while he was speaking, I stroked the coarse strands of my hair and told myself that surely he wasn't speaking to me. I was a college sophomore, and until then no one, especially a man, had ever addressed me with such interest and genuine pleasure. My heart was beating so hard, I could feel it in my ears, and I was afraid he could hear it, too, but he just kept talking, mostly about all the places he had been and the others he wanted to see before he died—New Guinea, Bhutan, "She-cow-go," the bayous of Louisiana. He asked me lots of questions I didn't know the answers to.

"And you, I'm sure a young woman like you has many dreams."

I remember wanting to say something about happiness, such a strange word in many languages, but even back then I knew that it was never really a goal in itself. I took pleasure, hastily, from where I could because I sensed that it would never last. Instead of waiting for an answer, François told me that he had always wanted to see *le quartier français*. After another round of coffee, it was decided that he would accompany me back to New Orleans after my semester in France. It was the first time since leaving home that I felt I really wanted something. I must have given him some right answers because he suddenly said to me, "*Viens.* I will show you my city." He stood up abruptly, took my bag and my hand, and led me out into the street.

The sun was starting to spread across the wide boulevards, a light I had never noticed before that seemed to settle deep and warm into the bones of the city. I thought about calling Nicole so she wouldn't worry but instead spent the rest of the day with François, riding around in his miniature car, succumbing to his whims. I tasted everything I could, no matter how odd or disturbing: butter-drenched organ meats, crusty sour breads, cheeses covered with the softest gray fuzz. We ate the crispy darkened skin of duck breasts and drank lots of wine before crossing his favorite bridges.

I finally got on the train late and back to Nicole's in the suburbs, sick with what I thought was longing for François, but the next morning Nicole proudly diagnosed my liver as having its first *crise de foie,* a true French liver crisis. She happily made herbal concoctions from her garden and made me drink salty Contrex water for three days. When she decided I was better, she taught me to make pork rillettes and monkfish larded with fresh garlic and sprinkled with toasted fennel seed, crispy potatoes with shallots and parsley. She was a fabulous cook and had only sons, no daughters or nieces, so I let her teach me and initiate my unassuming liver into the wanton ways of the French culinary world.

François didn't call for a week, and when I did see him again, he was seated at a sidewalk café across from the Luxembourg Garden with two women, drinking small glasses of golden-colored wine. He waved promptly and stood up to introduce me. The women kissed me absently on the cheek and said something too quickly for me to understand; looks were exchanged. I envied them; they had been raised in this country, mastered a language of gestures to help them deal with engaging and singular men in a city where whole affairs were constructed or demolished with the slightest glance or nod of a head.

"Come, join us." François sat close to me and held my hand. One of the women, a North African with deep olive skin and huge black eyes, smoked endlessly, stopping only to sip her wine or shrug her shoulder every once in a while. While François conferred with the waiter, the women were quick to ask me how I had met their friend and offered a few words of advice. I'm sure they dismissed me as some naive *Américaine* who didn't know much about anything, and they were right—but for a moment I was someone else, momentarily happy, and I found everyone around me palatable and glowing. The waiters were unusually charming, and the toast-colored wine was like butter on my tongue. I drank while François gently stroked my thigh under the table.

The following morning would be the last time I'd ever see François. He picked me up early—it was still dark—from Nicole's and drove me to the outskirts of Paris to sell and bargain at the Saint-Ouen flea market. He showed me the difference between fake and real first editions, the value of certain artist's proofs, and which porcelain plates were *très recherchée*. I bought an etching from a South American shipwreck collection with the few francs I had. Over a sunrise *café crème*, he told me that he was off to Spain and Italy to search for rare books and prints.

"They have the best crostini with crushed chicken livers, salted anchovies, and the women . . . ooh la." He smiled. "You will come with me, *non?*"

I was about to answer that I would taste anything for him when one of the women, the dark, beautiful one from the day before, showed up at the café. I don't remember her name, just that her head was expertly wrapped in a printed silk scarf and she wore large dark sunglasses, even though there wasn't much sun to speak of. She ignored me and said something to François and left. I looked at him, waiting for something, but he just shrugged and lit a Lucky Strike.

I looked around, and everything seemed to move in slow motion. Midmorning light flooded the stalls of used and battered things; the smoke that escaped from François's nostrils crisscrossed in shadows across his face, rendering his eyes cavernous and hollow. He kissed me, talking the whole time, though no longer in English.

"*Tu es si jeune. Je ne peux pas l'expliquer. Je m'en vais bientôt.*" He embraced me and whispered something about my being so young, about not being able to explain, about having to leave, but filtered through the sounds of the rising babel in my chest, it could have been Latin or Sanskrit or some other ancient language spoken long ago.

I swallowed hard, nodded, and pointed at his watch. I told him that by the time he arrived at his destination, he would be the one in the past. "As for me," I said, finally changing the hands of my watch, "it will be a new day." I sounded braver than I was—I wanted to stay there forever, be loved by this strange and beautiful man in a country I was just beginning to discover—but I hadn't cried for anyone up until then, and I wasn't going to start for him.

I hated returning to Nicole's in Précy-sur-Oise, hated the idea of returning to the bankrupt sky and bleached sands of Florida's waterways. Nicole sensed this, so with her contacts, she arranged a two-month stint for me to work (where one of her sons was already) as a Club Med Gentil Organisateur on the Greek island of Kos. After that, I promised to return to the States in time for a new semester, and I did, hating my dismal dorm life of cardboard pizza boxes and overlit salad bars. All I wanted was to cross the ocean again and disappear into a copper pot, into the big *creuset* of France.

My family came to visit me in Florida once, and I returned to New Orleans for the holidays, but I knew it wouldn't be long until I would leave again. I had disappeared at age three, at seventeen when I left for college, eighteen to Europe, and then again my senior year, when I transferred my credits and enrolled at the University of Nice to study French language and civilization. I said good-bye, leaving behind my sister and brother, my parents and grandparents, promising I'd be back soon, not knowing that soon would be in ten years.

In Nice, I met Joachim, a Swedish political science major with ambitions of working for the United Nations. He was my complete opposite: pale, green-eyed, confident, and stubbornly convinced that he could change the world. When we met on campus, he said I looked like someone who had survived a shipwreck. But it was my lucky day, he claimed, because he was going to save me.

Not that I believed he could save me, but I liked the boldness of his declaration. We started out as friends and shared a rented flat in Vieux Nice, just behind the Cours Saleya, with a Dane and a German architecture student. Joachim, Teis, and Wolfgang had decided—three male votes to my one—that I would have the smallest room off the kitchen. After I'd spent several hours rearranging my new room, the roommates I had secretly dubbed the European Larry, Curly, and Moe summoned me.

"Vee are to eat," announced Wolfgang like a fledgling maître d'hôtel.

On the makeshift table in the living room were mismatched bowls and plates of boiled gray potatoes, stewed onions, jars of pickled herring, dented tubes of Kalles Kaviar, and hard brown bread.

"Vee three made it. Our first meal together."

They must have thought I was delighted since I remained speechless as they seated me at the head of the table. I managed a smile and thanked them. Chewing wistfully on a slimy onion, I closed my eyes an instant and recalled the sweet Vidalias from my childhood and recipes for thick and creamy potato salad, fried chicken, and corn bread.

When I opened my eyes, the boys had disappeared from the table and were leaning out the window. I joined them as they jeered at a street brawl below. Men in earth-colored clothes and lopsided berets screamed strange syllable combinations, shaking their fists at one another. One toppled another's stand of bright red tomatoes, kicked over some heads of lettuce, and, hand in hand with a beautiful woman, marched off through the crowd, disappearing through the arch and into the Mediterranean.

I was grateful for the uproar and encouraged by such excitement at a food market. I slipped on my sandals and, with the stooges in tow, rushed down the three flights of stairs and out into the street. The sun lit up the Cours Saleya like a culinary opera. Children danced around, tossing figs at one another while their mothers in brightly colored skirts flirted with the vendors. I immediately offered up a few francs in exchange for a basket and waltzed through the stalls, composing my own private aria filled with musical words: *fleur de courgette, asperge sauvage, cabri, jambon de Montagne, rascasse, cigale de mer.*

The boys were also excited and pulled out money to help buy kilos of tiny sun-warmed squash and fresh fava beans, lemons, bouquets of fragrant blush peonies. I courageously began bartering in broken French with the *marchands.* Most were happy to listen, patiently allowing me to finish a sentence, then offered up samples of warm peppery *socca* and sweet and savory *tourtes aux blettes,* a *pissaladière* of sticky caramelized onions and salty-sweet anchovies. Others tried to speak Japanese to my Asian face.

We went back to the flat, and without a word the boys scraped the onions and potatoes into a dish for the neighbor's dog. They waited impatiently, along with the poodle's owners, Jean-Philippe and his girlfriend, as I orchestrated my first French meal. I watched the Stooges' Nordic eyes light up as they popped yellow teardrops of tomatoes into their mouths and tasted my sweet pea salad with mint and bacon. They were a bit reluctant but enjoyed my omelet of wild asparagus dusted with fragrant thyme blossoms.

"Sublime." Jean-Philippe winked and slid closer to me.

I think I was happy and didn't even wince when the Dane lathered lingonberry jam on his portion of *fromage.* We finished off the meal with a tender salad of mâche, creamy Camembert *au lait cru,* and another bottle of red. The next morning, I was unanimously voted into the largest bedroom and allotted full command of the kitchen, and later, when Jean-Philippe came by to take me for coffee, I started to relish the subtle powers of knowing my way around a kitchen.

CROQUE-MADAME

This is basically a really decadent ham-and-cheese sandwich with an egg on top to elevate it from a monsieur to a madame. Substitute thin slices of grilled chicken for the ham. I like my egg sunny-side up so I can swirl the cheese sauce into the warm yolk, but poached or over easy eggs would work as well.

Butter
4 slices sourdough or pain de mie *(white sandwich bread)*
4 slices good-quality cooked ham (or chicken)
Dijon mustard (optional)
1 cup grated Gruyère or Emmentaler, divided
1½ to 2 cups Mornay sauce
2 sunny-side-up eggs

Heat a large ovenproof skillet over medium high heat. Butter bread on all sides and top 2 of the slices with ham (sometimes I add a smear of Dijon). Top with half the cheese and cover with remaining bread slices. Place sandwiches buttered-side down into the skillet, pressing gently with back of spatula. Let cook about 1 to 2 minutes or until bottom is lightly golden. Top with Mornay sauce and remaining cheese. Place ovenproof skillet in oven and broil 1 to 2 minutes (be careful not to burn) or until golden and bubbly. Top, with a fresh sunny-side-up egg and serve hot. *Serves 2.*

Mornay Sauce

J usually make this in a nonstick saucepan, which makes for easy cleanup.

2 tablespoons unsalted butter
2 tablespoons all-purpose flour
1½ to 2 cups milk (whole or 2 percent)
¼ teaspoon salt
⅛ teaspoon fresh-ground black pepper
Freshly grated nutmeg, to taste
¾ cup coarsely grated Gruyère or Comté (about ¼ pound)

Melt butter in a heavy-bottom saucepan over medium high heat. Stir in flour and cook, stirring constantly, about 1 minute (do not let brown). Add milk, whisking constantly. Bring to a low boil and cook, stirring constantly, about 2 minutes more. (Once it boils, if too thick add more milk.) Season with salt, pepper, and nutmeg. Remove from heat and stir in cheese.

~~~~~~

SPRING PEA SALAD WITH MINTED CREAM AND GRILLED CHEESE TOASTS

If you make this out of season, frozen peas can be substituted. I also like to add fresh fava beans (cooked and peeled).

> *2 cups fresh, shelled English peas*
> *1 cup fresh snow peas (about ¼ pound)*
> *3 slices prosciutto or Canadian bacon*
> *1 cup crème fraîche*
> *½ teaspoon fresh lemon juice*
> Fleur de sel *and fresh-ground black pepper, to taste*
> *2 to 3 tablespoons julienned fresh mint leaves*
> *Grilled goat cheese toast*

Cook English peas 1 to 2 minutes in salted boiling water. Add snow peas and let cook 1 more minute. Shock peas in an ice bath and let drain. Cook prosciutto in a hot pan until crispy. Remove from pan and reserve. Combine crème fraîche, lemon juice, *fleur de sel*, pepper, and fresh mint in a bowl. Add peas and stir gently to combine. Let chill in refrigerator about 1 hour. Top with crispy prosciutto and serve with grilled goat cheese toast.

GRILLED GOAT CHEESE TOAST

$\mathcal{M}$ake this with almost any cheese you have on hand, but I like to use chèvre such as a young, fresh white Crottin, or try Rocamadour or a fresh Saint-Marcellin. Slice country bread or baguette and grill or toast lightly. Rub with garlic, if desired, and place cheese on top. Broil for a few seconds, sprinkle with some fresh herbs and/or a drizzle of good olive oil, and serve hot with spring pea salad with minted cream or your favorite green salad.

V

FIVE SIMPLE WORDS

꿍

I ALMOST DROWNED ONCE WHEN I WAS SEVEN, AT A BIRTHDAY party for my friend Kathy. Everyone knew how to swim, it seemed, except me. But I stood in line with the other kids and, in turn, jumped off the diving board and into the deep end. I could see Kathy's mother and all my friends above the water, and I wondered if they could see me as I was starting to go down.

I still remember that sinking feeling, the slow sensation of losing air. I sometimes think of this when I'm flying thirty thousand feet above the earth, in a jet transporting me to another part of the world, farther away from my point of origin. I wonder sometimes, if I had actually drowned that day, how long it would have taken my adoptive parents to forget about me.

Instead of returning to the States after my last year at the University in Nice, I left for Sweden with Joachim. Perhaps since my adoptive father's family is from Norway, I headed north instead of east.

"When are you coming back?" I remember my mother asking when I called from a pay phone along the Promenade des Anglais in Nice.

"I don't know, in a year maybe," I replied, and shrugged, watching the Mediterranean crash into the black rocky beach below. Her silence said it all: She didn't approve, she wanted me to come back and live close to home. She didn't understand why I would study in France, why I was living in a foreign country. I was momentarily homesick and blurted out that I would try to come home for Thanksgiving.

"Where are you going to live?" My sister was still in high school, and maybe my mother thought I was proving to be a bad influence, even though Suzy and I hadn't been close in years. "Where are you going to live?" she repeated.

I think she knew I was moving in with Joachim, and obviously, there was no wedding in the near future. Marriage was the last thing I was looking for. I didn't need a ring to escape, just a valid passport.

I knew when getting my first Swedish visa that I wasn't really going in the right direction, but at least I had the illusion of going somewhere, and I think I believed that Joachim could make me feel that home was somewhere close.

It was in Stockholm, however, that I discovered the first of many places I would never quite belong. I could speak French fairly fluently at this point, but no one in Sweden wanted to know if you could do anything better than they could. So the fact that I couldn't speak Swedish well quickly endeared me to Joachim's family and many friends.

At Sunday dinners, his father or brother-in-law (who had studied in the States) made a point of sitting next to me, not to make me feel more welcome, but to show how well they could speak my language.

"Did you know that Sveden has the highest rate of literacy in Europe?"

"No, I didn't." I'd smile, crunching into a mustard-sweetened herring.

Joachim and his brother-in-law would then often go into a

litany of all the high-quality products that come out of the great country that is Sweden—Volvo, Ericsson, Saab, Esselte.

"Vee are proud of being Swedish," someone would affirm. "But vee can English probably better than half of the kids in American high schools."

I'd nod agreeably, not wanting to correct them. Instead I cracked a hard round of *knäckebröd* in two and smeared it with a squeeze of liver paste. We did this every Sunday. Just a few more shots of schnapps, I'd remind myself, coffee, and maybe a few lines from an ABBA song I could never quite remember and I'd be home-free.

SOON I FOUND part-time work at the International School, teaching English and basic French to the awkward and privileged children of diplomats. I also signed up for Swedish language lessons, but Joachim, who liked speaking English, "the international language," told me I could get along perfectly fine without Swedish. But English had been my first language of survival, and I was determined to survive in Sweden, too.

Joachim liked to eat but didn't like to cook, so he'd go out drinking after class and sometimes not come home until dinner was already too cold to eat or it was too late to reheat. Every day, I'd try a different dish from one of his mother's cookbooks—recognizing words like *potatis, äpple, soppa, bröd* and learning new ones like *Jansson's frestelse,* a warm potato temptation with anchovies, onions, and cream. Sometimes, though, after too many boiled potatoes, I longed for Louisiana heat, dirty rice, shrimp Creole, or even a simple fried egg sandwich with a dollop of mayonnaise and lots of Crystal hot sauce.

When I wasn't teaching, I was obsessed with watching Brazilian soap operas subtitled in Swedish so I could learn other words away from the kitchen: *älskar, andra, behöver*. I learned to say with a certain Brazilian fierceness that "João was out of the hospital, in love with Rosita, and drinking all night."

Once, after two days away from home, Joachim came back. I was seated at the small kitchen table, in a half sleep, watching layers of snow pile up outside the window, a pot of lukewarm gumbo on the stove and a few shots of vodka in my blood. I accused him of having his own Rosita at the corner bar.

"*Jag vet att du älskar henne.*" I know you love her, I mispronounced.

But it wasn't Rosita he loved, he assured me, taking off his boots and making his way into the kitchen. "It's windy-eyed Kim," he sang, lifting the lid of the gumbo pot. "I'm hungry."

He lit the gas to high, then turned around to tell me that he also loved Johanna, a girl he had introduced me to once. Someone from his study group. Before I could say anything, she appeared in the kitchen—perfectly on cue—and of course I remembered her. Tall, big-boned, with midnight blue eyes and lots of swinging hair. She was beautiful; she looked nothing like me.

"*Hej.* I'm Yo-hana," she said, smiling. Her voice, like crushed ice, didn't quite match the sleekness of her body. She turned to Joachim, who fed her a spoonful of my gumbo. "*Lite salt.*"

She sprinkled some salt into my dish and stirred the pot, asking me something about how I was surviving the winters. But I was already standing at the hall closet, putting on the warmest clothes I could find: stockings under my long brown skirt, Joachim's thick wool socks, a mismatched pair of mittens, a red scarf, and a black wool cape. I grabbed my purse and started toward the door.

"Where are you going?" Joachim and Johanna asked almost in unison, frowning like a pair of disapproving parents.

My face turned hot, as if I had been caught in the act of something I would have a hard time explaining. All I could do was shrug and bite the inside of my cheek to stop the tears from clouding my throat, stop myself from turning back. Joachim tried to hug me, but I turned abruptly and he stuffed a phone card in my hand instead.

Looking back, I don't even know why I took the card. Who was I going to call? I certainly wasn't going to call him. I knew hardly anyone in Stockholm, and with the time difference, if I had tried someone back home in the States, it would have been an alarming hour to ring.

I didn't know where I was going, either, but I felt relieved stepping out into the thick snow that night, letting the cold air slice into my lungs. Wandering the streets, I thought of my father—my adoptive one with the Scandinavian roots. I longed for his Minnesota story, the same one of having to walk miles in snow to get home from school every day: "Up a hill . . . both ways." He told it so often, my sister and I mouthed the ending with him, rolling into laughter. My father never laughed much when he talked about his childhood, so I liked the story, because it was one of the rare and tender moments he shared with us. But I hated it, too, because it always ended in a lecture about why we should appreciate the smallest of what we're given. I always wanted to shout that I wanted the big things, lots of whatever there was in life, even if I knew back then that I wouldn't know what to do with so much.

I must have sensed even before that last evening with Joachim that I wasn't going to find the "lots of whatever" in Sweden. A country proud of being neutral, proud of its many islands and its cold surrounding waters. A country where all the clichés are true—the people and sky both dark and drunk in the winter and prematurely happy and drunk again with the slightest promise of warmth and sun. A place where strangers keep to themselves and the scent of foreign spices is considered suspicious.

I walked across the bridge into Gamla stan, old town, until I found a bakery-café that was just about to close. They let me in, and I ordered a big cup of hot tea and pointed to the last puff pastry roll stuffed with whipped cream. I dug out some coins from the bottom of my purse to pay and found a postcard I had bought some time back, a photograph of a wilted smorgasbord and a smiling blond girl holding a glass cup of mulled wine.

There were only two other people inside the café, sitting at opposite ends of the room, trying to stay warm. I sat at a table somewhere between the two and started to write my sister on the back of the card, wondering if my family missed me at all, but I drew a snowflake instead. The sweetness of the white cream filling made my teeth ache, and suddenly I was sorry that I had left the gumbo with Joachim. I imagined him in the kitchen with Johanna, her small, perfect nose crinkling as she inhaled the salty, spicy stew.

AFTER LEAVING JOACHIM—my visa hadn't yet expired—I decided to stay on in Stockholm a little longer. I may have been drifting, waiting for my life to begin. And even though I had no concrete reason to be there, something kept me from leaving right away.

I soon rented an apartment from a woman named Berit. When I spoke to her in broken Swedish, her name came out of my mouth sounding more like "Beirut," but she didn't seem to mind.

"Sometimes," she said in Swedish, showing me through the different rooms filled with packed boxes, "life is like a knocked-out city."

There was nothing harsh or exclamatory about her comment. As she showed me how to work the two beautiful *kake-lugns*—tiled heating elements, one in the living room, the other a sea-colored tower in the bedroom—she went on to explain that she was a Lutheran minister and that her girlfriend had just broken up with her, that's why she was moving and renting out her apartment. I nodded, following her around, taking in the bouncing sounds of her voice.

"And here is the kitchen," she said, sliding open the window. "There's an elementary school." She pointed. "And the communal laundry room. Lots of sunshine through here. It's a good place to simmer and think."

As I was paying her the deposit, she said she liked me because I wouldn't be trouble, because I was quiet—maybe a loner, like herself? I lied and told her that I had many friends in the city. I then explained that I had found a rhythm to my Swedish existence: free language lessons for immigrants on Fridays at the Gullmarsplan location, workout and sauna at Friskis & Svettis (Healthy & Sweaty) on Tuesdays, and teaching on Mondays and Wednesdays.

I think I wanted routine and order, things my parents and people like Joachim had tried to teach me but knew I'd never be good at. Maybe I wanted the illusion that if I had control over the timetable of my life, I could avoid emotion and the uncontrollable details like sorrow and love and absence.

A MONTH OR so later, I started teaching at the Berlitz School on Kungsgatan. It was there I met a poet named Charlotte. At first, we were reluctant to meet each other, everyone having told us how well we would get along. Finally, we met for tea. She was dressed in a bright green tunic and wide-legged pants, nothing like what any of the Swedish girls our age were wearing.

Conversation came easily, in Swedish at first and later in English. We compared our favorite words and poets, cities we longed to visit. Meeting her was like finding a mirror, and we searched silently, wondering about the darkness inside each of us that compelled us to write.

Also at Berlitz, I met Kajsa. Aside from being an aspiring model—she had just landed a modest contract—Kajsa free-lanced, tutoring students where I used to teach, at the International School, in Swedish and theater.

"As if these kids needed any more drama in their lives." She told me stories of the different families, where they were from, what they ate. She spoke always in her precise and throaty way, using her big rusty features to emulate her idol, Bibi Andersson. Kajsa made me laugh. She was a good distraction and helped me pronounce the strange bubbling sounds of the Swedish language.

Over spiced tea and pickled herring sandwiches one day, she told me she had been making extra money translating brochures for L'Occitane, a French perfume and soap company. I hadn't heard of it. The founder, Olivier Baussan, she went on to explain, had started it in a small town in Provence years earlier, and they were expanding, going international. They needed someone to do the English translation. He was a good friend of hers, and she had met him while on vacation in Portugal the summer before. That's the summer Kajsa was breaking up with Lars. Before I could ask her, she said she really liked Olivier when they met, but she was still in love with Lars.

Anyway, she continued, Olivier was coming to Stockholm to look at store locations, and he'd be in town only one night. She thought I should meet him and see if maybe he would hire me to translate the new L'Occitane brochures from French to English. Why not, I told her. I truly had nothing better to do.

Kajsa, who subsisted on tea and hard bread, insisted on cooking that evening. I don't know why, but I offered to bake a cheesecake—New York style. I bought a hard-to-find springform pan and graham crackers and improvised with a jar of lingonberry jam to top the cake. I stood in line at Systembolaget, the government-run liquor store, to buy wine and randomly chose a 1985 bottle of red rioja. At the time, I'd never tried Spanish wine and didn't know what to look for in a "good bottle." But as I handed over my crumpled 100-krona bill, I felt that my life suddenly depended on it.

It was the end of November, so the sun had barely risen and already set by the time I was to be at Kajsa's. I wore thick stockings, knee-high boots, a dark velvet skirt with a gray sweater. Bundled in a hat and coat, I walked the ten blocks from my place to Kajsa's. The weight of the cheesecake and the bottle of wine, the crunch of ice under my boots, all suddenly made me feel hopeful. I had a purpose, small as it was. I was taking a familiar path to meet someone new. I was just twenty-two years old, and everything seemed possible.

Before I made it to the top flight of stairs, I heard music coming from Kajsa's. It wasn't what she usually listened to, it was melancholy and rich—something I recognized but had never heard before.

It was Olivier who came to greet me at the door. He took my hat and coat and bent down to take a look at the bottle of wine. I regretted my ignorance and wished I had bought French instead.

"*C'est une excellente année,*" he remarked as I handed it over. His smile was sudden but not mocking. I could feel him taking me in as he closed the door. I knew Kajsa's place better than he did, but he showed me to the kitchen as if he had been living there his whole life. I followed, concentrating on his voice. He spoke in slow, deliberate cadences, carefully repeating words we might not understand in French.

Kajsa had attempted a carrot-mushroom ragout but had overcooked the pasta into mush. She laughed it off and pulled out dark bread and a triangular block of nondescript cheese as we savored the wine. It was delicious, and Olivier told me again that my choice had been, in fact, a very good year.

Olivier didn't talk excessively, but when he did, he told us about his latest projects for L'Occitane, which included sponsoring a sewing circle for pregnant teenagers in Burkina Faso. He told us about the magic of the shea tree and his new line of products using the butter from the shea nuts, his seven-year-old daughter, and briefly about a pending divorce. Mostly he talked about his love for Provence and the foods of his region. He talked of recipes, his hazel brown eyes lighting up at the taste memory of creamy *bourride,* green and black olive tapenade, garlic-and-anchovy-rich *anchoïade.*

I studied him discreetly. Small, wire-rimmed glasses sat on the bridge of a straight and handsome nose. I stared at him when I thought he wouldn't notice, as he changed the music again from Kajsa's rock to Schubert's trios. He wasn't at all the type of French man I had imagined falling in love with when I was a student in Nice. Olivier was tall, lean, and exceptionally graceful, so sure of his space and position in the room, in the world, that even his movements, at times almost feminine, were in perfect sync with his solid legs and thick-soled shoes that kept him firmly grounded. He caught me watching him and tilted his head, as if, in turn, to both study and question me.

I suddenly felt small and inadequate, lacking words in his language that would render me seductive and beautiful—

perfect syllables to answer that I too was falling and that yes, I too wanted something more.

Instead, I rambled on in my mediocre French about the translation I would do for him and how Stockholm was just a random stop in a long line of places I wanted to visit. I soon excused myself and thanked Kajsa, refusing Olivier's offer to see me home. In turn, he insisted we make plans to meet the following day before his late flight back to Paris.

THE NEXT MORNING, after my workout at Friskis & Svettis, Olivier met me and we walked to my favorite bookstore in Gamla stan where I used to go on Sunday mornings, when it was the least crowded. I pretended to read Whitman but was watching Olivier instead. I couldn't help but want to know him better—a French man in Scandinavia, joyous among the crooked rows of dusty, neglected books that I loved so much. I watched over the edges of *I Sing the Body Electric!* as he fingered pages, letting his large smooth hands run down the spine of each book. He spoke very little English, but I managed to understand that something important was happening.

He bought a copy of *Gilgamesh* and *Leaves of Grass* for me, and then we quietly slipped out of the shop together.

"Je n'aime pas le froid," he said, shivering.

"I don't like the cold, either," I answered in French, thinking in English how no one ever gets used to below zero.

It was freezing, and he had to be at Stockholm Arlanda Airport in several hours. But we continued along the dark stone streets of the old city and ended up in a café for gravlax, boiled potatoes, and squat glasses of cold, hard Absolut. Then we walked along the river, not really knowing where to go, just knowing that we couldn't bear to separate.

He held my hand all the way back to my apartment, neither of us really saying much. We listened to the rhythm of our steps echo in a country where neither of us belonged. He wanted to stay and take the next morning flight back to Paris, but I whispered he should go. There was both tenderness and joy in the way he told me good-bye, a promise of many more arrivals and departures to come.

Olivier flew me to Paris the next weekend. We met at the Hôtel du Jeu de Paume on the island of Saint-Louis in the heart of the city. He had reserved two rooms so there would be no misunderstanding. But all I understood was that I was meeting a man in a foreign country, someone I knew very little but who I sensed would be of immeasurable importance in my life. We ate fresh Vietnamese basil rolls on the street before going to the theater, where we sat in the dark, the electricity shooting out between us. And I savored the way he brushed the nape of my neck with just the tips of his fingers.

We dined on a late supper of oysters on the half shell at a grand brasserie in Montparnasse. It wasn't until years later, stopping in French coastal towns like Bouzigues and Cancale, that I understood this: Naked and eaten in its unaltered state, the oyster is the perfect food. Olivier tipped the first oyster into me, a taste so cold and sweet—it conformed perfectly to the shape of my mouth and tasted suddenly of the sea. We drank white Sancerre, a few bites of a steamed whole turbot with a side of beurre blanc. Later, walking the streets of the city, we tried to catch a cab, but it was late and I started to get wet with Paris rain, so we went deep into the underground, and that's when he kissed me for the first time, his tongue fitting perfectly the shape of mine, there deep down in the rush of the Paris métro.

Olivier flew me to London to spend a weekend in Bath, to Venice to celebrate my twenty-third birthday at Harry's Bar, where we ate John Dory and artichokes, capellini baked with ham and cream. He flew me to Nice, and we drove to the Moulin de Mougins, where I had my first taste of black truffle, a small one stuffed into a squash blossom and a larger whole truffle baked into an individual dinner roll. And he came to Stockholm almost every weekend after. Since he had shared custody of his daughter, it was easy to have her for a week at a time before leaving to come and stay with me. But when he was with me, I could tell how much he missed her. He'd call Laure just before her bedtime. I remember envying the tenderness in his voice, the longing as he sent small kisses through the invisible wires to his faraway daughter.

Our courtship began in the winter, so we hibernated, staying in bed for hours at a time, making love until I was sore and raw. After, we read to each other—poems from the elder Milosz, Tagore, Neruda, Södergran—imagined houses he wanted me to live in, places we would visit, foods he wanted me to taste. Olivier would rearrange my bookshelves, adding new editions in French he thought I should read. "You need your own bookstore," he commented one morning while I was still half-asleep. Um-hmm, I nodded, not really daring to say much more. Yes, I loved books but had never even entertained the idea of owning my own shop one day.

Sometimes I would surprise Olivier and meet him at the airport so we could ride the shuttle together back to the city, his hands already between my legs, his mouth already tasting of mine. Before his arrivals, I would go to Konsum and Systembolaget and stock the fridge with wine, red and black caviar, fish and vegetables, crisp bread for our erratic feedings. I would doze off, then drift in and out to the thick scent of stocks Olivier had simmering in the middle of the night. I'd find him in the half-lit kitchen, half-dressed and smiling like a mad *chef d'orchestre,* tasting Champagne as he conducted shallots to reduce down into red wine and roasted perch filets and steamed Chinese cabbage for a 4:00 a.m. meal. After a taste of cheese or bittersweet chocolate and several spoonfuls of ice cream, we'd fall back asleep, clinging to each other, just as the sun was starting to splinter across the winter sky.

He always brought me gifts from his travels: aged balsamic vinegars in hand-blown glass, mud-stained *bogolan* cloths from Mali that we used as bedspreads, vials of lavender essential oil he had distilled himself. And boxes and boxes of individually wrapped mild soaps from the L'Occitane factory in Manosque. Milk, almond, sandalwood. They scented his clothes and skin. He shampooed my hair with *lait aux céréales,* new products he was creating. I loved our private bathing ritual, how he doted over me in the shower, massaging my scalp with essences he had chosen so carefully.

After our time together, when he'd have to fly back, there was a hole in my heart, a gap so big that I was afraid it would divide us. But he would send packages, always including something to sweeten my tongue—Italian dried fruit cakes, Spanish almond confections, small boat-shaped cookies from Provence, and always a heavy linen cream-colored envelope with Swedish kronor to pay for phone bills. We'd talk at least three or four times a day, our ears pressed hard into the receiver—as if we could possibly get any closer—whispering about the next time we would touch each other or why we had to say good-bye. I'd fall asleep with the phone cradled on my chest, crumbs of orange blossom cookies pressed between my body and the warm sheets.

Neither of us really knew what was happening. Olivier used words like *femme de ma vie, reine de mon univers.* Sounds I repeated to myself, not translating them on purpose but wanting so deeply to understand. It didn't matter that I was in my early twenties and that he would soon turn forty. His body was strong and firm, and all that really mattered was that he wanted me. More than anything, though, is that with him I felt the least lonely. One night in his sleep, Olivier held me so tight that I almost couldn't breathe, and I remember thinking that in another life we could have been twins—he my exact and perfect opposite.

The rare weekends Olivier didn't come, I'd go back to the little world of out-of-print books, first editions, and talks with Mats, the owner. We had become friends, and I felt that we were linked because he had been a witness to my beginnings with Olivier. Mats would brew hot, milky tea, and we'd spread cloudberry jam on thick slices of potato-flour bread. Sometimes I'd meet Charlotte and listen to her talk of Milton, her Jamaican lover she had met around the same time I'd met Olivier. I liked her because she was quiet, a loner like myself. Other writers would come and go to the bookstore, and while Mats discussed Tranströmer with them, I would drift off and wonder if Olivier was ever going to come back. I knew he was real because of the marks he'd leave on me: my oversensitive skin red from his morning stubble, the churning in my stomach from the anxiety of being in love, and the resulting weight I had lost—parts of my former self left as a trail if ever I needed to find my way back.

But he always came back, and always with more gifts, more love, more reasons to make me feel I wasn't so alone in the world. After the sixth month of weekends and good-byes, he showed up at my apartment with a one-way ticket. He had dreamed this moment, he said. Dreamed these five simple words: *Prends ton passeport et viens.* Get your passport and come.

JANSSON'S FRESTELSE
(SWEDISH POTATO TEMPTATION)

This dish is offered up as part of the holiday smorgasbord in Scandinavia but comforts anytime with the rich combination of potatoes baked in cream and the surprise of the sweeter, milder anchovy found in Sweden. It would be a shame, but for a less decadent version, substitute ¾ cup whole milk for the crème fraîche. Also, fresh thyme and Parmigiano-Reggiano or Comté cheese would be good additions.

> 1½ to 2 pounds Yukon gold or russet potatoes, peeled and
>   sliced
> Salt and fresh-ground black pepper, to taste
> 1 medium yellow onion, sliced
> 8 to 10 oil-packed flat anchovy filets
> 1 (8-ounce) container crème fraîche
> 1 cup heavy whipping cream
> Fresh nutmeg (optional)

Preheat oven to 375 degrees. Place half of sliced potatoes in a lightly greased baking dish. Season with salt (use less or omit, depending on amount of anchovies) and pepper. Cover with onion. Finish with layer of remaining potato slices and top with anchovy filets. Add more salt and pepper, as needed. Combine crème fraîche and cream in a small bowl (sometimes I grate fresh nutmeg and add a little more pepper to the cream). Pour cream mixture over potatoes, adding more cream to cover, as needed. Bake at 375 degrees for 45 to 50 minutes or until potatoes are tender. Cover with foil if potatoes begin to brown. Uncover and bake another 10 minutes or until top begins to crisp and turn golden. Remove from heat and let sit 5 to 10 minutes before serving. *Serves 6 to 8 as a side dish.*

ALMOND-SAFFRON CAKE

I was initially inspired by a Swedish holiday saffron yeast bun traditionally baked to celebrate Santa Lucia, but this cake is more straightforward and has taken on a fragrant life of its own. I've incorporated the richness of almond paste and sour cream. Confectioners' sugar yields a light batter and a tender, airy cake. *Note:* I highly recommend gathering and measuring all ingredients before starting to bake. Also, I've made this with a hand mixer, but a stand mixer just makes it so much easier. Toast any leftover slices, smear with your favorite ice cream, and top with fresh seasonal berries. I also drizzle toasted leftovers with fruity extra-virgin olive oil and eat it with cheese, such as aged Mimolette, Spanish Manchego, or Fromage Blanc.

⅓ cup milk

Generous ½ teaspoon saffron threads (.01-ounce jar)

Grated zest of 1 orange (about 2 teaspoons) (reserve juice)

2 cups all-purpose flour (stir flour before measuring)

1 teaspoon baking powder

½ teaspoon baking soda

⅛ teaspoon salt

1 cup butter, softened

1 (8-ounce) can almond paste (not marzipan), about 1 cup (can also use 1 [7-ounce] tube)

1 cup confectioners' sugar

5 large eggs

1 (8-ounce) container whole-fat sour cream

Preheat oven to 350 degrees. Lightly butter and flour (or spray with cooking spray) 2 (8-inch) round cake pans. Heat milk in a small saucepan over medium heat. Add saffron and zest. Bring to a low simmer, remove from heat, and let steep. Sift together flour, baking powder, and baking soda into a large bowl. Stir in salt and set aside.

Beat butter and almond paste together at medium speed until creamy, about 3 minutes. Gradually add sugar and beat until fluffy, scraping down sides. Add eggs, one at a time, beating just until blended after each addition. Gradually add flour mixture alternately with sour cream, beating at medium speed just until blended, beginning and ending with flour mixture. Add in saffron-milk mixture, beating just until blended (no need to overbeat).

Pour batter into prepared cake pans. Shake pans gently or use spatula to smooth tops. Bake at 350 degrees for 25 to 30 minutes or until tester inserted in center of cake comes out clean. Let cool in pan on wire racks 5 minutes. Remove from pan and serve warm, dusted with more confectioners' sugar or drizzled with the reserved juice of 1 orange (about ⅓ cup) combined with 2 to 3 tablespoons powdered sugar. *Makes 2 (8-inch) cakes.*

VI

FIG OF MY IMAGINATION

ॐ

I PACKED UP THE FEW POSSESSIONS I OWNED IN THE EMPTY boxes saved from Olivier's care packages and took the shortest path from Stockholm to Provence, leaving only the slightest trace of my having ever passed through. I had nothing to regret, except my newest friend, Charlotte, who like myself appeared shipwrecked and had found the soft-spoken Milton, the Jamaican banker, an anchor disguised as love.

All the times I've changed cities and countries, I've left a trail of things behind—clothes and worn shoes, crumpled maps with highlighted borders to tell me concretely where I am. I keep books and music, postcards. Over the years, I've also kept tasting notes, menus, and jotted-down recipes, clues as to what I crave that may help me know who I am, better understand how food has the power to ground and comfort in times of disarray.

Then there are photos, life captured in a time warp. Here's a picture of Grammy and Poppy on a sky lift one summer in the Smoky Mountains. My parents, preadoption, tanned, lingering on a white hotel balcony in Hawaii. There's a picture of my young mother smiling, with her arms open to the world; another photo of the two of us sitting on the ledge of a stone fountain in an Asian garden. I'm an awkward, skinny orphan leaning toward the young woman for shelter, but there's distance between us—my new mother afraid to touch me. A photo of my sister and me in Tiffany blue leotards and soft white ballet slippers, Suzy with one hand on her hip, head tilted, smiling and waving at the camera. There are two pictures my grandmother recently sent, one of me, age four, sitting in a miniature folding chair, legs crossed, concentrating on the newspaper headlines; another of me in my first pair of American running shoes. On the back in her flowing handwriting she writes: *"You never took these off in the beginning, not even to sleep."* I have the urge to call my family when I look through the photos, but the distance built up over the years is not just geographic.

I keep all these images in a black linen box that I've promised myself to sort out later, into a real family album so one day there will be proof that I was part of one. This is my delusion— that I can create my own history, even randomly chosen, if I believe in it enough.

Olivier is obsessed with the camera. I, too, have taken up the habit. Look, focus, click. It's addictive, this focus, focus, click, again and again. I understand nothing about the measuring of light or film speeds, but I like this time frame, life frozen for just an instant. One of the first gifts I offered Olivier was a 1952 Leica, made the same year he was born, found in a shop in Stockholm. It took me hours of teaching, months of saving up, but it was worth it. No one, he said, tears in his eyes, had ever known what to give him.

There are so many images of our early times together. Here's one of us on our first weekend in Paris, on the island of Saint-Louis, like the only lovers in the world. Here we are on Santorini, July 1993. Olivier photographed me from the hot black sands of Perissa as my body slipped in and out of the ancient sea. There are photos of Spanish roads and half-lit mornings in port cities. And then the images of the stone house, Olivier's pride, called La Fare on the outskirts of the village of Pierrerue in the High Alps of Provence. We've got stacks of color and black-and-white prints from my first month here.

HERE I AM leaning against the smooth kitchen island, squeezing lemons, crushing ice with fresh flowering thyme to bring to the workers. I'm not really looking at the camera—I kept thinking of water, remembering the Aegean just a few evenings before. I had cut my left thumb and was sucking the blood so it wouldn't turn the lemonade pink. Just in case, though, I floated a few wild strawberries into the glass pitcher. I couldn't find any Band-Aids in the kitchen, and as I wrapped my finger in layers of thin cheesecloth, I realized that if there was an emergency, it could be a problem. I didn't really know where anything belonged yet. It was my first attempt at making anything in Olivier's kitchen, my second time in Provence, and our last day alone before the beginning of our new life together.

Earlier that morning, in the azure cool of the bedroom, I kept waking at different hours, each time blinking away the haze of disembodied voices and watery spaces of port cities— Stockholm, Marseille, Pusan, New Orleans. I felt for Olivier in the dark, the warmth and solidity of his body to remind me who I was and why I was there instead of anywhere else.

I remember the blood starting to soak through the cheesecloth and wanting to call to Olivier, but he was circling the house—a tiny *hameau* built during the French Revolution— instructing Serge, the caretaker, as his wife, Sophie, hung batches of hot white laundry to dry in the sun. Olivier and Serge were checking water filters and air vents. Olivier, in his subtle yet determined way, demands everything be perfectly restored by the end of summer. He's ordered extra shipments of ocher powders from the nearby town of Rousillon to color-wash the walls and beechwood to build shelves for my office. The three villagers he hired from the local bistro were setting large cream stones up the walkway. They kept watching me, though, through the glass doors, as if for some sign of truth to the rumors they had heard over pastis about who I may be: l'Américaine, l'Asiatique.

They turned, tools suspended, as I walked toward them in my big black Jackie O sunglasses. I was wearing a bright white bathing suit, happy that my skin was brown from Santorini sun and trying to be cool and exotic. But as I offered them lemonade, my makeshift Band-Aid slipped off and bobbed in one of the glasses. *Merci,* they nodded, sincere, wiping sweat from their foreheads and taking huge gulps. They smiled, looking me up and down, but before they could say anything else, Olivier suddenly appeared and clasped my wounded hand: *Viens, mon amour.*

We walked past Serge, whose back was to us, but from the look on Sophie's face, we could tell he was reprimanding her again. Sophie managed an embarrassed smile in our direction, the same one from that morning when I walked into the kitchen and saw them for the first time, speaking to each other in harsh, hushed tones. Serge introduced himself, then quickly left to buy fresh bread and croissants. They had been preparing for my arrival—Olivier always with his careful planning had sent a telefax from the island. Sophie handed me a glass of freshly squeezed orange juice. "From Flor-eed-a," she announced proudly in English, and then went on to tell me in French that she's part Russian, speaks some English because her father is American—a UFO specialist living isolated in Missouri. And that she and Serge ran away together to Tangiers when she was

fifteen, where she aborted several times before keeping their
son, Aden, and later Lenin, and now Lulu. I wondered why she
told me all this my first morning here in Provence, but she did,
carefully braiding her long dark blond hair while waiting for a
pot of hot Yunnan to steep for Olivier before he came into the
kitchen. Sophie said it all in a hurry—the thrust of words not
quite matching the movement of her lips—relating a dubbed
version of her life.

Sophie waved at us, and her small, callused hand in the air
was like a child's. She's beautiful, yet flawed. Serge is her scar,
her birthmark—a short man from the north with pudgy hands,
a big heart, and an even bigger appetite for oily *frites* dipped in
thick mayonnaise and lots of draft beer. Olivier waved back and
tapped his watch—a sign for Serge to keep checking water pres-
sure and pumps—and continued to lead me to the swimming
pool that's finally finished. The outdoor kitchen, however, is
still under construction, so we stood among chipped tiles and
ripped-opened sacks of cement, holding hands overlooking the
village of Forcalquier deep in the valley. Beyond are fields of fat
white asparagus and overripe cantaloupe that sweetens the air,
like stewed chocolate, and makes my stomach turn.

"What's over there again?" I asked Olivier in French, taking
off the oversize glasses, pointing beyond the forest. I can't quite
situate myself on the map, never could.

"Still disoriented?" Olivier laughed and lifted my long heavy
hair, bending down slightly to kiss the nape of my neck. I could
feel him swell as he pressed his pelvis to my lower back.

"The Alps are that way, right?" I pointed to the far north-
east. I remembered then that to the south was the Mediterranean. To the west, the Atlantic Ocean, and beyond, the family I
hadn't seen in almost two years.

"How do you feel?" he asked me in French for the third time that day, turning me around gently to face him. "I want you to feel at home. I'm giving you my office. I'll have a desk and more shelves built. Your books will be here soon."

I started to tell him about my dream the night before, the one I often have about the darkness and the fat rat that comes home faster than *Omma* does, but I am trying to be light and multicolored like the Provençal countryside and not tainted like my sleep.

Instead, I buried my head in Olivier's chest and inhaled his odor. I remembered this smell from the first time we had met in Stockholm and loving it about him—instantly, unwittingly—the scent of the earth he comes from, this landscape of lavender and ancient olive trees, ripe citrus, and the Mediterranean Sea. I wondered, if I smelled like a country, which one it would be.

"Je veux tout t'offrir." I want to give you everything. Olivier swept his arm across the valley as if it were his kingdom. Suddenly I wished I had my camera. Photograph Midas, the local industrialist who had recently sold his local perfume and soap industry, transforming it into a multimillion-dollar golden enterprise. But he stood there, with the goofy smile of a teenager, in his leather Jesus sandals and cutoff blue jeans, staring, almost afraid to touch me.

"Tout," he repeated. Somehow, I thought, he'll never realize that the everything he wants to give me will never take away the nothing that I've always had.

"Sit," he told me. "We will celebrate, and then I will take you to the *marché;* we still have about an hour before they start packing up." Olivier walked over to the outdoor kitchen, took out a bottle of chilled Ruinart from the refrigerator. He raised the bottle to me, about to speak, when the phone rang. He answered, and in the distance, shrugging his shoulders in apology, he watched me.

"*Pas de problème,*" I mouthed. I can wait. I walked over to the deep end of the pool, balancing myself along the edge. "*Tout,*" I said out loud, trying to pronounce it like Olivier, sweeping my arm across the kingdom. I could hear the tension rising in his voice, although he wasn't close enough for me to hear exactly what he was saying. I glanced over at him, watched as he paced and kicked around clay tiles. His legs are strong from years of cycling the hills of Provence. I dipped my toes in the pool. The water was cool. I stretched out in the hot Provençal midday, starting to feel hungry with promises of the open market, ripe blueberries for a chilled soup I've been wanting to make, succulent olives, and sweet ham shaved from the bone.

The cold of the glass bottle on my neck brought me back as Olivier sat next to me at the edge of the water. He took my hand in his, examining my cut thumb. "It's better now, but you'll have a scar."

"I always do," I told him.

"I love that about you," he whispered, sucking my thumb. "Always a trace. Like a map." He glided his wet finger along my legs, outlining the mosquito bite marks around my ankles, and traced his finger to the ugly birthmark on my inner calf. As he leaned over to kiss it, the phone rang again. "*C'est encore elle.*"

He told me softly that Dominique wanted to drop off Laure a week early for the rest of the summer. She was driving back from Italy, and that was probably her calling again. He had decided that we would go and pick up Laure at her mother's, down in the village, when they returned, in about two hours. I leaned back on the grass, gently rolling the damp bottle back and forth over my tanned stomach.

I nodded. What else could I say? He popped open the

Champagne and poured two glasses. He dipped his forefinger into my glass, touched the back of each of my ears with a drop of the cold liquid, and offered a toast. Olivier winked, and I could feel everything melting, the space between my legs. I leaned back and closed my eyes, ready for him to kiss me, but he filled my mouth with a sweetness I had never known before, deeper than honey. I opened my eyes to a handful of fresh fat figs dripping with their own milk. He whispered that we would roast them with red wine, taste them with acacia blossoms he would fry and powder with fine sugar.

I looked out toward the unfinished outdoor kitchen. The air was hot and dry, with just the slightest wind. I could see the tips of the Alps far, far in the distance. I pushed the hair off my face, and the sweetness from the wild figs stuck to my fingers and lips. I licked them again, willing myself to memorize that full-mouth flavor.

<hr>

FIGS ROASTED IN RED WINE
WITH CREAM AND HONEY

12 to 18 fresh figs (ripe but firm)
½ (750-ml) bottle red wine
3 tablespoons honey
1 cinnamon stick
3 tablespoons sugar
2 tablespoons thick crème fraîche (or heavy cream)
Garnish: fresh mint leaves

Remove stems from figs and cut a small X in top of each. Place figs cut-side-up in an ovenproof pan. Pour wine over. Drizzle with honey. With a knife, scrape cinnamon stick over figs, and add stick to pan. Roast figs at 375 degrees for 20 to 25 minutes or until figs are tender but not falling apart. Gently remove figs, using a slotted spoon, and place on serving dishes. Place pan over medium high heat, stir in sugar, and bring wine to a boil; let cook on high heat about 7 minutes or until syrupy. Remove from heat. Stir in crème fraîche. Spoon wine and crème fraîche mixture over figs. Serve warm (or chilled). Garnish, if desired. *Serves 4 to 6.*

CHILLED BLUEBERRY SOUP

Add 1 or 2 teaspoons of this to a glass of Champagne or Prosecco for a sweet summer sparkler; use to top crêpes, pancakes, or ice cream; or serve for dessert in chilled espresso cups.

> *6 cups fresh blueberries, divided, or 2 (12-ounce) bags frozen*
> *blueberries*
> *4 cloves*
> *½ cup liquid honey*
> *1 vanilla bean, scraped, or 1 cinnamon stick*
> *1 tablespoon fresh lemon juice*
> *3 tablespoons crème de cassis*
> *1 tablespoon balsamic vinegar*
> *Garnish: lemon or orange zest, crème fraîche*

Rinse blueberries and place all but 1 cup in a large pot. Add cloves and stir in honey. Split vanilla bean lengthwise, scrape seeds into pot using tip of knife, and add scraped bean halves (or scrape cinnamon into pot and add stick). Add 1 cup water and stir.

Bring to a boil, reduce heat, and let simmer about 10 minutes. Strain, using back of spoon to crush berries, through a fine sieve, into a bowl. Discard solids. Let soup cool. Stir in lemon juice, crème de cassis, and vinegar. Add more honey, as needed. Chill in refrigerator 4 hours and up to 2 days. Serve in chilled bowls with reserved 1 cup fresh blueberries. Garnish, if desired. *Makes 3 cups.*

VII

STICKS AND STONES

෪෨

$\mathcal{E}$verything I own—a few African handbaskets, mismatched terra-cotta dishes, some vintage New Orleans Jazz Fest posters, clothes, and books—has finally arrived from Stockholm. I take refuge in the boxes, locking myself with my past in the office Olivier has insisted I take as mine. This writing room he designated is a medium-size, beautiful space in the center of the main house. I like the big square window that looks out onto the immense sunflower fields to the east, but this room, my office, is the only path from the inside of the house that leads to Olivier's wine cellar. Olivier has also set up a thick beechwood table as a desk and added his father's cane-seat chair he insists I use as my own. "So, when you write poems and stories, you can think of him. He would have loved you . . ." The chair is big and uncomfortable, but I accept it, not wanting to disappoint Olivier.

Already, too much time has passed since we were alone together in Sweden, Italy, especially Greece, sunbathing on Santorini, sharing quiet suppers of feta and grilled octopus, drinking pine-scented wine as we overlooked the volcanic traces of the past, the landscape of centuries before us, and wondering if this was real—our having found one another. But I am doing more than surviving. This is my new life, a reinvention of myself. I clean closets, dust shelves, organize my books and photos.

Outside, the workers have almost finished setting the stones. I hear their foreign babble carried by the rustle of a wind they call mistral and the familiar cadence of Olivier's voice. Somewhere on this property, I remind myself, is the person I love—I have always loved. Before, I imagined every place a temporary space, a waiting room for somewhere else. Even when I met Olivier, I wasn't thinking home or happiness, I was just learning to be a young woman with a multistamped passport, wondering which fear is greater, losing what I have or actually having what I want.

I'm afraid to think I may fear having everything.

These past few months, I've met so many new people, but I concentrate on getting to know Laure better and the rest of Olivier's family—his mother, Giselle; brother, Alain, and his wife, Annie; his sister, Pascale. There are many friends, some with names I can't quite pronounce, and a variety of local misfits, curious people in the village who want to know who I really am. Olivier has incited gossip since selling most of L'Occitane and becoming a millionaire. I try to ignore the rumors that I'm pregnant, a gold digger, or simply an exoticism for the rich industrialist.

So far, those Olivier has introduced me to have all been chosen carefully. He presents me as a treasure, to be protected from scrutiny and jealous acquaintances who frequent Dominique. For now, I also concentrate on perfecting my French. No one here speaks English anyway, except for Sophie, who whispers a few words to me in confidence, usually about Serge's drinking. And Laure and Lulu, who like to pretend they speak American, dancing around random phrases like "sweet dreams," "bye-bye," "cookies and milk."

★   ★   ★

OLIVIER AND A man I've never met before are laughing together by the pool. Or rather it seems Olivier's trying to unbury the laughter from deep within his friend. Laure and I come down the hill, barefoot, our toenails shiny with the same pale pink polish from Laure's *jeune fille* makeup kit.

"*C'est Thibault! Un nouveau cerf-volant pour moi, pour moi.*" A new kite, for me. Laure runs to the man and jumps in his arms. She kisses him and then grabs the kite he's holding. Just as she goes to grasp the string, the kite starts floating up into the sky.

We all watch as the thin sheets of rice paper and bamboo— bright reds and deep browns—in the shape of an Eskimo bird mask flap away from us. Thibault pulls the string again, and the bird swoops down just above the child's head, within her reach. She shrieks with silky pleasure.

Olivier introduces me to his friend. "Tee-boe," I pronounce. He's a few years younger than Olivier and hungry looking. He stands lopsided, one leg slightly longer than the other. He stares at me, his eyes the color of afternoon thunderstorms. For an instant, I feel my own paper-thin weightlessness.

"*Je suis enchanté,*" he whispers.

I, too, am enchanted. His scent rises and mixes with the fragrant fruit trees. He smells strongly of something familiar, pungent and pleasant at once—like something retrieved from deep in the earth after a long time.

Laure jumps down and takes Thibault's hand, leads him proudly up the hill to fly the kite with her. I watch as he limps alongside. She is running and laughing child's laughter with a strange, funny-smelling man who can delight with wind and skies, and I watch her, suddenly wishing I were paper and wood, attached to the earth by a string. I take Olivier's hand in case he has sensed the slightest ambiguity in my thoughts, but he hasn't; he never does.

"I've invited Thibault to stay for dinner. He lives in the hills beyond the route d'Apt, makes these one-of-a-kind kites for a living. I'm trying to help him out." And then, as if he had never thought it before, Olivier adds, "I need to take care of him, like a brother."

I nod yes because I understand his words, even though I don't know this strange longing invading my bones and my blood. He smells like Grammy's refrigerator. "Your sister's coming, too," I answer distractedly. "And your friend, that woman you sent me to meet in the village—"

"Flora?"

"She's asked me to take her to the clinic in Marseille tomorrow. Is it cancer?"

He nods. "Where's her new lover, what's-his-name?"

I shrug. "I told her I'd accompany her."

"Are you going to be okay driving to Marseille?"

I nod. Olivier knows I hate to drive. I am always getting lost in this new landscape, am hesitant when it comes to on-ramps, tolls, and merges.

THE FIRST TIME I met Flora, last Monday morning at the market in Forcalquier, I was to stop by her studio and drop off photographs from our trip to Greece that Olivier wanted framed by Flora. She has known Olivier and Dominique for years. According to Sophie, Olivier has saved her many times in this life, and although Dominique tries to get information about Olivier from her, he knows that Flora's loyalty to him is unfailing.

Before I could find her studio, I stopped along the way, intrigued by a short, thick woman wrapped in layers of bright silks and linens, bickering with another dark, feisty woman at the olive stand.

"*Puta!*" the dark woman yelled, and spat at the ground. "My husband will lose a television over this, that two-timing prostitute of shit." She stared at the crowd that had gathered as if she were about to cast a spell and then disappeared instantly. I pretended to be sampling the green and black tapenades the olive vendor was promoting that day.

"*Ahh, bah voilà* . . . You must be Keem," the colorful woman said, pointing to the photos. "*Enchantée.*" Flora kissed me on both cheeks and apologized for the scene as she paid for a large wedge of *fromage d'abondance*. She turned to me and smiled, and then, shifting her produce in the basket to fit the cheese, she frowned up at the sky. "I just can't seem to make her understand that it's her husband's love that can save me," Flora said in her Provençal-accented French.

I must have looked confused, because Flora went on to explain that she had been seeing the Portuguese woman's husband, Jean-Marie, for several months now. "But it's not what you think," she added quickly, lowering her eyes.

I didn't know what to think as I walked with her silently through the village. Children waved, and various people called out, "*Flora, ça va mieux aujourd'hui?*" She waved back, smiling. I remember being struck by her lack of dramatic intonation, as if everyone knew that only love could remedy the disease that had already eaten away at one of her breasts and was now spreading to her lungs.

OLIVIER AND THIBAULT go through my room to the cellar to choose the wines for dinner. Laure's up on the hill, tied to the end of the bird mask, skipping along to the child's music in her head. She stops for a moment to wave at me. A half-erased moon is already pressing itself into the sky, although it's not quite night. How much closer it appears on this side of the ocean.

Of those Olivier trusts, I'm most drawn to and amused by Flora. Tonight, instead of a crazy hat, she shows up for dinner wearing a turban of muted colors. Her hair's slowly growing back after the second round of chemotherapy treatments, and she is always radiant, laughing despite the cancers growing slowly in her body, the stains spotting her lungs. She's abundant in her flesh, and tonight she's wearing a bright blue djellaba with slits up both sides to reveal thick, muscular calves.

She arrives carrying a basket of wild scarlet strawberries and black *trompettes de la mort* mushrooms. She offers me a picture-less frame made of opalescent razor-clam shells. That's what she does, builds frames of every material she can find—chicken wire, metal from broken fences, and chunks of broken stone— to capture what other people want enclosed. Then she holds out the palm of her hand and asks me to close my eyes. I smell something musty, irregular to the touch.

"Une truffe." A summer truffle, she explains, marbled cream on the inside, not as pungent or prized as the black winter truffles. Olivier takes it from me, kisses Flora thanks, and places the gift in a jar of arborio rice.

Everything about Flora points to the sky, one earring like a shooting star. Even her voice is lifted, floating toward some unrelenting god of good health. Her arms are solid, and as she hugs little Laure and Lulu, I too long for my mother, real or adoptive—one whose shape I can't recall, the other whose touch is of distant kindness and disapproval.

Flora has what my grandfather would call spunk, joie de vivre. She's what I would have wished a mother to be—

courageous with the qualities of a dying heroine. "Men," Flora told me that first day at the market, "sometimes don't know what to do with so much abundance in a woman. They don't know where to store all the love we have to give."

She and Thibault forgo the customary kiss, clasp hands instead and exchange knowing looks before joining us. Thibault's not laughing like the others, but staring. I can feel his presence from across the room but I pretend not to notice because they're all here—Sophie and Serge, Lulu and Laure, Flora, Pascale, and Olivier—gathered around me, expectant, as if I'm here to breathe life into the main artery that is Olivier's house. Instead, I offer up smoked duck breast slices wrapped around almond-stuffed prunes to accompany the apéritif. Olivier's glowing as he pours generous portions of cold Prosecco, some with wild peach pulp for Bellinis. The phone rings in the glass-enclosed alcove, and I rush to answer it.

"*Puis-je parler avec Laure?*" It's Dominique, asking for her daughter. The few times I've answered the phone when she calls, I immediately passed it over to Olivier or Laure. But tonight I feel different.

I make the first move. "May I ask who's calling?"

"It's . . . uh . . . Laure's mother," she responds, caught off guard.

Olivier knows immediately from my tone and whispers, "Tell her that Laure is playing with Lulu."

Somewhere deep inside, I enjoy telling Dominique that her daughter is unavailable, no matter how imperfect my French.

"*Passez-moi Olivier.*" Then I want to speak with Olivier, she says in that clipped Parisian accent I'm still trying to emulate. I hold the phone out to him, but he refuses to take her call.

"*Bien,* tell *my husband* that I need five thousand francs tomorrow to send to Laure's school before the start of classes, and he can throw in a couple thousand more because I want to buy some new clothes." Just when I think it's over, she adds, "Oh, and I'll stop by next week to get more of my things. My panties and bras, I trust, are still in the dresser?"

Olivier's explaining something to his sister as I hang up the receiver. I decide to take a deep breath, swallow the last drops in my flute, before opening my eyes again. They're waiting for me in the other room. I can hear their watered-down voices coming to me like an undertow. Her panties and bras have been in an upstairs room for over a year now since she moved out. I never allow myself to go in there, but I did, once.

"*Ça va, Kim?*" It's Thibault. His hand's on my shoulder, and I freeze, inexplicably wanting to go to him for some sort of comfort. Why didn't Olivier just take the call? "I'm sorry if I've frightened you," Thibault continues. I look at him, not really understanding. "I know you. I mean, as if from some other time . . . Never mind . . . I can't explain. It's like the birds I draw in my mind."

The phone rings again, and Thibault gestures to answer, but I take the phone before he does, determined to be unyielding if it's her again.

"*Allo?*"

"Kim Sunée?" It's an American voice. "What time is it over there?"

"Grammy?"

"Are you all right? Where have you been?" She yells to my grandfather that I'm alive. "Your mother says she hasn't talked to you in a while."

I shake my head, almost wishing it had been Dominique instead. "Olivier and I were in Greece. Didn't you get my postcard?"

"Sweetheart. When are you coming home?"

I want to answer that I am home but instead ask, "How's Poppy? What's he cooking right now?"

"I need your address again. Those French words are so hard." My grandmother pauses as she always does to hum and worry. "If you don't come back soon, we're just going to have to come over there and get you. Do you know I bought a new address book just for all the times you've moved? Let's see, there's Nice, Stockholm, Aix-en-Provence, and now this place called . . . Pierrerue?"

Pascale is lighting candles. She gestures for me to join them. I motion back to start without me.

"Grams," I say, "we're getting ready to have dinner."

She pauses to sigh heavily and hands the phone to my grand-father. "How's my chowhound?" he booms, and I am immedi-ately back in his kitchen. "I've made crawfish pies and stuffed artichokes with crabmeat."

We send kisses to each other over the phone, and Grammy gets back on to say that my parents have been talking about wanting to come to Provence and that she and my grandfather will also try to make a trip over. "It's so far . . . I don't know if I can make it all the way there."

Just when I am about to remind her that they made it to Ire-land and London three years ago, that I would love for them to visit, Olivier comes to me, holding out a piece of baguette drip-ping in olive oil. He puts it in my mouth and takes the phone to tell my grandmother in his soft, elementary English that "*allo* . . . yes . . . good . . . we . . . uh . . . call back yesterday." He nods, says, "Bye-bye, I tell to her," and hangs up.

Before I can object, Olivier is gathering us all at the table, directing everyone to their seats.

"How are things going?" Pascale asks, scooting in next to me. "My brother"—she nods in Olivier's direction—"even with the best of intentions, can sometimes be . . . overwhelming?" She laughs. "Always starting this project, helping out some artist or other. But he's in love, openly . . . we've never seen him so happy . . . not like our father." Before I can respond, she glances at Thibault, who is settling in next to Flora. "That man intrigues me. Always has," she whispers.

I'm not thinking about Thibault, but his scent of freshly dug earth suddenly sends me to the truffle Olivier placed in the rice jar. I wonder how long it needs to stay in there to fully penetrate the grains with its chewy aroma.

"So," Thibault says, smiling at Pascale while talking to me, "Olivier tells me you're a poet."

"Not really," I mutter. "But I do miss writing workshops, you don't really have those here in France, and I try—"

"*Elle est ma petite poète,*" Olivier answers. I cringe. My little poet. He raises his glass to propose a toast. "*J'aime le hasard. Le destin.*" Chance. Destiny. "*A la poésie.*" he says, smiling. We all raise our glasses.

"*A l'amour.*" Thibault raises his glass.

When Sophie gets up to start serving the first course, Serge stands and I'm thankful that there will be some comic relief.

"My turn." He clears his throat, letting out a roaring belch. "To this soon-to-be-finished construction site," he says, raising his glass. While he has everyone's attention, he starts recounting Dominique's latest ploy—her attempts at shaming Olivier into giving her more money. He tells the story as I imagine him holding court down at the village bar—the rich man's caretaker as the others buy him drinks in exchange for his embellishments. "She's telling everyone"—he hesitates—"that Olivier has to give her the house. This house that I take care of—that Olivier paid for"—he looks around and fixes his watery green eyes on me—"and that Kim is now the mistress of."

"But she never really lived in this house," Pascale protests, and for an instant I think she's talking about me. "She only wanted Olivier to buy it if she could have an apartment in Paris—*quelle petite bourgeoise!*" Pascale puts her lips together and puffs out an air of disgust, shaking her head.

"Children, go play outside," Sophie commands.

"But what about dessert?" Lulu whines.

"*Allez!*" Flora stomps her foot, and Laure and Lulu scatter away like frightened crows.

Serge lifts another bottle of Bordeaux—the Calon-Ségur I like that's rich and creamy—and gestures to Olivier, who nods approval before opening it. Serge smiles at me and proposes a toast—"To Keem." I want to disappear, but I also want Serge to continue. I want to hear it all, no matter what it will cost my heart.

"She says that Laure loves this house and won't understand why her mother isn't in it with her—why a stranger is in her mother's place, and—"

"And she told Laure that she didn't even have enough money to buy her candy at the store," Sophie interrupts. Serge shoots her a look. "I heard her the other day at the bank," she adds, passing the basket of bread as I serve seared scallops and confit of shallot with a saffron beurre blanc.

"*C'est délicieux,*" Thibault exclaims, sopping up the bright yellow sauce with his bread. "If she's as good a poet as she is a cook . . ." He winks at me.

My face feels hot. Olivier, on the other side of me, laughs lightly, shaking his head, opening a bottle of Condrieu. "*Incroyable.* I've got it all under control. I've already talked to Laure about most of this. She's eight . . . she understands a lot more than we think."

The children dart in and out of the room.

"Papa, can we have dessert now? Kimette made American cookies just for the kids." Laure leans into me, licking her lips.

I am grateful for her gourmandise. I bring out the warm chocolate oatmeal cookies on a platter for the children while Sophie clears the cheese plates and serves apricot *clafoutis*. Olivier opens a bottle of *vin cuit*, Domaine de Cazès. The apricots are tart-sweet against the creamy custard. I swallow the amber liquid of wine, hoping it will flood me fast.

After dessert and prune *eau de vie*, Pascale tells us good night. Thibault follows shortly after, lingering softly on each of my cheeks after kissing the others good-bye. I lead Flora to one of the guest rooms, my favorite with hand-rubbed ruby walls. I lay out a white linen nightshirt and fresh ecru towels.

"What time do you want to leave in the morning?" I ask, placing a small glass and an unopened bottle of Volvic water on the bedside table.

"I don't—but I have to be at the clinic for ten. The treatment lasts five hours, you know."

I nod.

Flora begins to undress slowly, hiding herself behind the door to the bathroom. When she's finished putting on the nightshirt, she slides quickly into bed, pulling the covers up to her neck.

"I'm cold—it's freezing in here." Flora's cough is thunderous.

"There's a warm breeze, but I'll shut the window." I go to turn off the light, then sit at the edge of the bed, tucking the covers snugly around her feet and legs. She looks like a mummy.

"*Merci, Maman,*" Flora jokes.

The kids burst into the room, smelling of sweets and sweat, to kiss her good night.

"*Bonne nuit, Flora,*" Lulu says, rubbing her eyes.

"*Bonne nuit, les enfants.*" Flora hugs the children to her one last time, and when she thinks they've left, she slowly unwraps the turban to reveal a thin fuzzy layer of hair, the only visible sign of her illness. The children let out a squeal of shock. Sophie calls for Lulu, who runs out of the room, gasping. Laure tugs at my hand, backing toward the door, staring at Flora's head.

"*Tu viens?*" Are you coming? she whispers, keeping her eyes fixed on Flora.

"Your father's going to read you a story tonight, I'll be in later."

She hugs me, burying her eyes in my neck. I whisper not to stare, not to be afraid, and send her on her way.

"Keem," Flora says before I leave the room. I wonder if I've forgotten something, an extra blanket or tissues. "Thibault," she says, suppressing a cough, "he likes you, very much."

I feel myself blushing.

"I've known him for many years. He's a charming, isolated soul." She hesitates. "He needs love, like all of us, I suppose, but sometimes he looks in the dangerous places."

I shake my head. "Let me know if you need anything else," I tell her.

"*Allez, bonne nuit.*" Go on, good night.

When I make my way back into the kitchen, I see Sophie from behind, her shoulders trembling in the last of the candlelight. When she hears me approaching, she turns to the wall.

"Sophie?"

"*Ça va, tout va bien.*" Her lovely brown eyes are swollen and thick with tears.

"I loved the dessert you made tonight—the best *clafoutis* I've ever tasted," I offer. Sophie tries to catch her breath but starts crying again as water fills up in the sink. "I'll rinse off the plates. Go on. Zorah's coming early tomorrow to clean."

"Ah, Keem—" She sighs deeply. "I speak English with you now—no one understand except you, okay?"

I nod, turn off the faucet, take the dishtowel from her, and lead her out of the kitchen into the night. We stand for a moment in silence, watching the sky.

"You know what it means to love someone even if it is no more possible?" She looks at me and then begins to laugh. "But of course not. You are so young, and Olivier is so in love with you." She lights a hand-rolled cigarette. "He is my age, Olivier, but I am so old already."

We walk past her house and down the hill to the pool, sit at the edge with our feet dangling in the water. Sophie leans down to rub her feet. Her ankles look unusually swollen, bruised. She catches my eyes and blows smoke rings to distract me. We watch them one by one float up into the air.

"You see that?" Sophie asks, pointing to the rings. "That is my life with Serge—light like smoke, but also toxic." She laughs again—a delightful, resigned laughter that puts me at ease.

"Sophie?" Serge's voice is a sharp sword. Sophie jumps up and puts out her cigarette. *"Soph— Au lit, tout de suite."* To bed, immediately.

"J'arrive," she yells. She blows me a kiss from the dark. "Tomorrow, I make breakfast for you and Flora before you go to the doctor." She stops and turns to me. "It is very nice to have you here . . . in the house. It is good for everyone."

On my way back up to the kitchen, I hear Olivier calling for me, too. "Laure wants us to tuck her in." Laure's and Olivier's voices come to me from the open window. "You're getting too big, I can hardly carry you anymore." I see Olivier silhouetted against the curtain. He feigns a minor heart attack, almost dropping Laure, which sends the child into an uncontrollable fit of laughter.

"I'll be up in a minute," I answer, reaching to pick a few plums.

The cool night air feels good on my face. I spread out my arms to balance myself in the wind. My head is full of wine and the movements of the evening—Olivier always making sure everyone knows his place, his unquestionable way of making the world turn in his direction. And I must call Grammy back after Olivier so quickly ended our conversation. I hear my grandmother's voice telling me she'll come and get me if I don't come home soon. I allow myself a small tipsy moment to believe that this could be home, that here is where I can make a difference. And maybe a place where I can begin to belong.

ON OUR WAY back home from the clinic in Marseille, Flora asks me to take the small roads along the coast. Highways make her sleepy and sad. "You never know if you're coming or going," she tells me, rolling her window all the way down, opening her mouth wide to gulp the fresh summer air. The high wind lifts her spirits, whips her magenta scarf playfully, but she coughs instantly. *"Merde."*

I push the central control button to roll her window halfway up. "Dr. Eskandari warned you about catching cold, Flora," I remind her, and regret it instantly. She pops in a cassette tape she's brought with her. *"J'ai deux amours,"* she sings charmingly off-key. She lights up a cigarette, inhales once, watching me out of the corner of her eye. I pretend to sing along as Flora finally tosses the cigarette out the window and rests her head back an instant.

I like being on the road but am afraid when driving; that's why Olivier bought me the tank—a 1986 Saab injection—a wink to our meeting in Sweden. Charcoal gray and, although not brand new, undeniably solid and reliable. But with Flora in the passenger seat, I am not as afraid, I feel strong and responsible. I want to impress her, although she's the one who gives me directions.

"Cassis," she says out of the blue. "Has Olivier taken you to Cassis yet?"

I shrug.

"*Allons-y*. A small port town with tons of outdoor cafés."

Because of the latest tests, which seemed to confuse the doctors, they decided to reschedule her five-hour treatment and instead run a series of different tests, which lasted two hours. I know she can't possibly think of food, but I must admit, I wouldn't mind stopping in Cassis.

"You have to eat," she tells me, reading my mind. "I just need to sit by the sea."

The waiter leads us to a portside table for two. The water is many shades of blue agate and green, the *calanques* in the backdrop stark white and rugged. A multitude of leisure boats bob up and down, eager for their owners—older men in crisp whites with slim women in capris and tortoiseshell sunglasses. I am acutely aware of entering a life portrayed mostly in movies with subtitles.

"How do you feel, Flora?"

"I feel like shit." She laughs lightly, wrinkles tightening around her faded green eyes. It's the first time I've heard her complain. "I've got one breast. Hair like a newborn, and my whole body's polluted with all those chemicals they love putting through my veins." She studies the sea like an impenetrable watercolor. "Let's have some wine," she says, summoning the waiter. "A bottle of Cassis blanc."

Flora wipes the rim of her glass, jingling the multicolored

bangles on her swollen wrist. She sips the wine, not really drinking. I know she's trying to have a good time, for my sake.

"Flora, maybe we should get back—"

"There are lots of things you shouldn't miss," she says suddenly, not really even looking at me. The waiter brings menus, but I shake my head. I'm ravenous but refuse to eat in Flora's presence. *"Si, elle mange."*

She whispers something to the waiter, who nods and returns promptly with the bottle of wine and a small white dish of black olives. The wine is crisp and lingers brightly on the tip of my tongue. The waiter reappears with a platter of freshly opened sea urchins, small rounds of bread and cold salted butter, and then a first course of lightly roasted scallops with the coral still attached, salty sea flesh like thick pink commas.

"Tu aimes la bourride?" Velvety fish stew.

I nod slowly, still not sure if I should insist on driving Flora home immediately. The doctor said she needed to rest. But then the waiter sets down a fragrant bowl of whitefish, *loup* and *baudroie*, in front of me, with aioli croutons.

"Mange." Flora pours the rest of the first bottle of Cassis into my glass, then orders a rosé. *"C'est la fête,"* she tells the waiter, winking.

"Just like my grandfather, feeding me."

"How's your family?"

"I don't really know. My grandmother calls, sometimes my mother . . . I think they're going to come and visit . . . but no one else really . . . calls that often." I dip a piece of crusty bread into the warm saffron sauce, thinking of those across the ocean. As the wine gently floods me, my thoughts whip through me like a hot sirocco. "And Thibault?" I ask, surprised by my curiosity.

But Flora responds as if she's been waiting for the question. "I loved Thibault once. Many years ago . . ." Her voice drifts off. "He was living with an older woman. Much older."

"How much?"

"At least ten years."

I wait patiently but wanting more.

"She fell ill," Flora continues. "Actually she was schizophrenic, and the family put her in an institution, near Digne. They took all her money. I think he was relieved in a way. He couldn't stand not being remembered when she'd become someone else."

I nod. Not being remembered. "And you showed up?"

"We've known each other forever. Centuries and centuries. Olivier, too. Different circles, though." Flora sips her wine, rolls a piece of crust between her thumb and forefinger. "One day, after driving back from Digne, Thibault showed up at my door. I made him soup, and he slept for twenty-two hours straight. When he woke up, I drew him a hot bath and we . . . you know . . ." She takes a sip and then another of the cool rosé, which actually flushes into her cheeks. "To get it out of the way. Then we spent the next weeks smoking a lot and taking walks up to the observatory . . . have you been up there yet? We'd sit at the highest point of the hill and play games about the stars. Pretend they were people we'd like to see again . . ." Flora's voice drifts off, and for a moment I think she's censoring herself for my sake.

"Who did you want to see again?" I ask quietly. "The living or the dead?"

"For me, the living, without a doubt. The dead can stay where they are."

"And Thibault?"

"Definitely the dead. He lost his older sister. She was sixteen.

A car ran over her, right in front of him. He loved her"—she pauses—"more than any woman he's ever loved."

"Did you love him?"

"I did. I do. But Thibault loves his kites and birds, wind and paper, things of the floating world—I think that's why he likes you."

"Flora . . ."

"It's nothing to be ashamed of—"

"But Olivier, he gives me everything—"

"Nothing to do with it. You're a woman. There will be other men who will fall in love with you, if there's Olivier or no Olivier. And I suspect you'll do the same." She waits, daring me to object again. "That's the way it is. And Thibault coming to me after losing that woman doesn't mean he loved me more, or for what I was." She leans close to my face. "He loved me, I'm sure of it, but also and mainly . . . because I was a *continuation*."

"Is that what we are?" I protest a little too loudly. I lower my voice, concentrating on counting the veins pulsing in her temple, imagining the silent cells multiplying.

"When it comes to love. I don't mean convention or morals, but *un vrai amour*. We continue what others didn't finish or left behind. I hate to say it, *ma petite,* but it has nothing to do with *us*."

"And the day I met you at the market. Who did you say that woman was—the one who was screaming at you?"

"My lover's wife. *Une portugaise*. She's crazy. Throws a television out the window for every infidelity."

"Does she know you're . . . sick?"

"The whole village knows. But ever since I met Jean-Marie, I've been better. He makes love to me, *tu imagines* . . . to this mangled radioactive body." She pauses to touch her neck, her shoulder, her heart. "I'm not a monster. I don't want to take him away from his wife. I just want the bit of love he can give me. I'm barely forty years old, and I don't know how much longer I'll be around. Do you understand that?" she asks, suddenly exasperated.

I look down at my half-eaten bowl of food, no longer hungry. Perhaps she thinks I am too young, too healthy, too American, to understand any of this. We watch the flow of people around us arriving and departing, and I think how we all go where love is.

"Look at Sophie," Flora finally says.

"What about her? You mean Serge?"

"Men are crazy about her. But Serge has her under his thumb. He's the only man she's ever known."

"I noticed some bruises on Sophie's ankle. Do you think—"

"He used to be . . . intriguing, witty . . . before the alcohol."

The waiter clears my plate, returns with small bowls of lemon water and a clean napkin while Flora insists on paying. He offers us a digestif, and Flora accepts readily. I order an espresso before the long drive back.

Flora's sleepy now, so it doesn't matter if we take the highway back, she says. Halfway there, she asks me to stop at the rest stop, she needs to vomit. While she's gone, I hum along with Gainsbourg and Birkin on the radio. Her cell phone rings.

"*Allo?*"

"Who is this?" a man's voice asks with irritation.

"It's Kim. Flora will be right back."

"Tell her Jean-Marie called. I can't make it tonight." He hangs up.

When Flora gets back in the car, I'm still trying to figure out how to disconnect. "Did he call?"

I nod, handing her a bottle of water and a fresh napkin. She wipes her mouth and forehead, then sighs as I give her the message and shift into first gear.

"Did he say *why* he couldn't see me?"

I shake my head, silent, accelerating to merge. I take the highway, speed past villages and mountains. Flora sleeps on and off. The fading light over the hills in the distance plays games, shadows like forgotten souls. A light freeze and the cool mountain air from the hills of Provence make me want to drive faster and farther. Speeding until it all becomes a blur, hazy and white.

Flora snores with her mouth wide open, but when I pull into the gravel driveway, she jolts awake. The wide iron gate is open, swinging back and forth with the force of the mistral, blocked by a car I don't recognize. Flora rubs her eyes.

"*Merde. Elle est là.*" She's here.

"*Qui?*" Who, I ask.

"*Elle.*"

Just then I realize that *elle* is Dominique. She's in such a hurry, pulling little Laure along by the hand, I don't have time to realize what's happening. They both see me as I drive up, their eyes wide like animals caught in headlights. Laure looks at her mother pleadingly and then at me. Dominique flashes a wicked smile. I always imagined her beautiful from the pictures I've seen, but her face is weathered with hatred, creviced with bitterness, her short black hair wild in the relentless wind.

"*Monte!*" she howls. Her voice is cracked ice as she yells at Laure to get in the car. Dominique turns on the motor and revs the engine, but there's nowhere to go because she has to wait for me to back up in order to get out. I relish this small power I have over her but relinquish. She accelerates and speeds past, little Laure in the backseat of the silver Renault—her panicked face a blur as she waves to me from the half-opened window.

Olivier's in the kitchen on the phone. He takes my hand and pulls me toward him as he says departing words to his lawyer. Sophie stands up to greet me, hugging me longer than is custom. Serge offers hot tea, gesturing for me to sit.

"You must be tired," he says, patting me on the shoulder.

I look to Flora, who has understood immediately. She's holding the local newspaper, reading out loud. On the front page of *Le Provençal* is Olivier's face, smiling at the camera. PROVENÇAL INDUSTRIALIST WORTH MILLIONS. Flora shows me the continued article on page three. In the upper right-hand corner is a picture I don't recall. A charity event, the two of us, and a caption in French: "Olivier Baussan, founder of L'Occitane, and his new companion." I turn to Olivier, who's hanging up the phone, nodding.

"Olivier's furious," Serge explains. "That the paper would print something like this. Then Dominique showed up, came back from vacationing in Saint-Tropez, packed up Laure, and stormed out of here, screaming about wanting more money. *She's* furious. Humiliated."

Olivier sits with Flora, Sophie, Serge, and me around the table. The newspaper is spread open before us, like a battle plan.

"What's going on?" I ask Olivier. "Did you know they were writing this article?"

"They interviewed me when Indosuez bought L'Occitane. But that was ages ago. Serge brings me the paper this morning with my croissant, and—"

"And Dominique refuses shared custody, divorce, unless there's a lot more money on the table," Flora finishes.

"She read WORTH MILLIONS and saw green." Serge laughs.

"Don't you have a bar to go to?" Flora asks him, annoyed.

"I'm not worth millions, it's the company."

"What about Laure?" I ask. "I thought she was here for the rest of the summer." I take some magazines and newspapers, the only American ones I can get in this small part of Haute-Provence, and sit in the worn leather chesterfield on the other side of the room.

"Dominique just took her away. She showed up and told her to pack her things, poor Laure in tears . . ."

"That's one thing that I will *not* tolerate." Olivier gets up from the table and starts dialing from both his cell phone and the house line.

Flora, Sophie, and Serge sit around the table whispering, flipping through the paper, organizing a plan of attack. I don't want to read it. Instead, I flip through *Time* and other newsmagazines that Serge buys for me in the village sometimes. Photos of strange faces with a blur of headlines. MONGOLIANS HAVE TEN DAYS TO CHANGE NAME. CLINTON TALKS OF LOVE ON CHINESE RADIO. SREBENICA, FLOODS OF UPROOTED WOMEN AND CHILDREN WAITING FOR FURTHER NOTICE. One of the articles catches my eye: "Missing Children Often Kidnapped by Own Parents." There are several photos of milk cartons and weathered posters thumbtacked crookedly to trees and random walls.

LATER, OLIVIER'S LONGTIME colleague Marie-Claire and some lawyers arrive at the house for an apéritif. They convene like generals preparing for war. It's the first time I've seen Olivier this anxious and tired. Angry. He's acute and swift, and I realize that his wrath is to be feared. I leave them to go and sit in the other room. The phone rings several times before Olivier gestures for me to answer.

"*Allo?*"

There's silence and then the sound of ice cracking again.

"*C'est parfait. C'est la chinetoque? Passez-moi Olivier.*"

"*Il est occupé.*" He's busy, I tell her.

"*Je m'en fous.*" I don't give a shit. "Next time he'll be talking to *my* lawyers." The dead on the end of the line is a relief. I hang up the phone and decide to bury myself in bed. I take the Larousse with me to look up *chintok* in the dictionary but can't find it.

I slide myself between the cold bedsheets before Olivier comes to warm them up. I will pretend to be asleep when he comes.

"Kimette? *Tu dors?*" I hold my breath and listen as his footsteps echo into the room. Olivier sits next to me, his body finding the familiar dent in our bed. "I'm sorry for all this—"

"She won't take Laure far—"

"She likes money too much to go too far."

"Olivier, what's *chintok?*"

"*Chinetoque?* Did she call you that? *Putain!*"

"Tell me. I want to know."

He shakes his head. "It's vulgar. Pejorative for . . . Chinese—"

"But I'm not Chinese—"

"Of course not. But you're all the same to her."

I pull the covers up to my neck.

"I'll go see everyone out, turn the lights off, and I'll be right back." He kisses my cheek. "Are you crying?"

"Of course not," I lie, turning my back to face the wall. I just want to be alone. I know that Olivier can sense when I'm slipping away from him and sometimes even from myself. It's happened before, but he accepts the dark parts of me. He tells me, though, how he wishes he could take it all away—whatever it is that haunts me. He says he can make more than enough money but that when he feels the nightmares seep into my body at night and the way I clutch him close, he wishes more than anything to be an alchemist, to turn my darkness into gold—something precious that he can give back.

"*Chintok*," I whisper to myself when Olivier has left the room. Chink. Gook. Sounds of words that become swords. To Dominique I am an object, for Olivier a treasure. A precious chinoiserie. I try to sleep. Pray for sleep. I close my eyes. Sticks and stones may break my bones, but words will always hurt me. Beneath my eyelids, a kaleidoscope of colors and voices. The bright kites in the sky, jewel-colored wine with Flora, Laure's drawing of her new family . . . lopsided smiles on our round, happy Crayola-colored faces. I want to remember Dominique, the cold stone face, what she was wearing—something tight and maroon colored, surprisingly sensible shoes. "Go to sleep," I whisper. "Breathe." Prune-colored lipstick. She is the mother of Olivier's child; her deep-set eyes and jawline clenched like an animal about to pounce. Why her? And then I remember that night with Olivier in Stockholm . . .

HAVING DINNER ONE evening, he made the mistake of telling me that he was the one who'd wanted a daughter—Dominique refusing to ruin her perfect figure, "the ultimate triangle," she called it—and how he'd begged her, not out of love, but out of frustration and a need for regeneration. We were at our favorite restaurant in central Stockholm, and that was the night he had planned on asking me to come to France, but I never gave him the chance.

"How could you beg a woman you no longer love to bear your child?" I insisted on knowing, cutting into the bloody filet of reindeer on my plate.

"You can't understand," he told me sadly, shaking his head.

"Why, because I'm too young?" I knew I sounded puerile but couldn't stop there. It was the closest we had ever come to arguing.

"I just wanted a daughter before it was too late. And I don't regret—I adore my daughter. You'll see when you meet her. She's nothing like her mother."

"But you claim you no longer loved—"

"I never loved her in that way." Olivier took my hands in his. I wanted to believe him, and then I heard him say, "Please stop. You can't know." He lowered his voice. "You were adopted."

I got up before he could stop me, before he could take back the words. Somehow I found myself in the ladies' room. The metal door was cold against my forehead. Someone flushed, and the sound of water made me want to cry. I will not cry, I promised myself. I am made of steel and carbon. I made my way back to the table, and Olivier was sitting there, waiting. No more questions, I wanted to reassure him. I let out a deep breath, but before I could stop, I heard myself say, "So why did you marry her? Why did you live with her for so long? Was it because of her beauty, her perfect triangle?" I despised myself for such questions, such lack of control. But I didn't want lies— any misunderstandings.

"She wasn't beautiful really. Vulgar—big breasts, pouty mouth, sassy. It was a challenge, I guess. I don't know."

I could feel it rising in me—all of the things I hated about myself: the ugly childhood bruises on my arms and legs and the darkness of my hair and skin. I hugged my sweater tight around me. "And you like these, after all that?" I asked, pointing to my chest.

"Keem!" Olivier looked appalled, and I was instantly sorry.

"*Excuse-moi.*"

"I've told you. Dominique and I have lived separate lives for the past ten years. I thought I was stuck with her, so I plunged myself into my work. It's banal, but true."

The waiter brought more wine and hard bread. I took one of the rounds and broke it in two, spreading cold butter on both halves. I handed one across the table. "Olivier?"

He looked up at me, anxious, taking the bread. He had told me from the beginning that he would always tell me the truth because he knew what it meant to me, and he always said he had nothing to hide.

"Do you see me as Asian or a woman?" I traced my finger along the rim of the glass and then caught my reflection upside down in the spoon.

"Well . . ." He thought. "You're a woman, of course, so I guess I see you as Asian."

"You see me as *Asian*? And Dominique?"

"She's a woman." Olivier didn't understand what I was doing. Why I insisted so. "*Ça suffit.* I beg you." There were tears in his eyes. "Why can't you just accept that I love you?"

I wanted to, but I couldn't say it. I was fighting a private battle about who I was, an identity I didn't understand. No one else was going to fight for me, so I had to carry valiantly on. "In other words"—I paused while the waiter gave us the check—"I'm not first and foremost a woman."

I remember stopping myself from crying silently into my food and then later on at the apartment, in the kitchen, Olivier anxious at the stove, waiting for water to heat to make tea. I flipped through the UNICEF calendar with its monthly photo of a different child in the world, left behind for lack of love. September: a village in Sudan destroyed by famine. November: a smiling emaciated boy playing with his little sister in a refuse pile of used tires and stagnant water. Each square had become a day and an event without Olivier—the exhibit he is sponsoring in Spain, a business trip to Dubai, his daughter's birthday. With each swallow of hot black tea, I thought of all the things I might never be—a woman with a perfect triangle, a good mother.

THE LAWYERS HAVE left. Olivier comes to me with a cup of hot oolong and gets in bed, balancing the saucer on his lap. After a while, he lets me sip the soothing liquid. I feel my flesh warm and thick. He kisses me, gently at first, waiting to feel what I want, then drinks me in. I'm with him. I'm not alone. My body reaches to meet his, open and wet, wanting him so much, not gently but voraciously. He touches me in the darkest regions, takes sips of tea in between, and then dives back between my legs, his tongue hot with a rush I've never felt before. When he enters me, I realize that I want it to hurt a little, some rawness mixed with tenderness. More than anything, I want Olivier to love me until there's nothing left. I want him to fill me whole, to drink me up until I disappear, until I am no longer discernible as a race or a gender, but just simply an empty shape that needs defining, filling in.

THE MISTRAL HAS decided to return to us—the third visit this August—chasing everything out of its path and causing strange cloud formations overhead. Olivier and I are not alone. The child is finally back, after Dominique unexpectedly took her away when she read the article in the paper. Laure is here with us, where Olivier claims she is rooted and safe, here in the rocking house. Although Laure's not as voluble as before the uprooting, she seems unshaken. Like her father, she's as solid as the sediments that form the mountainside from which this house was constructed.

The child, like the mistral, whips in and out of the house, playing chase with little Lulu, hesitating before plucking ripe fruit from the trees. I see her from the kitchen window, trembling an instant in the wind before disappearing. She reappears—coming up from behind me—and mimics the wind as she blows on the back of my neck and plays with my hair. She kisses me sloppily, then jumps in and out of our laps. She is cranky, pulling on Olivier's fingers, knocking the newspaper from my hands. The weather section floats to the floor, lands open to an article about the consequences of past, prolonged winds. Years ago, the mistral lasted a record one month in this part of Provence, turning people mad with the howling in their ears.

The laundry moves in a wicked dance attached to an unrelenting string. And every night, the animals move restless in their pins, anxious lovers turn to each other for comfort. I listen to the wind tear away branches, like missing limbs, like the broken hearts and bodies of those we lose and continue to love.

Thibault arrives at the house with a bouquet of sunflowers and some red poppies for little Laure. He looks at me as if to speak but takes Laure in his arms instead, whispering to her until she giggles in delight. Then she jumps out of his arms to count the number of poppies in her bouquet. The three of us sit at an outdoor table, the wind dying down.

"*Ça va, Olivier?* Laure seems to be doing okay."

Olivier nods, smiles at his daughter in the distance. "Two weeks of hell and negotiations with Dominique—I couldn't track her down."

"Are you pressing charges?"

"Absolutely not, only for Laure's sake. It's all about money, anyway. I'll find a way."

"I'm sure you will," Thibault replies.

The leaves rustle in a moment of agitated silence. I get up to offer *l'apéritif.*

"Just a quick one," Thibault says. "I haven't packed yet."

"Neither have we. Where are you off to?"

"Indonesia. Kite and paper festival."

Laure comes back to us, jumps on my lap. "Tomorrow I'm going to Corsica with Papa and Kimette," she announces to Thibault proudly. "*Maman* said I could go with them, even though she said Spain with her is much better."

"Spain," Olivier repeats, raising his brows.

"*Maman* said that you told her to take me, but it was a surprise."

Olivier reaches for his phone, maybe to call his lawyers again now that he has discovered where exactly Dominique had taken Laure. There's so much I don't understand about this custody battle.

"Laure, come help me in the kitchen, *chérie,*" I say. "We'll put your flowers in water, too."

The child takes my hand. On the island, I set out a large round platter the color of faded sunflowers. Laure steps in rhythm and takes out cotton print napkins with tiny yellow-and-green paisley print.

"Do these go with?"

I nod and hand her a wedge of Parmigiano-Reggiano, a handful of fresh figs. I wipe the small glasses for Lillet, and when I turn around, Laure has already arranged everything on the platter. She has even added some fresh herbs and shelled walnuts.

"Do you think Papa will like it?"

"*C'est très joli.*"

She giggles deeply. I make a pitcher of fresh strawberry lemonade for her, and she follows me out to the table with the platter.

"Maybe Thibault will stay longer," she whispers giddily to me, setting the food before the men as they ooh and aah. She clasps my hand in delight. "Just like Kimette, eh, Papa?"

I pour the golden liquid into the glasses, but before we can drink, Olivier's back in the house to answer the phone. When Thibault finally stands up to leave, Laure jumps in his arms to kiss him good-bye.

"Will you bring me a surprise from the kite festival?" she asks, hugging him tightly. "And something for Keem," she adds, gesturing for me to come close. She hangs on to Thibault but leans over and presses her cheek to mine.

"Don't forget us," she reminds him, running after the car. "I'll be right here." She stomps her foot firmly on the ground. Thibault waves good-bye.

"Where's Indonesia?" she asks as we make our way back to the house.

"In Asia."

"How far's that, to the moon and back?" She points to the sky, to her chest, and to the sky again, her freckles turning darker as her cheeks flush with the thrill of traveling such distances.

TRUFFLES

Aside from *la brouillade aux truffes* (my favorite way to eat scrambled eggs) I also like to use fresh truffles, both summer and winter, in some of the following ways:

For a surprising dessert I ate years ago in Saint-Paul-de-Vence: Whip together 1 (8-ounce) container softened mascarpone cheese with 1 cup powdered sugar until light and fluffy. Whip 1 cup whipping cream and fold into sweetened mascarpone. Shave, using a truffle slicer or vegetable peeler, some truffle slices and stir gently to combine. Cover and refrigerate at least 30 minutes. Serve in small, individual dessert cups and taste with Sauternes wine.

To satisfy guests before dinner: Toast baguette slices. Drizzle with extra-virgin olive oil; sprinkle with *fleur de sel* and shave truffle slices over.

Thinly slice crisp celery ribs and toss in a bowl with extra-virgin olive oil, *fleur de sel,* and cracked black pepper. Shave fresh truffle slices over and garnish with celery leaves.

Toss cooked fettuccini (or other pasta) with cream and shave truffles over. Sprinkle with *fleur de sel*, a crack of pepper, and, if desired, Parmigiano-Reggiano.

Before roasting chicken, slip slices of fresh truffle under the skin. Reserve the pan juices to make a sauce and stir in some truffle shavings.

Slip a truffle slice between 2 very thinly sliced potatoes. Brush with melted butter or extra-virgin olive oil and bake at 375 degrees until crisp and golden. Serve hot, sprinkled with a bit of *fleur de sel.*

Add chopped truffles to hot potatoes mashed with cream and salted butter.

VIII

BODIES OF WATER

❧

OLIVIER WANTS IT ALL PERFECT—OUR FIRST SUMMER VOYAGE together as a family—so Laure gets everything she asks for at Marseille-Marignane Airport. She wants green-and-yellow Eiffel Tower lollipops, glossy magazines, *herbes de Provence* in a terra-cotta jar, a music box with a smirking sailor that spins and sings "La Marseillaise." She shrugs nonchalantly when Olivier says yes to the makeup bag, to the T-shirt. Yes. Yes to it all because he doesn't want any contradictions. Yes to happiness no matter what form it takes or how much it costs.

On the small plane, there are only rows of two. So, yes, Laure can sit with Keem. Yes, she can change to sit with her father. Olivier looks to me, but I'm staring out the window, ignoring his plea for complicity. What can a child possibly do with so much? I want to ask him. Why can't a father just say no? Just then Laure crumples in my lap, crying with indecision. She doesn't know whether to sit with her father or with me. I caress the child's head, check for fever for no particular reason.

"*J'ai faim.*" I'm hungry, she whispers.

Luckily, I've remembered to bring Prince chocolate-filled cookies and Lu vanilla wafers, a small paper bag of ripe golden plums. Laure takes the cookies, licking the cream greedily, dropping crumbs on my arm.

"I'll sit with you," she says. "Papa can see us from across the aisle." She waves at him, and a huge chocolate-smeared smile lightens her face because she has finally made a decision. She leans her head on my shoulder, taking my hand in hers.

"I'm scared of flying," Laure whispers, her hand clammy with clumps of wet chocolate stuck under the nails. "Sing me a song, Kimette."

I tuck the child under one arm and kiss her cheek, tenderly, the way I think a mother should. I wish I could hum something comforting, but there are no soothing songs in my memory, just the fairy tales my grandmother used to make up, substituting me for the heroine. She used to begin the made-up stories the same way: "Once upon a time there was a little girl, her name was Kim Sunée, and she was hungry . . ." But when I read the books myself, I always turned to the middle of the story, anticipating the wicked witch or the poisoned apple.

THE AIR LITTORAL flight to Figari Sud Corse Airport lasts only an hour from Marseille but is still long enough for both Laure and me to feel the pain in our sinuses, excruciating needlepoints pricking constantly at the temples.

"Yawn," I tell the child, rubbing her temples. "Soon we'll be in the sea."

She finally falls asleep, her cookie-scented breath warm on my shoulder. Olivier winks at me from across the aisle as he turns to find a more comfortable position and then dozes off again. I envy their sleep, this gentle state of calm, as I rub my clammy palms on a wet napkin, thinking about anything other than crash landings, bombs planted in suitcases, separatist attacks on the island I've been hearing about on the news every night. I think of Flora and how I won't be able to take her for treatments while we're in Corsica. I think of all the people who would come to Olivier's funeral if something happened to him. Dominique, triumphant, taking little Laure away from me forever. She hates that we're traveling together as a family, but Laure's the one who wanted to spend the rest of the summer with us, the way it was planned from the beginning. I am starting to understand more about children and their boundaries, their heightened sense of what is just and bearable.

The drive from the airport to Roccapina in the south of Corsica is curved and sensuous. There are asphodel and bright golden genet, huge chestnut trees with their leaves spread out like wilted stars. I tell Laure and Olivier to roll all the windows down—let the odors of the island ride in the car with us. Laure lets her hand swoop along the wind, waves out the window, clapping her hands with delight. Olivier squeezes my knee.

"I love this country, this island. It's my childhood."

"Mine too," Laure adds proudly, her head popping up in the space between Olivier and me. Her eyes light up. "Remember, Papa, when we used to come with *Maman* . . . but she was always sick."

I glare at Olivier and then say softly, "I thought you said you never came here with her."

"Once or twice, but she despises Corsica. *Trop rustique,* I guess. Not bourgeois enough."

"Papa, what's bourgeois?"

We speed past rows of holm and cork oaks, fields of flowering thyme and rosemary. Finally, we stop at the edge of the fragrant maquis; beyond are a long stretch of golden sand and the Mediterranean.

"Voilà, Pascale." Olivier shields his eyes from the sun,

pointing to his sister and the others. Pascale and her lover, Thierry, are digging a hole in the ground next to their tent to store food. Marion, Pascale's child from a previous marriage, runs up the hill to greet her cousin. She's smaller than Laure, with thin brown hair. She waves at us.

"*Enfin.*" She sighs and throws her arms around Laure to give her a big hug. She reaches up to kiss me and pinches Olivier in the stomach. Olivier feigns unbearable pain and falls to the sand. For a moment, the girls look at each other in horror, and then they burst out laughing.

Pascale, Thierry, and the others who have come for the month are walking toward us. From a distance, they are a band of tanned stick figures, their smiles awkward and polite. As they get closer, they're an ambulant color ad for Club Med, in various states of undress—exuding good health and abundant sex.

Pascale's topless, wearing navy-and-white polka-dot bikini bottoms and a straw hat on her curly head of short black hair. She's only thirty-six, but her breasts are heavy, sagging. When Thierry gestures to greet me, I realize that he's wearing only a T-shirt that reaches just below his navel. His sex is hanging, swaying now as he moves to kiss me on each cheek. I glance at Olivier, who doesn't seem to notice. The others are mostly naked, too, except for a man with a pair of goggles dangling around his neck, and his wife, Françoise, stunning in a loosely wrapped red silk sarong. She kisses Olivier and hugs him a little longer than necessary. Then she turns, studies me from the top of my head to the tips of my toes. I bury my sandaled feet into the hot sand.

"*Bien sûr, vous êtes Kim dont tout le monde parle.*" You must be Kim everyone's been talking about. Her thin-lipped smile never changes as she leans down to kiss me. There are about twelve of us—Olivier's brother, Alain, and his wife, Annie, Pascale and Thierry's friends and their kids—all laughing, welcoming us to their colony.

"Je t'aide." Let me help you. Thierry lifts the weighted-down backpack from me and the bottles of water.

"Bienvenue en Corse—l'île de beauté," says a man completely naked except for his Dalí mustache. "A bit overdressed, *n'est-ce pas?"*

I untuck my Wasa ship T-shirt from my heavy linen shorts, kicking off my shoes. Voilà, I want to say. This is all you're going to get, because I'm not exposing anything else. Olivier pulls off his T-shirt and slips his hand in mine as we follow the others to our tent site.

"Elle est américaine," one of the women whispers behind us.

"In *Amérique,"* a man says to me in English with a heavy French accent, "you see guns and blood, dead pee-ple on zee *télévision,* but no titties, no ass."

I step up the pace, not wanting to agree right away. More friends come to help carry the blankets and provisions to the campsite, a secret untouched part of Corsica, visited by a handful of those in the know—nature lovers like Alain and Annie, who have been coming to this part of the island for years. The sand, superfine sugar, shines like ground crystal. Small yachts dot the horizon. The sea is a brilliant turquoise, not like the gray gulf of my childhood. The sheer beauty of it all is too much to take in all at once. Pascale and the others have lined up the tents so that each one remains hidden just so among the trees, separate from one another to allow for privacy. Why the thought to so much privacy when everyone is walking around entirely exposed, I haven't yet asked.

The next few days pass as in a dream. The children run around, build sand castles, nap, pick asphodel and rock rose from the maquis. The men spearfish and dive for sea urchins. Everyone hikes, fishes, and swims naked. We roast whole langoustes and potatoes in the open fire, read piles of thick books. After the initial hesitations of disrobing, I am now like the others—in a state of nudity that I never imagined so lovely, even though I am aware of how different I am from the other French women who have low-slung breasts and boast a freedom about their sensuality that is so foreign to me.

But soon I forget that I'm American, that I'm Asian. I swim naked in the sea, learn to dislodge sea urchins, cut them in half, and carefully scoop out the orange roe, sucking it from my bare fingers. I taste *lonzu*, the herbs of the maquis, dip chestnut-flour bread in dark liquid honey from the island. I am in love with the sheer rawness of it all—the water and sand, my new life so different from the closed-in world of my adoptive parents' ways.

I want to go with the men to spearfish and photograph the underlife of the sea—starfish and *rouget*, sea stones—but it's understood that the women stay together, sunbathing, reading *Paris Match* and *Marie-Claire*. One of the women, Régine, reads an article out loud to us in French: "Johnny Halliday has found love again with the young Laetitia, age twenty. . . ."

"Don't they all, the older they get?" Françoise rolls her eyes dramatically, wrapping her red sarong around her head.

"And you, Kim? How old are you?" Régine asks, pausing to stare at me.

"*Un bébé.* You are . . . what . . . just twenty-three, twenty-four, *non*?" Françoise stares. "*Et Olivier,* let's see . . . he'll be forty, *non*?"

"*J'ai fini.*" Pascale announces that she has finished painting each of our portraits in vibrant watercolors. She has painted me in greens and reds, lying on the sand, curled up like a cat in the sun.

"*Pas mal.*" Not bad, Françoise remarks. "But she looks a bit skinny."

"She's thinner than all of us," Pascale says.

"*Elle n'a pas accouché, non plus.*" She hasn't had children yet, either.

The women look down at my taut stomach and firm, muscular legs. One of them notices, though, the stretch marks across my outer thighs. Pointing, she says mischievously, "*Peut-être qu'elle a des enfants et que personne ne le sait.*" Maybe she does have children and no one knows about them.

I explain that the marks are not from childbearing, but from hunger. I bite the inside of my cheek so my voice won't quiver and try to explain how the doctors told me that my body stretched in the same way as a pregnant woman's after I was taken to the States and fed as a normal American child. Françoise glares at me, then stands up and stretches, lights a Gauloises cigarette between her sun-spotted fingers, and marches off.

AFTER A WEEK of sun, saltwater baths, roasted fish, and spiny lobster, we explore the land and on a nearby abandoned property discover a freshwater creek. The water's cold and sharp like ice slivers on our sun-hot skins. I pour handfuls of it over my head and let the water run down my neck to my hardened nipples. I don't care anymore who is watching or looking, if anyone is at all. My body is mine. We swim, soap one another's backs with thick sea sponges. The women take turns washing the children's hair.

When we've finished, silence and satisfaction come over us. The children are worn out and nap on and off in the shade. We sit and tell jokes, slice thick pieces of coppa meat, and devour them with ruby-colored wine.

In the evenings, when the men return with dinner, we build

a fire and cook, tell stories and smoke. Before sleeping, we scrub ourselves in the sea. I like how the salt sticks and dries in soft white patches on our skin.

Olivier licks the salt off me in our tent at night, his tongue lapping my body like the tiniest of waves. We make love again in the early morning before anyone is awake, leaving the small flap to our tent open to the sea and the sun slowly rising. I want him. I want this way of life. I want everything he promises but will never allow myself to admit it. I want him open before me like a map of the world that I will hold in my hands, carefully folding and unfolding it at the creases, knowing that entire lives depend on such precision.

We fall asleep again, the howling of the mistral to remind me that I am part of this earth, that I am flesh and my body open to all the possibilities.

Toward the end of our stay, we celebrate Olivier's birthday. For some reason, he has requested jambalaya. We dress and go into the town of Sartène to buy long-grain rice, Corsican sausage, bell pepper, onion, celery, and garlic, a few spices. We buy fruit and sweets. In Corsica, most of the confections are made with chestnuts and honey. And I cannot get enough of Brocciu, a soft fresh local cheese.

Back at the beach, I stir the rice over the open fire while Pascale puts together a birthday cake of semolina that she cooks on the campfire and tops with peach slices.

"No candles," Olivier tells us. "We know I'm getting old, and already I'm so much older than my Kimette."

I shake my head and give Olivier a kiss on the cheek, tasting the day's dried sea salt on his skin. We have not showered properly in days, but I realize for an instant that I am happy, that this is a family who could accept me, flaws and all.

"Are you off to the continent right away, or will you visit more of Corsica?" asks Annie, Olivier's sister-in-law.

"Papa, can we stop in Bonifacio?"

"We'll see. We've got to get back for you to start your school."

"Maybe in Paris, eh, Papa?"

"Paris?" Laure's cousin asks. "Are you moving to Paris?"

Laure nods, shrugs. "I want to stay in Forcalquier . . . but *Maman* has to, for work."

"Laure, your mother wants to, she doesn't have to," Olivier corrects her. "But you know Kim and I are buying an apartment in Paris, so we can be near you."

I turn to Olivier, raising my eyebrows. He nods at me as if we had already spoken of this.

"Have you still got the house in Bonifacio, or has Madame B. claimed that, too?" Pascale asks. "If you haven't sold it yet, maybe we'll stay a few days."

Olivier nods. "I want Kim to see Bonifacio. We'll stop there tonight, fly out tomorrow, so it's free any time after. I don't think we'll be using it much anymore."

Pascale looks at her brother, stands up. "How about some wine?" she asks. "Kim, will you help me wash the glasses?"

I stand up, too, wrap the damp towel around my hips, and gather the plates and utensils to follow Pascale down to the sea.

"My brother," Pascale says while rinsing a glass, "has never been so happy."

"But Dominique—"

"A fake. He never really loved her. It was all about Laure. You should know, too, that the divorce is going to be difficult. She's going to try to get all she can and drag it out as long as possible."

I shake my head as if to protest, but I'm not sure why or what I'm fighting against.

When it's time to leave, Pascale and Thierry and the kids, Alain and Annie, kiss and hug us good-bye. A straw hat here, Laure's stray sandal there, and we're off. In the car, it feels strange to be in clothes again, even the thin cotton sundress I'm wearing. The leather seats are hot and steamy, and there's no air-conditioning in our rented Citroën.

"Papa, it's too *hot* in here. I don't want to sit in the back." Laure's voice is cranky with that same indecisive tone as on the plane, and then, like the child she is, she changes her mind. "I'll sit back here and sleep. Papa, that was the best vacation ever. When can we come back?"

"Maybe next summer, we'll see."

"With Kimette?"

"Of course."

"Look, I'm even as dark as her." She leans over into the front seat to compare her sunburned arm with my dark brown one. "See, Papa."

"Almost darker," I tell her.

"Ooh, la, la . . . ooh, la, la," she sings, lifting my arm in the air. She sits back in her seat with the headphones on, humming to her own music.

The heat makes me sleepy, and I feel relaxed with Olivier at the wheel, driving smoothly up and around the cliffs. I know that he knows where we're going and without him I'd never get there. As we get closer to Bonifacio, Laure starts complaining.

"I don't feel good, Papa."

"What's wrong, *mon coeur*?"

"Pa-paaa . . ." Laure lets out a heart-wrenching cry, tears that rise from deep within her belly. Olivier tries to comfort her with one arm while driving. I take her other hand and squeeze it. When she calms down, Olivier asks her what's wrong.

"*Maman*'s going to be mad I didn't call her."

"She knows we went camping and that we couldn't call—"

"But she told me I had to call her *every* day—" More tears.

"It's okay," I tell her. "We'll call her as soon as we get to Bonifacio." I give Laure some water and cookies and start playing a game. "I went to my grandmother's house and I brought an apple . . ." By the time we reach the letter *G*, Laure is stretched out on the backseat, snoring lightly.

"She gets like that when she's tired. Too much sun," Olivier offers as an explanation.

"Olivier, did it ever occur to you that maybe it's all too unbearable for her?" I ask. Olivier shifts into third gear, lips tight. I don't really know what I mean, so I say the first thing that comes. "This happiness. Your wanting everything to be so *perfect*."

Olivier accelerates, keeping both hands on the wheel, no longer slowing down to take the curves. "But it is," he tells me when we are high on the cliff. "Laure adores you. My family loves you, my friends. What's wrong with finally being happy?"

I don't have an answer. Obviously, Olivier has never wondered what he did to merit such happiness. As for myself, I anticipate daily what I will have to do to deserve it.

We don't speak for the rest of the drive to Bonifacio. When we arrive, I'm dazzled by the white cliffs of the town, the hollowness of the dusk-worn streets. The drive through the narrow, winding alleyways jostles Laure awake.

"We're here. We're here. Can we eat down by the water, Papa? I want pasta and calamari in that yummy sauce."

The white cliffs are steep, and I feel the vertigo come over me. A wave of nausea as I anticipate entering a house Olivier shared with Dominique. I roll up my window and lock the door; I don't want to get out. I also know before we get to the house that I will ask Olivier questions. So many of them, about his life before me, why he loves me now and not someone else. Questions about his past that will hurt me in the deepest invisible way, some that are sometimes better left unanswered. But I know that he's confident in his moves, his decisions. I try to remind myself that everything he does is toward our happiness.

Olivier parks the car in the impasse. The stairs leading to the front door are damp with peeling, water-stained blue paint. When he unlocks the door, my body tenses—my stomach tight with anticipation. Laure rushes to the phone to call her mother. Olivier makes his way into the entrance with me behind him. We drop our backpacks filled with sand and rocks and empty water bottles. I'm amazed at first how different this place is from the house in Provence—no beautiful African masks or oversize olive jars, hand-stained walls, and heavy quilts. I realize that it's not Olivier's style at all. Pale wicker furniture with floral-printed cushions dominates the main room. There are matching thick rugs and silk plants in white ceramic pots throughout. Hanging on the brightly painted blue walls are strange erotic drawings of tree-men. Olivier sees me staring at them.

"Do you like those? A Polish painter friend of mine and Domin—"

"I hate them," I say flatly. "I don't want to be here," I whisper so Laure won't hear. "This isn't your house."

"Of course it is. I just let *her* decorate it, to appease her. But it's mine, not hers. It's ours, yours and mine. Listen, we're only staying one night. Laure wanted to stop here."

Later, after tucking Laure into bed, I tell Olivier that I don't want to sleep in any of the bedrooms, so he pulls the cushions off the sofa and we line them on the stone floor, cover them with musty sheets and a cotton blanket. He's exhausted from the drive and falls asleep quickly, his body wrapped tightly around mine. During a few moments of restless sleep, I dream that I am a warrior, an invader, but I can't fight because my body is swollen with hollow eggshells. In another dream, my adoptive mother's in Germany or Switzerland, in Joachim's house, looking for me under the covers, in the cabinets. And then later in a New Orleans shotgun, she's scrubbing floors, waterproofing the walls and all of our clothes.

In the morning, I hear water running and realize that Olivier's in the shower. The scent of his vetiver soap mixed with hot steam floats to me from the bathroom. It sounds like a group of children outside the window, playing tag or ball. I roll over, hungry for sleep.

Under the sofa, shadows and dust. I blink. I stretch my arm to discover some papers, credit card receipts, a little girl's sock, and a few photos. There's one of a woman caught in a half turn. I flip it over. Dominique, 1982. I turn it back around and blow off the dust to better study the photo. Her profile is perfect, a straight nose slightly upturned, large brown eyes with long lashes, and short dark hair. She's sitting at a café in a port city. It could be Saint-Tropez or Cassis. She looks like an actress, a *vedette,* waving to some distant admiring crowd. I look around nervously. I want to keep the picture for some reason; maybe it will help, help me understand why Olivier married her in the first place and why he loves me now. Outside, the children's cries get louder, more rhythmic, lulling me back to sleep.

*I'm eleven, twelve, and grounded all the time, grounded because I read things that aren't for my age—*Love Story *and* The Bell Jar. *I'm grounded because I want to wear powder and have lips the color of seashells. I'm grounded for the mess in my room, but I must keep everything, especially the books with drawings of girls who have curly hair the color of faded strawberries. Mine is more like burnt chocolate milk. The strawberry girls are always smiling, and boys like them.*

I look in the mirror and touch the smooth flat skin beneath my faint eyebrow. Why don't I have eyelids like the other girls at school? I'm happy when they let me play games or jump rope with them, but when it's my turn, they sing this song:

> *Kim Kim comes from the moon,*
> *came to earth but landed too soon*
>
> *One, two, three, four*
> *Jump, jump, don't touch the floor*
>
> *Kim, Kim landed too soon*
> *Maybe someday she'll go back to the moon*

CHOCOLATE CAKE WITH
MASCARPONE-CHESTNUT CREAM

In Corsica, chestnuts are abundant and found in both sweet and savory recipes. Chestnut cream is sweet and can be baked into breads, used as a filling for crêpes and cakes, or frozen into ice creams.

8 ounces good-quality bittersweet chocolate
½ cup unsalted butter, softened
1 cup confectioners' sugar
3 large eggs
1 cup all-purpose flour
1 teaspoon baking soda
¼ teaspoon salt
1 (8-ounce) container sour cream
1 teaspoon vanilla extract
Mascarpone-chestnut cream

Preheat oven to 350 degrees. Melt chocolate in a microwave-safe bowl at high for 30-second intervals until melted, or on stovetop. Stir until smooth.

Beat butter and confectioners' sugar at medium speed with an electric handheld or stand mixer, about 5 minutes or until well blended. Add eggs 1 at a time, beating just until blended after each addition. Add melted chocolate, beating just until blended.

Sift together flour, baking soda, and salt. Gradually add to chocolate mixture alternately with sour cream, beginning and ending with flour mixture. Beat at low speed just until blended after each addition. Stir in vanilla. Pour batter into a lightly greased and floured deep 9-inch round cake or springform pan or a 9×13–inch glass pan. Bake at 350 degrees for 28 to 30 minutes or until tester inserted in center comes out clean. Let cool in pan on wire rack 5 minutes. Remove cake from pan and let cool completely. Serve with a dollop of mascarpone-chestnut cream.

MASCARPONE-CHESTNUT CREAM

*Y*ou can double this recipe and use leftovers to stuff fresh figs or crêpes or smear on toasted bread and top with chocolate shavings for a sweet snack. All I really need for this is a spoon.

> 1 (7-ounce) container mascarpone, softened
> 1 (8.75-ounce) can crème de marrons (chestnut spread)
> ¾ cup chilled whipping cream
> 1 teaspoon grated lemon zest

Beat mascarpone and chestnut spread together at medium speed, about 3 minutes or until light and fluffy. Beat whipping cream in a medium bowl until soft peaks form. Fold whipped cream into mascarpone-chestnut mixture. Stir in lemon zest. Cover and chill in refrigerator until ready to serve.

IX

THE MONK'S TABLE

ॐ

*S*OMETIMES I HAVE TO REMIND MYSELF WHERE I AM. SITTING in my writing room, after swimming forty laps, I jot down in my journal: Tuscany, by way of Nice (warm peppery socca, buy chickpea flour) and Genoa, a quick business trip to Lausanne and Neuchâtel (frame poster from the Musée d'Ethnographie), a bike tour near Laguiole and dinner at Michelin-starred Michel Bras, a stop at Eugénie-Les-Bains for a rose-petal steam facial and *cuisine minceur* (lamb rolled with foie gras) . . . and finally back in Provence. Our days and nights are dense, and now already Olivier has us packing up again.

"Just a suitcase for a few days in Paris," he suggests. "Eventually we'll want one set of clothes for the city and another for the country."

It is the last days before Laure is to start school in Forcalquier. The minute we arrived back from Corsica, Dominique started calling again, claiming at least 50 percent of everything, even though she and Olivier were married under the separation of property and goods, a technicality I don't quite understand about French marriage laws but that Olivier explains means he doesn't legally owe Dominique much more than child support. Because of this foresight on Olivier's part, she calls at odd hours, leaving ranting messages demanding large sums of money with outrageous stipulations. She thinks that moving to Paris with Laure—taking his daughter out of his beloved Provence—is a way to punish Olivier. So because of Dominique's threats, although nothing has been decided, Olivier and I will be on our way as well to start looking at apartments. I tell him if we move to Paris, I might join a writers' workshop I found at the British Institute and take lessons at Le Cordon Bleu.

"Why?" he asked. "You're already my favorite chef."

I don't have an answer. Instead, I fold scarves and gather shoes, thinking of Dominique. Olivier's mother told me how much Dominique liked to spend money, lots of it, at Cartier, Yves Saint Laurent. I don't quite understand her financial frenzy. She gets everything she asks for and doesn't need to work. Money for me is like directions, disorienting, especially this new currency that comes in bright and oddly shaped pieces of paper. Monopoly money. But it is a necessity, so I have to learn a new exchange rate, percentages, count in a new language.

Olivier tells me not to worry about anything. His colleague and partner of almost twenty years, Marie-Claire, receives our bank statements, balances our accounts, deposits money whenever it is needed.

"Let me take care of everything," he said again as he kissed me good-bye this morning, driving off with Serge to a town called Ganagobie just a few kilometers from here. "You just worry about what you want to cook tonight—we're having guests—swim some laps, and enjoy all this."

After several seasons with Olivier, it doesn't get any easier, trying to learn to be a *social* being. I am still uncomfortable as the hostess in this huge house that isn't mine. And I don't want to fight him, but the more he tries to do or give, the more the earth feels tilted and heavy, slipping away in deep, thick layers.

It is difficult not to feel like an impostor. I think of the poem my mother accused me of copying from somewhere so many years ago. I can write my own poems, but is it possible that this isn't the life I'm supposed to be living?

For now, I want to try to savor the last moments of summer. So I buy more glossy food magazines—*Saveurs, Côté Sud, Cuisines du Bout du Monde*—and delve into more new recipes. It seems there are always people to meet, some with accents I can't quite understand, but it doesn't matter because the menus I create seem to transcend any need for translation. If anyone thought me an impostor, I learn more and more that you can't fake it in the kitchen—it is here I suspect that I just may actually be good at something.

For tonight's meal, I am deciding between serving whole legs of lamb—which I like to sear, cover with rosemary, thyme, and tapenade, and wrap in fresh bread dough to bake in the oven—and roasted *cabri* with anchovy-and-garlic-spiked caramelized tomatoes. But I'm not sure who's coming or how many, so when Olivier chooses rabbit, before leaving with Serge, I agree. I still make him quarter it, though, because he likes the head intact. I threw it away the first time.

"No, no . . . that's where all the flavor is," he said, laughing. He picked it up and rinsed it off, then added it to my earthenware dish where I had gently placed the saddle and hindquarters.

He watched as I melted butter and whisked in strong Dijon mustard, crème fraîche, before pouring it all over the rabbit, soaking the head and covering each protruding eyeball with a black olive before adding sprigs of rosemary and a crack of black pepper.

"*Tu m'épates.*" How do you know how to cook rabbit? he wanted to know.

I shrugged, because I really didn't know, and directed him

to scrape the carrots and potatoes to roast in the oven. He kissed me gently on the side of the neck and scraped vegetables clean as though it were the most important job in the whole world.

But more than rabbit, my job this week is to pack, cook, and enjoy the rest of the time here before starting another life in Paris. Tonight I will also sear duck breasts with fresh raspberries and balsamic vinegar. I start to make a batter for small muffins of olives and Sauternes, but I keep thinking of Olivier, why he chose today to go with Serge and visit his father's grave. Fernand is buried high on the hill of a monastery, and Giselle and Pascale, although family, must obtain special permission, because they are women, to visit the grave.

Later, Sophie and Lulu come to help set the table for lunch, carrying a market basket full of fresh baguette and herbed *fougasse* breads, fresh peas. As we start to peel fava and cranberry beans, Olivier and Serge pull up to the front of the kitchen with an enormous table loaded in the bed of Serge's truck.

"What'd you buy now?" Sophie asks, shading her eyes from the sun.

"A monk's table, for us."

"I don't see any monks around here," I tell him.

"But imagine," Olivier says, his eyes lighting up, "the history . . . the meals associated with this table."

Some of Serge's friends from the bar are there to help carry it into the kitchen. It takes five of them to haul the long wooden table from the back of the truck.

"It seats thirty," Olivier announces proudly.

"What's a monk, Papa?" Laure skips around the table.

"Thirty hungry mouths around that table. *Ma pauvre*, you've got some work ahead of you." Sophie gathers the pods into a bag and hands me the bowls of bright green and marble-colored beans.

"We can't help it if everyone always shows up at mealtime." Serge winks at me. "So, what's for lunch?"

"As if we didn't have enough room, enough guests?" I tease halfheartedly.

Serge and the guys go off to Sophie and Serge's. Olivier opens a bottle of red.

"You know, they made my father mayor of Ganagobie," Olivier says, not really talking to me. "Even though he was a journalist. He died young. Only fifty-two. Cancer. Drank too much. Loved too little." He gets up to stretch his arms and take a deep breath before continuing. "I feel young, but still, I'm older than you. I need to stay in shape. There's so much I want to do. I'll be fifty-two in . . . *twelve* years." He pours two glasses of wine.

I don't really want one, but I take it anyway. He sits across from me, dusting off the end of the table. He's mentioned his father many times before but always briefly. "Your parents . . . they weren't divorced, right?" I ask.

"No, but Fernand had a mistress for many years. Giselle was too busy taking care of us kids, wanting to be an artist. It was different back then."

"How, people don't have mistresses anymore?"

"It's a terrible life . . . cheating the heart. Doesn't tempt me whatsoever. I had to make a decision: stay with Dominique because of Laure or leave, continue to love my daughter, and also love a woman"—he looks up at me—"the way I want to—wholly, fully. Not in hiding." He gulps down the wine and pours another glass.

"Did Giselle ever know?"

"Of course she must have known, felt it. But didn't want to know. I want to know everything . . . about you. I have nothing to hide from you ever. No secrets between us, okay?"

I nod, knowing this is impossible. How can he know every-thing about me when I don't even know myself?

"This wine is delicious, isn't it?" he asks, holding the glass up to the light. "Maybe we should serve it tonight. It will go with the rabbit and duck."

I am relieved to be talking about more familiar subjects. "So how many people are coming?"

"Well, we have Pierre and Louise, Gérard, Flora, Thibault, the usual suspects, oh, and Nelly and Louis will be here any minute now—driving down from Paris—"

"But don't they know we're leaving soon to go up there?"

"They can stay. Sophie and Serge will take care of them. We'll be back soon."

NELLY AND LOUIS Pons have known Olivier since he first started buying Louis's paintings ten years ago. I met them at the sum-mer theater festival in Avignon. During intermission of a per-formance of *Semelé*, Nelly roared, *"Robert Wilson est un pur génie, la fille est trop grosse, par contre."* I told her I thought the woman was beautiful. She scowled but smiled charmingly after I agreed with her that Wilson was a genius. She waved to the conductor, claiming, *"William Christie est aussi un homme incroyable."*

She looked wistful, as she often does when talking about brilliant men, including Louis. Nelly is, Olivier explained, a *pied noir*. Black foot, a French citizen born in Algeria. When I met her, I knew what Olivier meant when he said, *"Elle a dû être très belle."* Beautiful, or had been, years ago. Even bitterness and age have settled comfortably into her features, sharpening them with a rich sadness.

I saw them again at one of Louis's exhibits. Louis stood off to the side while Nelly held court with various gallery owners and collectors, spending most of her time with the *nez* of Chanel, discussing Jacques's latest scent, convincing him to let us all smell Allure before finalizing it.

Nelly had been anxious about me liking them, but more important, about me loving Louis's work. More than her or the paintings, though, I liked Louis immediately; it was like reuniting with a long-lost relative.

"*Et toi, Kim? Tu es heureuse?*" Louis asked. I thought his question so strange, asking me about happiness, but before I could open my mouth, he winked.

SPREAD OUT ON the newly polished monk's table are clear glass carafes of wine and water, loaves of Moroccan bread baked by Zorah. Olivier passes around Roquefort-stuffed celery sticks while I unmold warm miniature green-olive-and-Sauternes muffins. There's a big bowl of orange couscous, chilled ratatouille-stuffed cabbage leaves, green pea, fava, and mint salad, duck breast with raspberry-balsamic reduction, three different purées: sorrel, saffron-carrot, and celery root. Bright green leaves of tender mâche and wedges of aged Laguiole and *chèvre frais*. For dessert there's *fromage blanc* sorbet with candied ginger and warm *tartelettes* crowned with golden Mirabelle plums.

The first to arrive is Pierre Magnan, an aging mystery writer from Manosque. For his wife, Louise, a beautiful small bird of a woman, I have made a batch of fresh melon soup. She loves these melons from Cavaillon, sometimes seeded, slightly chilled, and filled with the finest port.

Other guests show up, along with acquaintances we didn't know would be coming. They stay for drinks and invite themselves to dinner. I scramble to make more salad, set out more cheese and olives. Olivier doesn't seem to mind the extra ten people who have decided to stay. He is impressed and beaming when I'm complimented by everyone. Even Nelly seems content and offers a toast in honor of *la cuisinière.*

"*Ma chérie,*" she says, her mouth full, "you two should open up the house . . . start a table d'hôte . . . one of those luxury bed-and-breakfasts. The house is way too big for just the two of you."

"That's a great idea. We'll rent out three of the bedrooms," Olivier says without missing a beat, "have it listed in the *Guide des Hôtels de Charme.* Sophie and Serge can run the daily tasks of the bed-and-breakfast. And when Kim and I aren't traveling or in Paris"—he pauses to wink at Laure—"we'll cook meals for the table d'hôte, meet with guests, teach Provençal cooking." He looks at me. I'm silent but smile reassuringly.

"But what about my room, Papa?" Laure pipes up. "What if I have to go to Paris with *Maman?*"

"Your room will always be yours." He pours more wine. "This project will really just be an extension of our regular dinners at the house," he continues, looking my way.

Olivier gestures for Sophie to grab a pen and piece of paper, and soon there is talk of seasonal menus, summer berries, truffles in the winter, mushrooms in the spring and fall. I do love the passion for the distinct seasons here in Provence and the singular flavors each one promises.

"Winter's the best," offers Pierre's wife, Louise. "Show them how to find truffles. Like you showed us last year."

In season, the *rabassier* comes to the property with his *chien truffier.* Last winter, I went with the hunter to our special oak trees, where the dog unearthed truffles, big, black, and abundant. The hunter sells his share at the market for 5,000 francs a kilo. But we store ours in fat glass jars of arborio rice for fragrant risotto. Or I place them gently in a bowl of yard eggs, allowing the porous shells to take on the deep scent of the earth.

For a first course, I like to crack the eggs into the top part of a *bain-marie,* stir them ever so slightly until they are just cooked. Then I swirl in fresh salted butter before plating the soft *brouillade.* There's always a moment of silence as we all watch Olivier shave big black paper-thin moons of truffle over each serving, an extra slice over mine. Then a round of applause and an "Ooh-la-la" from Olivier as the last bit of black gold disappears into his mouth.

"And Sophie would have to quit her job at the nursery school," Olivier decides. Serge and Sophie like the idea of a shared project with Olivier, but I'm not sure their relationship can sustain being together all day and all night.

Olivier then brings out the bottle I bought him in Nice a few weeks back, a slim antique glass olive oil bottle. He told me he had been thinking about olive trees, *oliviers,* and the history of the olive route. "This," he says, holding up the bottle to everyone, "is also going to be the start of another project."

I'm not sure what he's talking about, but I welcome any new projects after L'Occitane, both for his sake and in the hope of allowing myself room to pursue my own writing.

"And in Paris," Olivier announces, "I think our Kimette is going to open a bookstore."

I look at Olivier, surprised. We talked about it briefly when we first met in Stockholm, but never with any certainty. Before I can ask any questions, Nelly stands up.

"To the happy couple," she offers. "If *I* were so lucky . . ."

We all raise our glasses, pausing to look carefully into the eye of each toasting companion. I look around, and yes, there are exactly thirty of us around the monk's table, exactly as Olivier envisioned. But no matter how many people, I know with Olivier on my side, we can tackle criticism, jealousy, any and all new projects, even if some of them are just ideas he needs to throw out there, maybe to test us, test himself. But I know, too, that none of this will last. Nothing ever has. As I look around at the guests, somewhere deep inside I also sense that sooner or later there will be a last supper.

After dinner, Nelly pulls me aside to whisper that ever since the sale of L'Occitane, just before his meeting me in Stockholm, Olivier has wanted to focus on family and love, aspects of his life he never paid attention to before me. "And I just want to let you know that before you and Olivier leave for Paris, I'm going to ask for a small loan. You don't mind encouraging him, do you, *chérie?*" She smiled.

This is the third time this year. I don't say yes or no to Nelly, but I know that between her, Dominique, and who knows how many other people asking for loans, donations, and, most important, time, Olivier will have to eventually say no. Olivier, who likes playing the father figure, always tries to find a way to help someone. It is a strange reversal of roles, but I sense that I will have to learn to be the protector, the reasonable one.

Thibault lifts his glass and winks in my direction. Nelly watches carefully as Olivier leans into me, and when he places his arm possessively around my waist, I am filled with the realization that there is something both desperate and hopeful about our love, and I feel invincible for just a small but tightly wrapped-around moment.

Sometimes when Zorah is cleaning the kitchen and the guests have all slipped away into their rooms, I go out into the cool night and stop to pick a ripe purple fig. I open it in two and scoop out the flesh with my tongue, letting the milk run down my chin.

Tonight I walk past the fig trees down to the vegetable patch, close the makeshift gate behind me, and stretch out among the summer vegetables. I am taken with the richness of the soil and how quickly things grow in this garden. I break off yellow flowers from the young squash that I will stuff tomorrow with goat cheese and pluck fresh mint leaves for a tea custard recipe I dreamed I would make. I think about Fernand, Olivier's father, never having allowed himself to live or love fully, how the number 52 plagues Olivier, feeding his obsession with our age difference and his inconsolable need to produce and create.

Olivier opens the gate and sits next to me. "You know, I've been thinking about olive oil. I want us to start something . . . I need to start something else, since L'Occitane. Remember the bottle I brought out tonight? What if we searched for the best olive oils in the Mediterranean. We'll go to Spain and start there," he decides, excited again about a new enterprise. "Then we'll go to Greece, Italy, find the best olive oil producers."

I recognize that look in his eyes, what I've come to understand as his immeasurable need to leave a legacy. His father's disappearance at such a young age has made his desire for immortality even stronger. His energy excites me, but at the same time his life is in such sharp contrast with my own—I have done nothing of value, of legendary proportions, as he has. Yes, I'm young, he continues to remind me, but he also firmly believes that being his companion, sharing his life, is enough for both of us. I do not know yet how to say that it's not. There are other things he needs to do that are important, he has said again and again, like finding roots for me.

"We'll trace the route of the *olivier,* the olive tree," he continues, "and, I've been meaning to tell you . . . we've got to go to Hong Kong and China soon for L'Occitane."

I press my cheek to the ground, to bring myself eye level with the rows of salads and tender shoots of peas. I am suddenly struck by the profound realization that I have no earth, no history of my own. And without a past, how can I possibly build a future, especially with a man so deeply rooted, so sure of where he is from, and so confident about his every move? In contrast, I am sometimes a three-year-old orphan again, a young woman still trying to make sense of the ground beneath her.

"You know," he says, stroking my hair, "maybe there's even something in Asia with your namesake, like the *olivier* in the Mediterranean for me, something that leads back to you. We'll see. I think we need to stop in Seoul on our way to Hong Kong."

"I don't know, Olivier, I don't speak the language—"

"You'll learn. We'll get you a Korean tutor, surely with the university in Aix or Marseille, we'll find someone."

"I don't have any way of knowing if I even have any family—"

"You always said you had a brother and that you talked about your Korean grandmother."

"Those are memories," I remind him. "Things my American family said I *talked* about. I have no way of knowing or finding them. I don't even know my real name, only what I told the policemen at the station."

"Well, then that is your name. Chong Ae Kim. You said it. Don't worry. I'll make all the arrangements for the trip. All of it. *Tout.*"

"*Tout*, not *tu*," I whisper. Everything is possible, even if I've never allowed myself to say it before. As for now, I want to stay here forever, my body pressed so close to the earth of this new country, fragrant and rich.

A WEEK OR SO LATER, while one of the carpenters is building some chairs for the upstairs terrace, I ask him to follow me into the kitchen. He admires the craftsmanship of the long heavy oak table, sliding his hand along the smooth edges, caressing the legs.

"*Elle est très belle.*"

Very beautiful, I agree. "*Je veux que tu m'en coupes un tiers.*"

He looks at me, frightened almost. "*Pas possible.* I would never cut a third of it off. It is a pure *sacrilège.*"

"Fine, then *you* come and cook dinner for thirty people tonight and tomorrow night and the next and every night until—"

"When do you want it done?" he asks, the saw high in the air.

The following night, with a third of the monk's table cut off, there are only eighteen of us at the large table and six kids at the smaller one. Olivier doesn't mention the table at first, then concedes and says he actually thinks it looks better, he was thinking of having the same thing done.

Nelly has invited a friend of hers, Gianna, a gallery owner, and her anorexic poodle to the house. The last supper, I realize now, is nowhere near as I roll out pastry dough for a raspberry tart and prepare the meat filling for *pâté en croûte*. While coring pears to stew in chestnut honey and Chianti, Olivier walks into the kitchen.

"Do you still want me to roast the lamb?" He looks at my pastry, eyes the slightly imperfect decorative leaves. "This is gorgeous. I love smelling your cooking when I come in. So much better than what I can do."

"Olivier, you know you're a great cook."

"Dominique hated the kitchen. She thought cooking was a ridiculous waste of time."

Nelly glides in next to me, starts stirring the pot simmering on the stove. "*Chérie,* is that rice pudding? Gianna's dog is allergic to dairy, perhaps we could have something else for dessert."

"This isn't for the dog," I reply dryly, taking out the spoon and covering the pot before placing it in the oven. "Besides, you told me he had an eating disorder, like Gianna. We're having stewed pears." I shut the oven and go back to trimming the dough.

Nelly huffs her shoulders and snaps a green bean in two. "Hmmm. A bit too al dente," she says, chewing thoughtfully.

The knife in my hand, fortunately, needs honing.

"I guess it'll do," she decides.

I roll my eyes at Olivier.

"I saw that, Kim," Nelly says. "Why have you been so rude to my friends? I invite them for dinner and you hardly talk to them."

"I got up at six-thirty this morning, after the big dinner last night, to go to the market, and I've been standing in this kitchen all morning cooking for them." My voice is higher than I want it to be.

"No excuse. You and Olivier with everything you have and poor Louis and me struggling like we do." She breaks into a hysterical rage of tears—something I imagine only seasoned actresses capable of—and then starts to hyperventilate. "Do you think it's easy being an artist's wife?"

"Nelly, calm down," Olivier says. "I just gave Louis a check this morning for seventy thousand francs. He can give us the painting whenever he's ready."

"*C'est vrai?*" she asks, batting her moistened lashes. "He didn't tell me. Louis . . ."

THE NEXT DAY, Nelly and Louis, their friend Gianna, and her dog do not show up for lunch. I spend the afternoon out on the back terrace. It's an odd time of year. The fields are turning brittle and brown. The stink of rotting cantaloupe penetrates the air. I am once again faced with the onset of this in-between time, this season before the fall. The abundant rows of sunflowers with their heavy bowed heads remind me of my own forgotten prayers, my folded, tired bones.

Nelly has left a note of thanks to Olivier and a P.S. informing us that she's not speaking to me anymore, not until I come to my senses. Whatever that means.

"*Kimette, fais un effort,*" Olivier says, holding out the letter, sitting next to me in the sun.

"Why do you insist on taking her side?"

"I'm not. It's just that she relies on us, we're like family . . . you're like a daughter she never had."

"Well, she's not like a mother I would ever want to have. She's demanding and dramatic. We cook for all these people, she invites anyone she wants . . . Where does she get off—"

"*Elle est hystérique.* She's jealous. And Louis is an important artist."

"I know. I love his work, but why do you always have to defend her? She takes and takes."

Olivier stops to take me in his arms. "My Kimette. Do you realize that before meeting you, I had everything—this house, my family, my friends, my career—but not love."

"Do you realize I'm just twenty-four years old and trying so hard, to be the hostess, the cook, the stepmother, the confidante—"

"But you're all that and more—"

"*Ça suffit.* I'm nobody. I haven't done anything with my life. I'm not even myself, much less what everyone thinks I am."

"Stop it. You're perfect, just the way you are."

"You're not listening." I take his hand in mine and pause for a moment. "Olivier, I love you and everything you've wanted for me, but this is *your* house, *your* family, *your* friends. It's *your* perfect life."

"But . . . I've given you a new life. My friends, my family . . . they all love you . . . they've adopted you like their own."

Suddenly I can't find the words in any language to tell Olivier that it's not an honor to be "adopted" again and again and that he can't just order me an identity, create an instant history. He doesn't seem to grasp that my past is the one thing he can't conquer or fix.

"I cook all day to have these glamorous dinners—a show we put on for your friends and family—as if everything's perfect. It's not. The divorce proceedings. It's going to take forever, and . . . Dominique—her phone calls and stories she's spreading. You know there're still rumors going around that I'm your pregnant *mistress*. I thought everyone knew that you were separated before we even met?" I get up to go inside. "You know how awkward it is sometimes when we go to the market in the village, everyone either staring and whispering or pretending to be your friend."

"Okay, okay. We'll take a trip to Spain, the Costa Brava, if you want, or Venice. You love Venice. We'll go to your favorite restaurant. Keem," he calls, following me into the house. It takes a few minutes for my eyes to adjust to the change in light. "I thought you enjoyed this. Convivial dinners, just like your grandfather. It's *who* you are."

"I do enjoy it, but you're not listening to what I'm saying." I grab a handful of magazines and newspapers and start flipping through the pages.

"I'm doing what I can," Olivier says, lowering his voice. "She's on a rampage right now . . . it's her pride. It's not about me. It's my name, what I represent. *Écoute,* I just need to wrap up some things here and then we'll be off to Paris. I'll take you to have a nice dinner, just the two of us."

"I'm sick of food, too. *Ras le bol.*" I open a bottle of water and drink down three hard gulps.

"My Keem. Just a few more days, we have a few more dinners to host this week, and—"

I fold up today's *Libération* and toss it onto the counter. "You know what, I'm like all the other laborers in this country. I am officially *en grève.* On strike," I add in English for emphasis.

He looks genuinely surprised, and for an instant I reconsider my act of social protest to strike. As I make my way out of the kitchen, I hear him yell something about Harry's Bar and the Hotel San Daniele, maybe we'll bring my family over here.

I go to my office, scan the shelves, and make a mental note of books and authors I want to read again: Woolf and Rilke, *Turtle Island,* Didion. And other books, new editions of Freud in French and a copy left from one of our summer guests, a book by someone named Lacan I find on one of the bookshelves.

Later, at dinner, Laure and Lulu, Serge, and Olivier are at the table. After two months of nonstop friends, Sophie and I set out leftovers in mismatched pots and pans directly from the stove onto the long wooden table. No silver, no dishes. No more cooking for the masses. No more diversion by getting on a plane and escaping to some luxury hotel against the backdrop of a beautiful landscape.

I reheat leftover summer vegetable gratin, steam some couscous with a pat of salted butter, unwrap half-eaten wheels of cheese and set them on the table as well.

"*Bon appétit.*"

"Where are the forks?" Lulu asks, not sure if she should laugh or not.

"Voilà." I hand her a basket of bread. She looks at Laure nervously, and they both begin to giggle when Serge takes a slice of baguette and scoops a mouthful of minted squash into his mouth. "Or, use your fingers." The kids shout with joy and dig into their food. Olivier looks at me as if I've gone mad. "Have you forgotten? I'm on strike, *chéri."* I kiss his forehead, then grab a handful of blueberries and pop a few in my mouth.

"Me too." Sophie takes my wrist and we run out of the kitchen, race down to the pool. We untie our sundresses and slip off our sandals before diving into the cool water.

"Swim for your life!" Sophie screams, doing the backstroke.

"For your sanity!"

After, we sit on the swing wrapped in thick blue towels, and I watch Sophie hand-roll a cigarette. Moonlight shines down on us, blue and golden on our moist skin.

"I've never felt so free!" Sophie shrieks. She towels her hair dry and pulls at the scabs on her forehead. She said she fell the other day. "It's healing, *non?"*

"How's it going with Serge?"

She shrugs, lights a match.

"Sophie, you don't have to put up with that." This is the first time I've mentioned the unmentionable. "You know Olivier will end everything with Serge—"

"No. He would be devastated. He hasn't had a drink in weeks. He's been trying." Her voice gets softer until she's sobbing into her wet towel. "Promise me you won't fire him, that Olivier won't."

I put my arm around her shoulder, and we sit like this for a long time.

"Do you think Flora's going to hold out much longer?"

I shake my head. I don't know if any of us will, I want to tell her. Instead, we gather our clothes in silence and trudge back toward the house, guided only by starlight pooled in soft patches along the rocky path ahead.

FLORA'S BEEN IN bed at four in the afternoon the last few days. Much to Nelly's disapproval, I've designated one of the guest rooms as Flora's alone. She won't eat much lately, except for rice pudding that I make in large batches and that she sometimes washes down with shots of single-malt Scotch. Or she eats purées and desserts, anything sweet and smooth that soothes her craving for tenderness. She no longer wants me to read to her. She wants me only to recite poems, short ones that I've written or poems of love by Neruda, Roethke, a few lines of cummings, Rich.

"Has he called?" she asks quietly as I sit on the edge of the bed one afternoon. The room smells of alcohol and the inside of plastic medicine vials. I get up to open the windows. Flora squints. *"Ferme tout,"* she orders. Close everything.

"You need some air in here. And no, he hasn't called, Flora. It's been weeks, and you've got to—"

"What, give up? You're always the one telling me how hope is important." She scoots herself up against the wall behind her bed, looking pale and remorseful. "I'm sorry." Her eyes cloud up, and her shoulders start to tremble.

"Flora, I went to his house this morning, on my way back from the market. I knocked on the door and—"

"Did *she* answer? Was she there?" I shake my head, thankful that I don't have to lie.

"Well, what did he say?"

"He wasn't there, either. So I went to the café, the one by the fountain, and . . ." I want to tell her that he loves her but that he can't face her death. A coward. I sat at the table with him.

Are you here to accuse me? he asked, staring straight into my eyes, jaw quivering.

I shook my head. I wanted to say that I just wanted him to go and see her one last time. But before I could ask, he was already sobbing into his murky pastis, claiming softly that he didn't want to kill her by not being able to give her all his love, that all he wanted was to share a little bit of it, that he couldn't save her, and in that case he was worth nothing. He had done what he could. *Un rien, un vrai vaurien,* he called himself. A true, worthless nothing.

And then I found myself screaming at him, shaking him by the shoulders, shouting that all I was asking was that he come and kiss her one last time. Not to just disappear as if she had never existed.

I remember feeling suspended, as if I were suddenly someone else, as if he were suddenly everyone who had ever loved and left. I was so close, I could smell my own perfume sweating off of his body. In his dilated pupils, I swear I could see myself— a madwoman, a floating country, a long-forgotten language.

ORANGE COUSCOUS SALAD

This dish lends itself to many different combinations. Try adding grated zucchini or carrot, toasted pine nuts, lemons instead of oranges, fresh snow peas, fresh summer tomatoes . . . the possibilities are endless. You can also substitute bulgur wheat for the couscous.

1 cup water
1 (10-ounce) box medium-grain couscous
¼ cup extra-virgin olive oil

1 teaspoon salt
½ teaspoon pepper
½ small red onion, thinly sliced
2 oranges
2 tablespoons chopped fresh flat-leaf parsley
2 tablespoons chopped fresh mint leaves
1 cucumber, peeled, seeded, and chopped
1 cup golden raisins, currants, or chopped dates

Bring water to a boil. Pour couscous in a large bowl and add water, stir, cover with plastic, and let steam 5 minutes or until couscous is tender. Fluff with a fork. Stir in olive oil, salt, pepper, and onion. Let cool slightly.

Zest both oranges. Juice 1 of the oranges. Remove white peel of second orange and chop. Add zest and chopped orange to couscous. Stir in parsley, mint, cucumber, and raisins. Cover and chill in refrigerator 1 hour and up to 2 days. Taste and rectify seasoning by adding more salt and pepper, olive oil, and juice before serving. *Makes about 4½ cups.*

TIPSY MELONS WITH PROSCIUTTO

Halve 3 small ripe Charentais (or other summer) melons. Discard seeds. Slice a small piece off bottom of melon so it will balance on a plate without wobbling. Fill melons about a third with good-quality port wine. Chill until ready to serve. Grill slices of country bread or baguette, top with fruity extra-virgin olive oil and *fleur de sel*. Serve with thin slices of *jambon de Bayonne* or *prosciutto di Parma* or *Serrano*.

X

HEART, APPLE, KNIFE

T'S ALMOST AUTUMN, AND WITH THE CHANGE OF SEASONS, Olivier always decides something of unprecedented proportion. Backing the car out one morning, I find a twelve-foot sculpture by an artist friend in our driveway. It's nothing we would ever buy, but the friend was *emmerdé,* in the shit, and needed the money fast. We are also preparing for a huge anniversary party at the house for all the employees of L'Occitane, and there are more last-minute business trips to book . . . Not that Olivier needs falling leaves to make decisions, but there's something in the air. Flora senses it first.

"So, what has he decided today?" she teases as she slices fresh fennel bulb and plump leafy brussels sprouts. "To buy a small island nation and employ all its inhabitants?"

I shrug and crunch into a pear.

"Thibault's coming to lunch. I invited him," she reminds me. Today is one of her better days, and seeing Thibault always cheers her up. "I think he needs me."

I crush hazelnuts to sprinkle on the fennel salad. When Thibault arrives, he and Flora sit out under the linden tree, speaking in soft, hushed tones as I try to concentrate on garnishing the plates with shaved Pecorino, a drizzle of olive oil.

At the table, Olivier announces that he has found the perfect spot for the poetry bookshop, the one he mentioned when we first met way back in Stockholm and again at dinner this past summer, the one I have never let myself hope for.

"Where?" we all want to know.

"That's a surprise." He smiles.

"Keem, locked in a bookshop?" Thibault says, concerned.

"What's the name going to be?" Sophie asks, popping open a bottle of beer for Serge.

"Something symbolic of poetry," Flora answers.

"And of the poet," Thibault adds, a bit sarcastically, it seems.

We go through a list of possible names, including French and English, recite characters from Greek mythology. Somehow we go from Pegasus to wings, *ailes.* I like the idea of wings and flight.

"*A Tire d'Ailes,*" Olivier says.

Flora and Sophie and the girls seem to like it. Thibault thinks it is not simple enough, pretty enough, for me.

Ah, tier-dell, I pronounce. Her tears? "What does it mean?" There is no real translation for it, but from what I can gather, it means "On the Wing." Flight, poetry.

"*Oui,*" Olivier confirms, nodding toward Thibault. "A Tire d'Ailes . . . it's perfect for Keem. That's what we will name it."

"Won't you have problems with the working papers, a visa for her?" Thibault asks.

"Marie-Claire has already got that worked out. We've got it all covered." Olivier opens a bottle of wine. "Now, the other news is that the parents of our Kimette are coming to France."

I look at him. "Why didn't you tell me?" I need time to prepare for such a visit. I haven't seen my parents since Thanksgiving over two and a half years ago, a quick trip home

I promised them just after I had announced I was moving to Stockholm.

"I'm telling you now . . . I'm having tickets sent as we speak."

THE DAY BEFORE my parents are to arrive, I drive to the *roseraie,* the wholesale rose nursery, not too far from Pierrerue. I pick out two hundred roses—porcelain cream, red, and the rare black ones—to place in vases all throughout the house. Perhaps out of guilt for being so far away or in my attempt to prove that my life is not a total waste, I want to make this the best trip of my parents' life. Olivier could have given me a bit more notice about their visit, but I'm as ready as I'll ever be. Sophie has made sure there are lots of fresh linens, and Olivier has brought home boxes of L'Occitane soaps and shampoos for their room.

At dinner the night before their arrival, Olivier says, "It's about time I met your parents. Even if they aren't much older than me. I'm grateful to them no matter what, for not leaving you behind in Korea."

I nod. "I wouldn't be here if it weren't for them." I scrape my half-eaten polenta and daube into the dogs' bowls. I can't eat. I'm nervous. I want my parents to like Olivier, Laure, Sophie and Serge, and Lulu. I want them to approve of my life here, of, as Olivier would say, my new adopted family.

MY MOTHER AND father make the journey from New Orleans to Paris, and from Paris to Marseille, where Serge meets and drives them the one hour from the airport to the house here in Provence. Laure and Lulu and the dogs, Gribouille and Noisette, run to the gate to greet them. It has been so long since

I have seen them that when they hug me tight, patting me on the back, it is bittersweet, awkward, the gestures somewhat misplaced.

Olivier and I show them around the property. My mother smiles, nods, doesn't say much else, a quiet grunt here and there, so I can't tell if they're excited, surprised, or just plain jet-lagged. I show them to their room, a beautiful renovated space in a separate building, and offer bottled water and newspapers in English, a map of Provence. It is odd to see them here, my parents as my guests.

"Why don't you freshen up and we'll get lunch ready."

My mother squeezes my hand and whispers, "He seems really nice, Olivier. And Laure is so cute. I guess she's kind of like my granddaughter?"

I nod, I guess so.

Since Olivier's English is lacking and only Sophie speaks it a bit, I spend the days and nights as constant interpreter, sometimes mixing up words, forgetting the simplest combinations in both languages. My parents prove to be gracious guests despite the language barrier and are quick with the *mercis, bonjours,* and *oui, oui, s'il vous plaît.*

As the days pass, I realize that there is something to being lost in translation. Here, in the distinct light of Provence, my father is no longer the sad, stern father I left so many years ago. I discover that he has a good ear for languages and prefers speaking with Flora and the girls, who hardly speak any English, whenever he can. They practice new words in English and French, and my father delights them with jokes I never knew he could tell.

My mother has quickly shed her tightly wound, nervous American self. She takes the market basket from me and walks through, bartering and gesturing for runny cheese and the best crusty baguette. She lingers over bowls of steaming sugary coffee and croissants that Serge brings back to the house fresh every morning. She buys silk and cashmere pashminas for both of us to toss around our shoulders against the cool of the evening. She and my father taste all the wines Olivier offers up, toast with him. He and my father smile and gesture and toast each other repeatedly. I think they like each other, how could they not? It's so much easier when words are filtered, gestured, half understood.

But just when I think I can breathe easy, we go to Aix-en-Provence one day, and walking through the Cours Mirabeau to the market, my mother asks me if this is how I intend to live my life.

"What do you mean?" I ask defensively, bracing myself.

"Well, have you thought about getting a job? Are you going to let Olivier support you for the rest of your life?" I look to my father, but he is too far away, engaged in a conversation with one of the cheese vendors.

"I . . . um . . . do translations for L'Occitane," I stutter. "I'm cooking all the time, traveling with Olivier . . . And . . . you know I write. I had some poems accepted for a local French journal recently."

"Writing isn't a *real* job," my mother reminds me. "Poets don't make a living at *poetry*."

I swallow hard, reduced to silence. Things have been going so well since they got here, too well; I should have been prepared for something like this. I want to defend myself but realize there's nothing much I can say. I want her to know that I'm trying as best I can to invent a life for myself, to discover that there may be a place, no matter how foreign to her, that I can call home. I realize, too, that she may be worried about me, but her tone is harsh and critical, always, and never counterbalanced with something more generous, never a hint of approval.

"Oh, look, there's Olivier." She perks up. "He said he would take us to the lavender fields on the way back, a place where we could stop and cut fresh lavender." She waves frantically at my father while Olivier gestures for me to come to him. He is standing next to an older Asian woman holding a bunch of fresh white anemones.

"I want you to meet someone," he tells me as I approach. "This is Madame Song."

"*Bonjour,*" I say, looking at Olivier, waiting for an explanation.

"*Bonjour,*" the woman says, smelling her bouquet of flowers.

"She's Korean," Olivier explains. "Madame Song teaches at the university here, and I thought maybe she could give you some lessons."

"Olivier say you go home to Korea, very nice."

Yes, I nod, looking around for my parents in the bustle of the market, in case they have overheard that we are going to Korea. I haven't had a chance to tell them yet. Madame Song is smiling, nodding, as Olivier sets up a time for me to meet with her. But I am distracted. I keep searching—somewhat frantically now—for someone resembling my parents. I don't want to lose them, but it seems there is not a trace of them anywhere.

OLIVIER HAS DECIDED on a February date to fly us to my homeland, back to another planet, as far as I'm concerned. We have a few months for me to change his mind, although I'm not sure where to begin. With Laure back in school and most of our friends in Paris for the *rentrée*—the mass return to the city after the summer season—the house in Provence is empty, and just for a few solitary moments, I enjoy the hollow echo of my steps on the large stone floors.

We've been on "the grape cure." Olivier claims it reestablishes our imbalances and protects throughout the harsh winter months. End October, early November, is the best time. The first day we drink only vegetable bouillon, followed by three days of grapes, and the fifth day back to vegetable bouillon. I lose three kilos, Olivier only one. We compare as he's packing his bags to fly off to Saudi Arabia.

"I told you wine doesn't count as grapes," I tease.

"It was a good try. Now I'll be eating for days on end with the Bedouins in the desert. And no wine."

"Do you have to go?" I ask. "Can't they come here?"

"They will. But Hamad wants to show me the shopping center where he'll franchise L'Occitane and then a stay in the desert with a renowned astronomer. It's polite. You'll be fine."

"But this house is . . . immense."

"Sophie and Serge are on the property. Flora's here, and I can have my sister come and stay in one of the rooms if you want."

"No, I'm fine." I want him to go, I want time for myself, but I can't sleep without him. I can't risk dreaming without him next to me, just in case.

"And tonight I have invited Madame Song, the Korean tutor from Aix, to come to dinner. She and her husband are coming at around eight. I asked Thibault to come, too. So that's four for dinner, Flora might join in as well, depending on how she's feeling."

I nod. "When are we leaving for Seoul?"

"We have to be in Hong Kong the first week of February to meet with potential franchise buyers. And Chinese New Year is on the tenth, so we'll stop in Seoul first."

"Olivier?"

He looks at me, waiting for the same question. We've been through it before, my not really wanting to go back. Nothing there for me. But he wants it, and I want what he wants, for now, even though I'm afraid to go, afraid that the plane will not quite make it, afraid of what I might find. Or not. But I don't tell him any of this—I do not want to disappoint him. I will go, secretly hoping someone will recognize me, perhaps tell me something I've been wanting to know. I shake the thoughts from my head. "What do I cook for Madame Song?"

Olivier smiles. "Who's married to a Frenchman? *Une bonne blanquette de veau,* made by a Korean American who lives in Provence, what else?" He laughs, charming in his attempt to steer me away from the fact that he is leaving me alone in this half-restored house that, as Serge put it, I am now the mistress of. He takes me in his arms, pulls me close, and kisses the top of my head. "What am I going to do with you?"

Veal stew for my future Korean teacher just doesn't seem right, and when Serge drives off with Olivier to take him to the airport, I flip through cookbooks. I can think of nothing Korean to serve but grilled beef and spicy kimchi, and where am I going to find that around here?

When Thibault finally arrives along with Madame Song and her husband, I'm ready but nervous. I've covered the outdoor table beneath the linden tree with an olive-printed Provençal tablecloth and pale green dishes, and in the center I've placed a small vase of lemon verbena and spearmint from the garden. I want to impress this Madame Song, make sure she has time to teach me my mother tongue. I've made a curried pumpkin soup with langoustine, veal loin stuffed with fragrant girolles, tried a last-minute gingered *panna cotta* that I hope will be set in time for dessert. I change clothes twice and finally answer the door wearing a long black skirt and a cream cashmere sweater.

Madame Song's a small woman with wisps of white hair that fall softly just above her rounded shoulders. When she smiles, handing me a bouquet of fragrant yellow freesia, her face is like shiny cracked porcelain. Her husband, Pierre, a French diplomat, is unassuming and soft-spoken, gentle when he greets me. I offer them wine, and Madame Song takes the glass from me with both hands, nodding and smiling.

Once we're seated, Pierre asks in French, "Are you South Korean?"

I find this a strange question since they already know. "Yes," I answer.

He looks at Madame Song, and they exchange what I hope is not a look of doubt. "You don't look full Korean—"

"But I am," I protest a little too suddenly. "If not, what am I?"

"*Où est votre mari?*" Madame Song wants to know where my husband is.

"They're not married," Thibault responds, and I glare at him.

"On his way to Saudi Arabia," I reassure Madame Song, ladling hot soup into her bowl.

She swallows the creamy pumpkin and nods in approval. "This very good, but you no cook Korean food?"

I shake my head and look down into my steaming soup.

"It's okay." She smiles. "I give you recipe for *bi-bim-bap.*"

I thank her and get up to serve the veal.

"Sun Ae, your family, in Korea?"

I shrug. "I was abandoned."

Madame Song stops chewing, and her eyes widen with dismay. "No possible. Korean never abandon children—"

"I was found at the marketplace. My mother—"

"Mother no abandon. Korean mother never abandon children."

"Then she lost me," I retort lightly, returning with the sliced veal. I forgot the *jus* and the chopped parsley garnish.

Madame Song seems to like the lost version better and leans back in her chair, her face a thick slice of pale moon. "Ahhh, yes, your mother lose you at market. And mother have many, many questions to answer when she get back to house and no little girl."

I want to laugh at the thought of my mother returning home after twenty-five years, reprimanded for having lost me at the marketplace, but then I realize there's something graver in what she's saying.

"You," she says, leaning in close to me, "no abandon. But very, very lost." She shakes her head, not out of pity, I think, but for emphasis.

"Do you remember your family?" Pierre asks.

"A brother, grandmother. Mostly my brother," I repeat as if to convince myself. Thibault looks at me from across the table, searching my eyes if he should change the conversation.

"So when will you go to Seoul? Olivier say you go soon . . . when we meet first time in Aix."

"In February," I tell her.

"Very, very cold."

"Yes, but Olivier has business in Hong Kong and China. He decided this was a good time."

"And what do you think?" Pierre asks.

There is an awkward moment of silence as I search for an answer, but I have too many thoughts about it all, too many apprehensions I don't want to go into at this first dinner.

The wind picks up with the first fall chill. I serve dessert and chamomile tisane, and finally, Madame Song and her husband thank me for dinner and make their way back to Aix. Before she leaves, though, Madame Song writes down her phone number and we make an appointment for our first lesson the following Wednesday.

Thibault helps me clear the dishes and then sits in the worn chesterfield next to mine, in front of the fireplace, a pot of hot lemon verbena steaming between us.

"You're quiet—"

"She's right. I was lost . . . and maybe—"

"There are a thousand maybes. She can't know." He scoots closer to me, but I stand up, throw some more wood onto the fire, slip off my shoes, and sit back down.

"I'm sorry if that was difficult for you. Olivier asked me to come . . ."

"I know, but . . . Olivier's not even here."

"I am."

I know he is, and I also know that it's time for him to go. I get up, start to clear away the cups.

"Was the bookshop your idea or Olivier's way to keep you . . . tied to him?"

I shrug, pretending not to understand his question. "I'm not a kite."

"Are you actually going to decide any of it?" he continues.

I grab his car keys and walk out of the kitchen, stepping out onto the wet grass, my bare feet pale in the moonlight. Thibault follows, but I can't look at him.

"Don't be afraid." He takes my hands in his, brushes them with his lips. He smells like fire and wood. "Kim," he whispers, "I want . . . to kiss you."

"Not here," I hear myself whisper back. "Not here" doesn't mean yes, but it doesn't mean no, either. I walk him to his car, an old blue Citroën, hidden behind the hedges and Cumberland rosebushes. I'm cold now and want to go to bed, dream of something else. Thibault pulls me toward him, and I think of Olivier, guided by the renowned astronomer, zooming in on us through a telescope in the desert.

Focus. I must focus.

Thibault's lips are wet and sudden. He presses his body to mine, and I'm weightless, struggling against the density of his hands as they keep me grounded, tugging at me like one of his kites. It is the briefest of kisses, but there's a strange rush in my veins. These are the games we play, longing for the dead and for the living. I want him, and I don't. He's my brother, my savior. I am paper thin and opaque. Restless and unattached. He's my string, my tie to another world.

I'VE BEEN TRYING to practice new Korean words every day. *Komapsumnida*, I pronounce, counting the syllables in my head. Olivier and I are on the streets of Saint-Germain-des-Prés, near our new apartment. After looking at a handful of places with the real estate agent, Olivier decided in five minutes that the fourth-floor apartment at 9, rue de Luynes would be ours. It needed renovation, but that, too, was decided swiftly. In less than a month, we were moved in, and now it's as if we have been living here our whole lives.

"Come on, try it," I urge Olivier as we walk to pick up Laure from her school, located in the Marais on the other bank. Friday afternoons in the city are bustling with Parisians on their way to Normandy, Provence, anywhere to get away from the city. But this weekend we're here with Laure. Olivier wants to take me shopping for our trip in two weeks. Summerlike in Hong Kong and China and winter in Seoul. Olivier repeats after me, *komapsumnida,* trying to learn politesse in my mother tongue.

"I give up. You're the one who can get us through. I can't even speak English."

"It's not easy. I haven't had that many lessons. Especially since we're spending more and more time in Paris. Madame Song has been very patient with me canceling lessons. Okay, listen: *Maum, sagwa, k'al, nabi.* Heart, apple, knife, butterfly. Try *I tabang arumdapkunyo.*"

Olivier repeats after me and then shrugs. *"Qu'est-ce que ça veut dire?"*

"I think it means 'It's a beautiful tearoom.'"

"Ah, *oui,* very useful." Olivier laughs and opens the door. "Let's go in here."

At the Guerlain shop across from the Bon Marché department store, we buy spicy Samsara for me and Eau de Guerlain for him. Back at the Bon Marché, we look at shoes, to see not if they are comfortable, but if he likes them on me. He loves to play Poupée. I'm his China doll. He buys me things I'd never buy for myself. We go to Issey Miyake, Pleats Please. Anything I want. All of this and more, but it always seems too much. I tell Olivier that I want a pair of boots, but the heel's too high, he decides.

"You look better in casual, not frou-frou," he tells me. "You're not a Chanel type. Gold chains on purses. That's all Dominique wanted. You're more raw linens and silks, ecru colors."

"But I like this purse," I lie, testing him, knowing he'll say no.

When we get to Laure's school, we spot her in the courtyard. She sees us and waves excitedly but stops to walk in sync with the other girls. They're coltish and fashionable, some in short skirts with high boots and others in flared pants and perfectly matched sweaters, whispering and giggling secrets to one another.

When we're a good distance from the school, Laure takes my hand. "No one else has red hair like me," she laments. "Not even Papa or *Maman.*" She peers in the window of the *boulangerie* where Olivier's purchasing *pain au chocolat* for her after-school treat. "Look—" She points. "You'd never know he was *my* papa." She says this catching her breath, as if the thought were both delightful and dangerous. Then she frowns. "Who do you look like, Kimette?"

I shrug. "Someone." I'm sure.

"Papa said you didn't know your real parents. *C'est bizarre, ça.*" She squeezes my hand, then pats it gently. "*Vraiment bizarre.*" It's her new favorite word. I realize that the child actually feels sorry for me, but I remind myself that she can't begin to understand how bizarre it actually is. Olivier steps out of the *boulangerie* smelling of sugar and yeast.

"Now don't eat too much. We're going to Nelly and Louis's for dinner tonight."

Ignoring her father's words, Laure takes the sweets from him, biting greedily into the sugary dough. I pretend to be looking for something in my purse to let them walk ahead of me. I follow Laure and Olivier, longingly. I study them like strangers, objectively, as if I were going to paint or photograph them. In my eyes, a portrait of a father and child, connected by the simplest of gestures—passing back and forth warm, buttery pastry.

In my head, there's *maum, sagwa;* in my heart, *ppang, nabi.*

TONIGHT, I'M WEARING a simple black silk dress with silver-and-brass jewelry Olivier brought back from various trips to Mali and Burkina Faso while I was living in Stockholm. Nelly greets us in a rush, her jet black hair smoothed into a tight chignon, her amber-colored eyes outlined in smoky blue kohl. She is breathtaking.

"La ménopause, qu'est ce que c'est affreux!" she whispers in my ear, fanning herself as she leads us in. Menopause has also caused her sudden forty-pound weight gain, she laments. On seeing Laure, she smiles. *"La petite, quel plaisir."* She looks me over and, with a breath of approval, whisks us into the living room. The whole apartment smells of cardamom and earthy cinnamon, something sweet. *"Une tagine de poulet aux dattes,"* she announces passing around cumin-infused carrot slices and large marinated olives.

"Where's Louis?" I ask, biting into a juicy *harissa*-spiced olive. She wipes her forehead with a frayed Hermès silk square and points to the cellar.

Laure takes my hand as we descend the spiral stairs to his studio. "It's always a little scary, but I'm not afraid," she tells me. "Papa, are you there?"

Olivier's right behind us as we duck into Louis's studio. He stands when he sees us.

"Salut. Laure, I'm so happy you came. *Comment vas-tu?* Kim, tu es très élégante."

"Merci, Louis."

"What a beautiful piece." Olivier's crouching down to look at Louis's latest object: a large wooden board painted teal blue with small pieces of chicken wire and shells, a stunning mass of feathers painted terra-cottas and gold. *Entre chien et loup.*

"It's always about the yes and the no," Louis explains. *"Oui ou non. Ici ou là-bas.* The pull in opposite directions, choices."

Laure bends down and stares at the array of lost-and-found objects: ruins of trees and bent metal rods, tiles from wrecks, dried rat heads, and misshapen wood pieces. *"Bizarre,"* she whispers to her father. Olivier stands next to me as I stare at a newly finished piece hanging on the wall. I can't keep my eyes off it, a rectangular-shaped light wooden background, three birds in the center, ochers and blues and pale pink. There's a wooden dial for a moon.

"*Ça te ferait plaisir?*" Olivier asks Louis how much. He holds up one and a half fingers. I look at Olivier. "It's our little system. *On l'achète.*" Louis takes the piece off the wall and wraps it loosely in Kraft paper. Laure grasps my hand, and as we ascend the stairs, I think of perches and flight, hope and feathers.

CHICKEN THIGHS WITH CINNAMON AND DATES

1 teaspoon olive oil

2 sausage links (such as Merguez, spicy Italian pork, or lamb),
about ½ pound

6 to 8 skinless chicken thighs

1¼ teaspoons salt, divided

¾ teaspoon fresh-ground black pepper

1 large onion, thinly sliced

3 garlic cloves, smashed and coarsely chopped

1 tablespoon fresh-grated ginger

1 teaspoon ground cinnamon

½ teaspoon ground cumin

½ teaspoon hot paprika

1½ cups low-sodium chicken broth or water

½ cup fresh orange juice

About ⅓ cup golden raisins or currants

2 to 3 carrots, cut lengthwise and halved on the bias

1 large orange, cut into 8 wedges
12 to 15 dates (preferably Medjool), pitted, or 12 to 15 large
*   prunes, pitted*
2 to 3 tablespoons chopped fresh cilantro
Garnish: fresh cilantro, toasted almonds or pine nuts

Heat olive oil over medium high heat in a large ovenproof pan or Dutch oven. (If using a tagine to bake in, a wide skillet will do.) Cut sausage links in halves or thirds, depending on length, removing casings if desired. Add sausage and chicken to pot in one layer; sprinkle with half of salt and pepper. Let cook about 5 minutes. Turn meat over, season with remaining salt and pepper, and let cook 5 minutes more. Remove chicken to a plate. (If using a tagine, place chicken and sausage directly in bottom of tagine.) Add onion to pot (if brown bits are stuck to bottom, add about 1 tablespoon white wine, water, or orange juice, scraping to loosen bits) and let cook about 5 minutes. Add garlic, ginger, cinnamon, cumin, and paprika. Stir and let cook about 3 minutes. Add chicken broth and orange juice, raisins, and carrots and stir. Pour onion-carrot mixture over chicken and sausage in tagine, or if not using tagine, place chicken and sausage back in pot. Add orange wedges and dates.

Stir, cover, and bake at 350 degrees for about 1 hour 30 minutes or until chicken and carrots are fork tender. Taste sauce and adjust seasoning as needed. Top with cilantro and serve with hot buttered couscous and *harissa* paste or coriander (or other favorite) chutney. Garnish if desired. *Serves 6 to 8.*

XI

WITH RESERVATIONS

ॐ

THE FINAL LESSON, AFTER NEW YEAR'S, WITH MADAME Song is spent perfecting "please" and "thank you," "I like the hot of the ginger tea," "the dumpling soup, please." This is ridiculous, but it's my fault for not being able to pick it up. I will it, but nothing comes back. And even though Olivier found Madame Song, he decided after just a few lessons that it wasn't necessary, especially after he saw how frustrating it was for both of us.

"You speak English and French, Swedish," he said. "That's two more languages than I can manage . . . we'll be just fine. You don't need to learn Korean after all." But I insisted on continuing, trying to learn words in my mother tongue if we were to survive a return visit to Seoul.

"Soon," she calls me, interrupting my thoughts. "I no understand. Your French fluent, no accent, and you no pronounce *Kurigo sajindo myot chang tchikko shipsumnida?*"

I try again to imitate her cadence, but it doesn't flow. She shakes her head and clucks her tongue like a mother hen.

"I'm not doing it on purpose."

"Of course not." She crosses her arms over her chest, unconvinced. "But I come all the way to Paris from Aix-en-Provence for your final lesson, and . . ." She stops to shake her head. "Why don't you just practice vowel combinations."

"Can't I just write the letters with the calligraphy brush instead?"

She tilts her head to one side and then the other, tapping her fingers on the tabletop, staring at me. I take a sip of my tea, hiding behind the steam. "You know, my husband and I were saying . . . ninety percent Korea people no look like you. Eyes different. Maybe, in fact you not—"

"Madame Song, I'm leaving for South Korea in two days, and I have tried my best. Would you care for some more tea?"

She nods. I pour and then dip the thick bamboo-stick brush in black China ink, poise myself just so over the large scroll of white paper. "You no get lost over there," she jokes. She smiles and leans over me, placing her hand gently on mine, guiding my wrist and fingers as I write *"Komapsumnida"* in large black swoops. The ink drips and dries in strange shapes, like shadows of missing faces. I stare at the blots, the variations in depth, willing myself to recognize them, understand the elongated forms and nuances of my mother tongue.

Laure and Olivier arrive at the door just as I am kissing Madame Song good-bye for the last time before our trip to South Korea. Olivier takes a picture of the two of us before she leaves.

"Un cadeau pour toi." Laure hands me a drawing of the three of us. Olivier and Kim on a jet and Laure waving to us from the ground. I thank her, and she follows me into the bedroom as I start folding clothes. "Where's Asia?" she asks, wrapping herself in one of my cashmere stoles. "Near Indonesia?"

"Yes," I answer. "Far, far away."

"Papa, are you coming back?" She pulls on a pair of my boots.

We both answer yes. The bell rings, and Laure wobbles to open the door.

"*Ma chérie,* are you all alone?" Nelly's voice is shrill, and I know immediately that she's in one of her hysterical states. I hold my breath as she waltzes into the room. Louis kisses me and whispers that Nelly is in "one of her moods."

"*Salut, Nel.*" I cover my open suitcase with a blanket, but as Nelly leans down to kiss me hello, she unearths a brown wool turtleneck.

"But, Keem. You can't possibly think of taking this to Hong Kong. *Non, non, non.*"

"It's my favorite sweater."

"Even if it is designer, this color doesn't go with you. You need bright, happy colors for such a . . . how do you say . . . sad journey."

"Sad?" I grab the sweater from her and fold it neatly back into the suitcase.

"Yes, you know. Going back to your roots, even though there is no one there for you."

"Is anyone hungry?" I walk past her and into the kitchen. "How about some pasta? *Olivier, un peu de vin, s'il te plaît.*"

Olivier pours wine while Laure does her homework and I make spaghetti carbonara, a salad of Belgian endive, oranges, and walnuts. Flora calls, and so do Thibault, Sophie, and my friend Charlotte from Stockholm, all to wish us good luck. Everything seems so final and tragic that I put on some bossa nova and dance around with Laure while waiting for the water to boil. She has traded my boots for my favorite sweater, the sleeves too long for her. She asks if she can keep this one, just until I get back. Of course, I tell her.

"So have you learned the words for shopping in Korean?" Nelly inquires during dinner. I shake my head. I can hardly ask the time. "You're leaving tomorrow, no?"

"Monday."

"Papa." Laure throws her head into Olivier's shoulder and then climbs onto my lap, sticks her thumb in her mouth. I assure her that we'll be back soon, even though I read in a recent issue of *Ça m'Intéresse* magazine that Korean pilots are undertrained and I've been dreaming the wreck, the crash, for weeks in anticipation.

After we've tucked Laure into bed, I brew up some aromatic tisane.

"Bon voyage en Asie." Nelly gives me a bottle of perfume, Yves Saint Laurent's Paris. "So you won't forget us. So you'll come back." She looks at me, and the gentleness in her eyes makes her seem momentarily concerned and quite old, even maternal. I hug her tightly.

"A très bientôt." Louis presses a square notebook in my hand, with a Bic pen drawing of me and the planets shooting out from my hair. There are open spaces for notes and photos.

"Write it all down, furiously. And good luck," he adds, winking at me.

ON OUR WAY across the continents to South Korea, I keep thinking of Madame Song back in Provence. I have her photo. I've glued it along with Laure's drawing onto the first page of the book Louis gave me. Madame Song looks like the 10 percent of Koreans she told me I resembled. Although I never really noticed the difference until she pointed it out, it's all I can think about now. And I remember now how Suzy always insisted she was not Korean because she didn't look like me. Her eyelids are smoother, less pronounced.

Laure, she claims, looks like neither her mother nor her father. "Maybe when I'm ten," she said hopefully, "I'll look more like one of them." But she looks a lot like Olivier—the same jaw and piercing way she stares at you when there's an idea about to take fruition.

Eight weeks of Madame Song's tutoring and I'm only able to confidently repeat the same words I've said all these years: *Omma, Abba, kundungi.*

Changing Olivier's mind about the journey was impossible. Every day I read him the articles from the *International Herald Tribune.* North Korea resistant to international inspections. Below freezing temperatures. I even called the American embassy in Seoul. "I'm American, but Korean . . . If there's a war or something . . . is everything okay over there?"

"It is today, February first, 1994, but you never know about tomorrow."

I recall the functionary's words as the flight attendant dressed in a red-and-blue silk dress takes cocktail orders. "A double for me, please," I remind her as I slip Lexomil under my tongue. When she returns with just one glass of Champagne, I mix it with another dose of Ivadal and wait for sleep.

We're only twenty minutes into the seventeen-hour flight from Paris to Seoul. When the FASTEN SEAT BELTS sign blinks off, I'm able to breathe a little easier. This is my first time flying Korean Airlines. Small, square-shouldered pilots in navy blue and red take turns walking up and down the aisles.

"Why aren't they flying the plane?" I whisper to Olivier, squeezing his hand. He's stretched out, putting on the massaging microfiber socks that come in our first-class complimentary bags.

"Some dinner and a nap and we'll be there in no time." He kisses my forehead.

During rice and fish, hot soup, and a blurry movie, I ask Olivier if I look like the flight attendants. (*Non.*) The pilot? (*Non.*)

An ancient Korean man walking down the aisle? (*Non.*) Then the little boy by the window? (A slight resemblance, *si tu veux*).

The captain announces that because of the conflicts in Afghanistan, we will have to take a longer route. I order another glass of Champagne and think of the stretch of continents below, how the earth constantly shifts and changes, and the wars being fought in the remotest regions of the world, the tiny battles inside.

Eventually I lapse into a half sleep and see my Korean brother who sometimes appears in my dreams. He is always warning me about the dark and the cold. There is a warm spot on the empty floor of our Korean house, built high on stilts. I am the youngest or smallest and must wait in line to sit on the spot. Sometimes he lets me cut. Together, as in the grim fairy tale, we are an exotic version of the blond Hansel and Gretel, minus the loving father to take us home.

Then they fell asleep and evening passed, but no one came to the poor children. They did not awake until it was dark night, and Hansel comforted his little sister and said: "Just wait . . . until the moon rises, and then we shall see the crumbs of bread which I have strewn about, they will show us our way home again." When the moon came they set out, but they found no crumbs, for the many thousands of birds which fly about in the woods and fields had picked them all up.

Many dreams later, we prepare for an evening arrival at Kimpo Airport. My throat tightens as we shuffle into a multitude of lines. I do as the others, remain silent, keep my head down—I want to blend in, be accepted across the border without being noticed, as if I've always belonged. When it's my turn, I show the immigration officer my American passport, offer an international smile—sincere but brief—in an attempt at discretion. It's the heart of winter, so I'm dressed in black boots, black cashmere coat, wool pants, and a gray turtleneck sweater. My hair is silky and straight under a knit hat. I'm cold and anxious and speak only when I am spoken to.

"Kim Soon-nay?" The immigration officer looks at me, raising his wide, sparse eyebrows. I nod, holding my breath. "American?"

I nod again and watch as he flips through the pages. Stamps from Athens, Geneva, JFK, Valencia, Marseille, and a Swedish work visa fan out like an animated travel log. The moon-faced man nods, adds his own black stamp, then jolts his head for me to pass.

Sweet victory. I've been granted entrance to my home country. I take a deep breath as Olivier is also allowed in. He squeezes my hand. I look around the airport as we make our way to the baggage claim, holding back the tears, not wanting to admit that I was half hoping someone might be here to greet me, acknowledge me as one of theirs.

In the back of the cab on our way to the Westin Chosun Hotel, Olivier whispers in my ear, "This is so exciting for you, for us." His enthusiasm is jarring. What could possibly be so wonderful about this cold, gray, silent city? But I feel guilty as he makes an effort to point out every brightly lit temple and square. I lean into him, thankful that he's real and solid and sitting next to me.

When we arrive at the hotel, the cabdriver grunts as Olivier pulls out dollars and francs and Korean won. He points to the revolving glass doors and lurches away, leaving us at the hotel entrance. Mostly men in dark business suits walk swiftly in and out of the entrance. Olivier checks us in, ignoring the thumbs-up from a Korean man in the lobby.

The next morning, February cold aches in my bones. Olivier

rubs my legs to warm them up as I recall dreams of crowded places and missing faces. They come back to me throughout the morning. We have breakfast standing in the street: cloudy soup with a side of fried dumplings and a thick red dipping sauce. The flavors are hot and sweet and dense at once. I devour the dumplings whole, burning my throat with this food I so long to remember. I stare at the faces through the steam. Are they staring at me, or is it just my imagination?

Later, another cabdriver drops us off at Folk Village—the memory park of a country, my country. It looks like a back lot of Disney World where they put the less commercial, less exciting countries on hold. There are artisans working diligently to reconstruct what Korea was. Merchants sell wooden tools, figures, and bowls and offer steaming ginseng tea. There's even a film crew, Korean Hollywood, filled with a tired cast of Korean warriors. I photograph a young girl leaning on her mother's body. Do I look like her? Olivier shakes his head wearily. "She almost looks real," I tell him, focusing in on the swan curve of her neck. "Not like the others who pretend to show us the past."

Walking along a trail, I freeze in front of a row of houses. They're built on stilts, just as I've always remembered, with outside heating devices. An old woman opens the door to one of them. She is ancient. I watch her as she slowly lifts a blue surgical mask off her mouth, the one I see many older people wearing to protect from the bitter cold, and calls after a little boy running toward us. He stops, waves at the woman, laughs, and continues in the opposite direction. I instinctively go to follow after him, but Olivier catches my arm.

"He won't come back if you chase him."

Later at the National Museum, we must wait our turn. It's below freezing, and children line up military style in the large perfect square. It appears they're on a field trip, but they're not smiling; gravity weighs down their faces, pulls down their shoulders, shutting their smooth eyelids to the outside world. Everyone seems so serious and sad here, or maybe it's just me.

The museum guards let us enter the stone cold museum, one by one. No one smiles, no one speaks. They listen to our footsteps echo, watch us as we take in the pottery and tools, costumes and weapons. There's a replica of a pharmacy filled with ancient remedies for memory loss and solitude.

In another section are glass-enclosed cases. There is one of a miniature version of a wall in Kach'ang village. I feel like a giant, standing above, looking down. Tiny women made of earth and clay carry baskets of heavy stones on their heads. Each year, they must circle the wall three times with the weight of the stones to protect their families against tempests, fever, and nostalgia. My body aches for them. The guards follow us around, trying to see what we see.

Our third morning, drinking fish broth and biting into crunchy rice cakes, I tell Olivier I want to leave. I know it's sudden and inexplicable, but I fear the truth—never finding anyone who recognizes me.

"You have to give it some time," Olivier says. "I know we can't really find your family."

I shake my head. "Maybe if I had contacted the Catholic Relief Services . . . it's on one of my documents . . ."

Olivier takes a sip of his soup. "I'm sorry. I should have been better prepared. I should have tried to find your family. What was I thinking?" He turns away, and I can't tell if he's angry or sad or mad at me, even.

"I never asked you to look for them," I say. "It's impossible. There's no trace, really . . . just these stupid papers, and . . ." I stop myself, breathe in the cold air to shock my system out of crying. "I'm sorry. It's the jet lag. And the weather. You've done so much already . . ."

Olivier kisses me and then hands me a piece of rice cake. "At least the food is really good."

I nod. The food is wonderful, both rustic and exquisitely presented. I love the spicy red pastes to slather onto grilled meats. Shiny earthenware bowls, hot with sizzling rice. "But I do want to leave soon," I remind him. "Time won't change anything. Look what happened last night."

Last night, we wanted to eat authentic food outside of the hotel. So the concierge scribbled down the name of a local restaurant in Korean for the cabdriver while the female hotel clerk seemed to delight in informing me in broken English that the only Korean women with white men at five-star hotels are high-end prostitutes. She looked me up and down, daring me to respond.

The cabdriver dropped us off at the restaurant. I was excited to eat Korean food and marveled as waiters brought tiny bowls of colorful kimchi and larger, steaming stone bowls of rice and beef to the tables around us. We waited and waited. Finally, a woman reluctantly gave us menus and disappeared behind a silk screen. We waited some more, and then she sent out a fat, laughing waitress, who pointed at us, pointed at Olivier, the white man at my side. She then called the others to come, look at us, and finally shoo us away. I wanted to shout at their round, scornful faces that I was just like them. That I didn't choose to leave, that it was all a mistake or a bad dream.

But because they wouldn't serve us, Olivier led me out of the restaurant, out onto the street, where, luckily, vendors were cooking thin slices of beef and bits of sweet, spicy omelet behind vapors of steam and starch. We walked a little farther and huddled together against the harsh Korean winter at the open-air counters and devoured half-moons of pan-fried dough, steaming bowls of rice-thickened soup. Olivier ate for both of us as I thought about the faces rejecting me.

Come, is all I wanted them to say. Eat at our table.

ON OUR LAST night, I dream of *Omma* again and again. I hear her voice hovering, like the helicopters that threaten to chop away at the air and swallow up the people from the ground below.

I open my eyes from sleep, uncurl my body, and sit up on the bare floor. "Shhh," my brother whispers, placing his finger over my lips. In the next room, a woman's voice as sweet as scented rice explains that it was all a mistake. I rub my eyes and blink away sleep to discover plump waitresses laughing. Omma speaks: "She's simply been lost all these years. Misfortune, everyone knows, misplaces people, but loneliness and persistence," she explains awkwardly, "brings them back."

Omma shuts the door firmly and quietly starts brewing water for tea and sweetened rice cakes. We'll have to share. I'm happy even to give my piece away, as long as I don't lose my place.

On our last morning in the city, we walk the streets of the main center. In a back alley, people dressed in bright blue, red, white, and yellow silks gather at an open altar, surrounded by rice offerings and multicolored ribbons. I want to bow, too, and pray with them to whatever gods unite them, but I stop myself because I realize that I would only be an intrusion. I wouldn't know how to kneel properly, haven't learned the vocabulary necessary to ask for blessing, forgiveness, and grace.

On our way back to the hotel, we take a detour through the antiques quarter. I want something to take back with me, something old and meaningful, anything that will prove that this part of the world exists, a vestige of my memory. Olivier hands me a beautiful papier-mâché box covered with multicolored cutouts. The ancient merchant and his wife speak broken French to us.

"*Boîte—*" She points enthusiastically. "*Cent cinquante ans vieux.*" One hundred and fifty years old, filled on the inside, she points, with stories written in Chinese. Stories of love and loss. "*Merci, revenez, bientôt, bientôt.*" Come back, soon, soon.

"*Komapsumnida,*" we repeat, bowing in her likeness, thanking her for such kindness.

WE'RE ON A Cathay Pacific flight. As the Boeing lifts its heavy body into the sky, we rise, too, our bodies floating above my birth country. Our next stop is Hong Kong, and I'm ready for anything as long as I can get out of here. I can't dream any language to make them understand that I had no choice but to be taken away the first time. But this time, I can choose not to stay.

This flight, for some reason, I'm not worried about bombs or terrorists. I want to be airborne. I know that I will fly and land safely somewhere, sometime, soon. I clutch the box to my heart, squeeze Olivier's hand. The flight attendant offers cocktails, but I shake my head. My throat's hot and swollen, and no words will come out. I scoot all the way into the back of my seat, letting my legs swing back and forth.

Because there are no formal records, because I was abandoned, I realize that Seoul is not where I can validate myself. I cannot look to this part of the world to see where I belong. No familiar faces, and certainly no one to claim me. I look out the window through the clouds, imagine the plane piercing the emptiness of the sky.

"You see—" Olivier points out the window. "This isn't really your home." Maybe he's right, but does he have to say it? Pronouncing the words just makes it more real. "Your home is here"—he points to himself—"with me."

"Good-bye, South Korea," I whisper, not really ready to say adieu. It gets smaller and smaller, and I look down to the people and buildings below, the temples and rivers and villages. Suddenly, I am one of the miniature women in the museum replica of the village of Kach'ang, circling the wall again and again, my body heavy with nostalgia, not strong or wise enough to ward off tempests, fever, and loss.

As we prepare to land in Hong Kong, the passengers wave to the late workers in the high-rise buildings on both sides of the arriving Boeing. One of Olivier's business associates, a half-Vietnamese, half-Chinese woman named Ling, will be there waiting for us at the airport. Another border to cross, and we're in.

"Everything is for sale here, twenty-four hours a day," Ling boasts as we make our way through tunnels from Kowloon to our hotel overlooking the bay. The waters of the city are silver, reflecting metal skyscrapers and jets. Ferries, shrimp boats, and flat-bottomed junks slowly drift in and out of the bay. There is so much to fill the eyes and nose here that there is little time for thoughts, no room for longing, and definitely no time for tears. When we arrive at the lobby of the New Harbour View, an Asian man stops me and asks, "You? Half Japanese, half white?" I don't think to answer and instead find myself shaking my fist at him.

"I'm not like you," I hear myself say in such a strange-sounding accent, not recognizing the sound of my own voice.

The food in China and Hong Kong is equally thrilling, but in both places I am claustrophobic with the rivers of people—they *do* look like me, but not one familiar face or smell or syllable among them. All I care about now is Chinese New Year in a few days, February 10, and all I want are colors and dragon dances and red lanterns. I can't have the Korean family I dream, so I want a movie poster version of this part of the world.

In the morning, Ling takes us on the Hong Kong Peak train to Victoria Park, and then I venture out on my own for a few hours while she, Olivier, and the others discuss business. I walk the streets far from the hotel, taking pictures of the open markets—macro shots of dried scorpion, pale starfish, and red roots shaped like withered men. I focus in: a cow's head with the skin ripped off, left on a garbage heap. I want to capture it along with freshly fallen ginkgo leaves and rotting Asian pears.

It's almost noon when I realize I must find a taxi to meet Olivier and the others for lunch. The air suddenly feels hot on my body; it wraps around me like a heavy gauze, making it harder and harder to breathe. Buses come and go, but no cabs. The heat thickens and swirls in my throat. A digital sign flashes: 24° CELSIUS / 95% HUMIDITY. Something's slowly seeping into my body, invading my lungs. My head begins to spin with the honking of horns and trolleys, people everywhere, all with someplace to go, negotiating and trading their lives away. I finally see a cab and rush out into the flood of Asians.

"Thank you," I mouth to the cabdriver. I shut the door, exhausted.

The cabbie, a small, older Chinese man, looks at me in the rearview mirror. "Thank *you*," he mimics in English. "You no thank you me." He spits and slams on the brakes. "Is that all you people know to say . . . thank you, thank you?"

I'm not sure if he's kicking me out, so I start to open the door, but he accelerates, cackles, and growls at me as we wind our way through the puzzling jigsaw of the city. My throat is starting to swell, and I can't find the words to defend myself.

Somehow I make it to the restaurant where Olivier's waiting for me, seated next to Ling. Her husband and father are there along with four Chinese investment bankers. Ling gestures for me to sit opposite her, but Olivier takes my hand and seats me next to him. Our table's in the center of the main dining room, filled with families and miniature kumquat trees hung with bright red and gold envelopes. We smile, nod, greet one another. Immediately waiters place multicolored dishes, saucers, bowls, and chopsticks on the large lazy Susan in the center of the table. I want hot ginseng tea, but before we can order, the waiter sets down a glass of cognac for each of us. Ling's father rises and proposes a toast for loyalty and prosperity in the Year of the Dog.

"*Gan bei,*" we all repeat after him. Bottoms up. The cognac soothes my aching throat. The waiter immediately refills our glasses with the same amber liquid as the first courses are served: hot-and-sour soup, smoked oysters in a dried black mushroom sauce served in an intricately woven basket of fried noodles.

"*Gan bei.*" We lift our glasses and drink. I try to whisper to Olivier that I think I'm coming down with something, but Ling keeps leaning in to him, interrupting our conversation. She swirls more cognac into my glass as her father leads Olivier to the large fish tank to choose the next course.

"What year were you born?" Ling asks me in her high-pitched French, leaning into the empty space where Olivier was sitting.

"In 1970, 1971?" I shrug. "More or less."

"*Un chien.* It's your year to flourish. Dogs are very faithful," Ling informs me, "but no good with dragons. Olivier is a dragon, no?" She lets out a tiny burp and then excuses herself to the banker on her left, who's also drunk. Someone spins the lazy Susan, and a few of the porcelain bowls go flying off the table.

"To the Bank of China," says a young woman dressed in last season's pinstripes, looking around nervously.

I read recently that the same architect who designed the pyramids in the Cour du Louvre also designed the Bank of China. To no one in particular, I whisper, "It looks like a knife in the heart of the city."

"Forget 1994. A toast to 1997," encourages another banker at our table.

When Olivier returns, my head is spinning. "I'm sick," I tell him.

"You've had too much. Just pretend to drink, and I'll help you with the rest."

"No, it's my throat." I swallow and can feel the saliva barely squeeze down. "And I think I have a fever."

"On second thought, drink the cognac," he responds, kissing my damp forehead.

Ling looks over at us, and I shoot her a canine smile. I excuse myself and find my way to the bathroom, clutching my stomach, my face dripping with sweat. I throw up in one of the toilets, the women scowling as I wash my face and gesture apologies.

The fish Olivier has chosen is plated with uniform slices of ginger and scallion. The head is cut off and offered to Olivier, but he declines politely, offering it to the eldest at the table. I'm amazed as Ling's father pops it in his mouth, whole, sucks and slurps, then spits out what he doesn't want. I turn away to see that everyone in the restaurant is doing the same. Men and women in custom-tailored silk suits and dresses sit, concentrating their agile tongues to separate the good from the bad, spitting out the inedible. There are fourteen courses and several bottles of cognac that I somehow manage to sit through. I do not want to make trouble—I do not want to embarrass Olivier.

THE NEXT DAY, my fever is up to 103 degrees. Breathing feels like a razor scraping the inside of my throat. Olivier gives me a bottle of essence of red thyme, distilled in Provence. I take a drop of the liquid on my tongue. It burns like fire and makes me gag.

"Maybe we should wait until you're better. You can't travel like this," Olivier suggests, wiping my chin.

But it's the Chinese New Year, I want to say. The Year of the Dog, and I will dig a hole to China if I must. I swallow another drop of the potent essence because I want it to cure me, whatever has crept into my body and shoots from my throat down through my chest. A Chinese pharmacist says I have the pollution in my lungs . . . bronchitis.

Olivier checks for fever: 104 degrees now. The pharmacist gives me watered-down root tea, offers dried scorpion powder ground into a fine mist to drink down with cognac. My whole body aches, my lungs heavy with congestion. One of Olivier's business acquaintances jokes that I am having an allergic reaction to Asia.

The next day, Olivier relents and we take the Kowloon–Guangzhou express train from Hong Kong across the border and into China. Ling has made arrangements for Olivier to meet a Chinese businessman, a possible supplier of bottles and plastics for L'Occitane, in Shenzhen, in the Cantonese region of China.

The Chinese businessman is waiting impatiently when we arrive. He doesn't shake hands or talk to us. He talks only to

Ling, who then translates, what I understand, from their gestures and facial expressions, to be a censored version. I don't catch his name, but he's much taller than Olivier, with big, pointy teeth. I secretly call him the Wolf. He drives us around in his shiny black Lexus, which costs what a Chinese laborer makes in a lifetime, he tells us through Ling.

"This part of the region is prosperous," he continues. "The people are becoming healthier, wealthier."

I can feel the heat rising through me, pushing up something in the back of my throat. I'm going to vomit again, but I keep my eyes fixed on the road ahead. The outside bumps by—a war zone, from the evening news broadcast. There's dry dust everywhere, and the light, it seems, has no direct source. Old men on bikes sell sugarcane on the side of the street, a child limps across an open running sewer and waves at us, a big toothless grin across his weathered face. Buildings are under construction, but they're nothing but big cement blocks with minuscule windows on every other floor.

The scaffolds here are amazingly precarious, made of dried sticks of bamboo. Their fragility reminds me of the houses I used to build as a child. Houses made of my grandfather's playing cards. I would set them on the kitchen table, creating a whole village, and then stomp by noisily to test the solidity of my construction.

The Wolf pulls into the parking lot of a five-star hotel in the village. "For tourists," he says proudly. A young man promptly arrives and opens the Wolf's door. They lead us into the hotel. The Wolf flashes a pointy-toothed grin, and all the girls behind the reception desk squeal as they line up in front of him. They are plump and shimmering in their gold lamé tops. They kiss him one by one as he slips a red-and-gold envelope into their eager palms. He says something, and one of the girls translates that the Big

One will return in several hours to take us for dinner. The Wolf doesn't say good-bye, just turns. I keep my eyes planted firmly on his back until he is swallowed up by the automatic doors.

We're taken to our room, which overlooks the city center. Everything in the hotel is five-star, on the surface—large meeting areas, overly polished light fixtures, and smiling employees. But the walls are a mud brown and the floors a powdery gray tile. In the bathroom, Olivier points out the large marble bathtub, a toilet with no seat, and a sink. *"Regarde,"* he says, pointing under the sink. I squat down to see that all the pipes have burst and are held together with worn pieces of masking tape. Rusty water leaks from around the toilet base.

Someone knocks on the door. Through the peephole, I can make out only a shiny black eye. I let in a young man from room service who is carrying a plastic tray with two mugs, two Lipton teabags, and a thermos of boiled water.

"Happy Chinese New Year," he wishes us. He sets the tray on the table next to the window, then opens the closet door.

Olivier pours tea while I take another drop of red thyme. I'm used to its burning, so this time it soothes me. Fever twists my body, aches in my bones. I take a sip from the thermos. Lukewarm water. I spit it out, take a deep breath, and close my eyes. I want to click my heels three times and be back in Paris.

"I want to go home."

"Soon," Olivier answers. I fall asleep in the chair and awaken later to the sound of gunshots and explosions. With every blast, my heart jumps. Helicopters swarm down low over the streets. The chop-chop sound of the blades reminds me of early childhood nightmares. Not a war, I pray. It's dark out, and from our window we see people lighting up the sky with fireworks and red fire bombs. Olivier shoots a photo quickly before powder and smoke fill the air. I cover my ears as another explosion pops. Don't let me die here, I think. Anywhere but here.

The phone rings, and I vaguely hear Olivier say, "We'll be right down."

"Do you think you can join us for dinner?" he asks me. "Maybe you should stay here."

I can't swallow, but I don't want to be left alone. I nod, take one last drop of red thyme. Ling and the Wolf are waiting for us in the hotel dining room. The Wolf is the only man dressed in a suit and tie. Olivier and Ling's husband are in dark pants and linen shirts. The three other Chinese businessmen at our table wear polo shirts and slacks with navy blazers. The Wolf picks his teeth and spits on the chair where Olivier is to sit. Olivier pretends not to notice and smiles. I don't understand these customs, especially if there is a business deal to be made.

The Wolf orders for us all. With each course, the waiters show it to him first, and if he approves, they set it before us. I ask for hot tea with lemon instead of the cognac they pour for everyone else. The meal slips before me in a blur: dried oysters stewed in oil, meat in a thick red sauce, peanut paste steamed in pale sticky buns. I notice that the Wolf doesn't eat. He watches us, and every once in a while he sits back to clean his nose or pick at his finely manicured nails. I can't chew or swallow but pretend to enjoy the greasy food set before me. I'm relieved when the waiters bring out hot bowls of soup. The steam feels good on my nose, raw from wiping it so much. I inhale but can't really smell it. I dip in the spoon and pull out a black marbled egg-shaped object. I bring it closer to see that it's furry. I plunge it back in before anyone sees me.

Olivier whispers, "It's the thousand-year-old eggs. A Chinese delicacy."

I push my bowl toward him. I suddenly long for Korean food—aesthetic, clean, and spicy, served in smooth hot bowls.

After dinner and toothpick time, Ling announces that we're going to celebrate the New Year. I perk up at the thought of petite women in traditional dress with plump red lips and paper lanterns, dragon dances. I want the China of picture books and movies, the clichés of Asia I have always fought against.

Ling leans close to Olivier, chatting on like a schoolgirl. But he hugs me close to him as we make our way out to the parking lot. I wonder how we're all going to fit in the car when a young man from the hotel runs out, the Wolf's car keys high in the air, then backs the big fat Lexus right up to where we're standing. The employee gets out, pops open the trunk, and places three large cardboard boxes at our feet.

We look at one another, puzzled. Is someone going to pop out of one of the boxes? Are we to applaud? Say thank you? The Wolf ceremoniously opens the boxes and pulls out long red firecrackers, places them on the ground between the car and the street. He takes his silver lighter and lights them one by one as he watches them shoot off into the night. After each explosion, he spits happily on the ground. I look around and there are no dancing dragons, just wolves, businesswomen instead of ladies in red dresses carrying lanterns. This is it? Suddenly I imagine the Wolf in a wide-brimmed hat and spurred boots, the lonesome Chinese cowboy kicking the West in its sides, except that his back is slightly hunched, and as he turns his head, light shines on his greasy, sweaty face, his pointy teeth becoming even sharper in the night.

THE NEXT MORNING, the Wolf sends a message for us to meet him for breakfast in the semiprivate dining room on the top floor of the hotel. Eight a.m. and already multiple trays of steaming bamboo baskets are rolled to our table. The same waiter from last night sets down a steaming basket in front of Olivier at the Wolf's approval. He lifts the lid: steamed black-footed chicken's feet with its claws in a thick red sauce. The Chinese are all watching him. Olivier lifts his chopsticks, bites into a foot, chews, and smiles. They laugh and raise their glasses in a toast, and then my heart sinks as the Wolf insists on rotten egg soup for the whole table.

Breakfast, thankfully, is cut short because Ling and the Wolf are eager to take us on a tour of the prospering village. We follow them through the winding streets covered with red confetti and discarded fireworks from the night before. At the marketplace, we see where all the produce from last night's dinner is sold. An old woman squats behind a cardboard box laden with shriveled oysters. Cut-up raw chicken pieces are spread out on the dirt floor. At every stand is a bowl of the black furry eggs. Children run around playing among broken branches and waste from trucks.

We stop in front of a baby, wrapped in green cloth and a dirty sweater, lying on the ground on top of a large white piece of paper. I can't tell if it's a girl or a boy, but surely it can't be more than six months old. I ask Ling to translate.

"Please take this child. I have no choice but to abandon my child."

I look around at the crowd gathering, hoping someone will come and help, but they are laughing instead, talking among themselves, reading the paper, buying produce, pointing at the baby, the sky, and the foreigners in their midst. I am compelled to run away with the child in my arms, run as fast as I can, but I start coughing hard, my lungs on fire now as I take the camera, point, and shoot, imagining already the developed image—a lost child and, along the edge, the feet of all those standing around waiting, expectant, paralyzed into doing nothing.

We walk back to the hotel along the lake. It has become the village dump. I photograph the floating chairs, electronics parts, and waste. This is what I will think of when I remember this part of the world. I start to focus in on a man squatting at the edge of the water but cover up the lens and stare at him with my naked eyes. He slices open the throat of a turtle, rocks back and forth as if humming a lullaby. I watch him watch it bleed to death.

THE ROAD LEADING out of China is shared by pedestrians, truck drivers, men on bicycles, chickens and turtles, a few private cars, and taxis. We're finally leaving, on our way to Hong Kong for an evening flight back to Paris. The fever is still high, but I'm dying to get on the plane.

At the airport, our flight is delayed. We're in Cathay Pacific's first-class lounge with Parisians clad in black, businessmen from Singapore and China, a few Australians, and a handful of Americans.

Olivier and I are finally seated on the top level of the jet. It feels like a small private plane. There's one attendant, it seems, for every three passengers. They smile demurely, offering caviar, fresh fruit, Champagne in abundance. All I can swallow is hot water with lemon, a drop of honey. I can't sleep, can't breathe. I try to restrain my cough while everyone snoozes in the cabin, stretched out comfortably in their seats, eyes masked, necks cradled in velvet pillows. We're pulled up into the sky, and I can feel my body instantly lighter, effortlessly slipping away.

When we arrive back in Paris, I could almost kiss the ground. Asia is such a far, faraway land. Coughing is painful and leaves traces of mucus and blood in my throat. At Roissy, we fold into a cab under the gray sheets of cold rain. When I see the driver's Asian face in the rearview mirror, I feel resentment rising in me for no particular reason.

"Où aller?" he asks.

Olivier directs him. *"En bas du boulevard Raspail et vers Saint-Germain. Rue de Luynes."*

"Rue de Lune?"

"Luynes," I correct him, irritated with his lack of understanding.

"You—" The driver points to me in the mirror. "You not one of us. Hair too shiny, too thin." When he grins, I notice half his teeth are missing and the other half rotting.

I cough into the back of his head, blow my nose like a foghorn, and throw the shredded Kleenex on the backseat floor. I lean into Olivier's body, let him stroke my forehead, which is damp with rain and fever, as we make our way back through the streets of Paris.

"I want to go home," I whisper. But the words get caught and sound foreign in my mouth.

"Ohh-mmma," the little girl calls. Her voice stretches across the village and bounces back into her heart.

"Ohhh-mmma," she cries. Everything is in slow motion. Her limbs ache with longing. Her brother reaches out to her, or maybe it's her grandmother. The market is gray with rats and picked-over fruit that nobody wants, leftovers that will rot for days.

She's sitting on a bench, legs dangling in midair, surrounded by vendors. She sits clenching a morsel of food tight in her fist, so tight, her knuckles are white and cold. She whispers to herself, "She told me not to move." She rocks back and forth with the words and rhythm to keep her warm. "She told me she'll be back." And then everything *speeds up. The sun goes away and leaves her in the dark with lights glaring from the port. Alone again and wandering, circling the market-place. Her head spins with directions and street clatter. Swimming on land, drowning in shadows of the disappeared.*

"Reviens, Omma." She hears her voice, like streaks of rain. "Come back. Come back."

Someone's shaking me, wiping sweat from my cheeks. *"Ça va, mon amour? Réveille-toi."*

When I finally open my eyes, a man's sitting on the bed, speaking a strange language. I try to answer but cough instead, and the pain takes me out of the dream. The dream. When I blink, my eyelids hurt. Olivier's staring down at me as if I were dead, and for a moment I think maybe I am. I touch my chest and head, try to get out of bed, but I'm soaked. Moisture drips down my back and sticks in between my thighs.

"The fever has broken," Olivier says.

"What time is it?" It's night somewhere. Everything is suddenly motionless as I lie back in bed and wait. Finally, the late night métro roars beneath the city. Paris, I sigh, pulling the sheets up to my chin. I'm in Paris. I watch Olivier disappear into the hallway. The light falls across the bogolan bedspread from Mali. The shapes are strange, masklike, mocking. I strain to hear everything in its exactness, Olivier as he steps barefoot into the kitchen, opens a bottle, and pours water into one of our green Moroccan tea glasses. The sound of water soothes me back into sleep.

A doctor is waiting when I wake up around noon the following day. I've never seen him before. Olivier must have called SOS Médecins. He's sitting in our living room talking with Olivier about the best helmets for motorcycle riding in big cities and which world city is the most polluted.

"Athènes est horrible. Mexico, très très pollué."

"Hong Kong," I say, coughing. It feels as though a piece of my lung is missing. I sound like an old man. Swallowed up in Olivier's bathrobe and making my way across the room, I feel like a ghost. I sit on the white sofa, next to the doctor, and prop my feet on the low wooden table.

"You shouldn't be barefoot," the doctor tells me.

"I'm sick," I claim. Leave me alone.

"Exactement." The French love it when they're right. The doctor prods and pokes me with his yellowed fingertips. His breath smells of cold tobacco and sour charcuterie. He tries to listen to my heart. I cough in his face. "Very bad. Bronchitis, chronic."

"I'm allergic," I whisper. To you, I want to say.

"To what? Asia?" The doctor slaps his knee as if he's just invented the most clever diagnosis. "You'll need X-rays." He scribbles something on a pad of paper, lights a cigarette. "And don't be surprised if you have scars on your lungs."

I SPEND THE day taking in the rich sounds of Glenn Gould playing the Goldberg Variations. I drink honey and lemon, a few sips of cognac minus the dried scorpion powder. Olivier stays with me all day. He keeps busy but is never far, drawing soap labels for a new line of products or designing furniture for another house, inventing ways to help the poor. His latest project is a sewing circle in western Africa. Nuns teach young girls to sew and the proper and useful ways of the condom.

"Il faut que tu manges," he says, leading me into the kitchen. He's always telling me I have to eat. I lean against the counter, watching as he expertly peels and chops leeks and potatoes.

"J'ai rêvé d'elle." I start to tell him the dream about my

mother, about the darkness and getting lost at the market. He sets the knife on the chopping board and listens carefully, as if for the first time. When I'm finished, he rinses the vegetables thoroughly, fills the pot with water, and then turns to me, checking my forehead for fever.

"Et ton père? Tu ne rêves jamais de ton père coréen."

"Non," I whisper. He's right. I never dream of my Korean father. I have no recollection of him. It's as if he never existed. "I guess I lost him, too."

The steam rises from the pot. Olivier stirs, adds salt, cheesecloth filled with parsley, bay leaf, and thyme, covers the soup with the lid. He takes my hand and pulls me toward him. He opens my robe and fits his arms backward through the sleeves so we're wrapped together. He smells like citrus and sandalwood, his country, not mine. We stand like this for a long time.

The soup's hot and thick. The fever's gone, but my throat is still swollen. I ache all over, inside and out. It feels as though my lungs are swelling. My bones are ripe and about to explode.

Dominique drops Laure off later in the afternoon. Laure rushes into the house and squeezes me hard. She takes off her jacket to reveal my sweater, the one she wanted to wear while we were away. From the sofa, in a feverish half dream, I listen as Olivier corrects Laure's homework, and I wonder if my Korean father likes math or music. I want to know his favorite words. I wonder if he remembers me, if he has ever touched or seen my face. I wonder, sometimes, which hereditary illnesses my parents have passed on to me. I pray that they are healthy. I wonder how tall my mother is, what is the shape of her tears, the scent of her landscape.

Sometimes, when I step out into the night, I wonder how long it takes for their eyes to adjust to the same hollow darkness.

Sometimes I compose letters in my head: We are nearing the end of the century, and I know that neither one of you is ever coming back for me. Wherever you are, I'm still a part of you. I'm the one whispering in your ear, wondering how we've let all this water come between us.

~~~~~~~~~~~~~~~~~~~~~~~~~~~~~~~~~~

KIMCHI SOUP

The success of this soup depends on the quality of the kimchi and stock, so use the best. You can make a vegetarian version by using good-quality vegetable broth in place of stock and adding tofu and a poached egg for protein. It's best made a day ahead to remove all fat.

> 1 teaspoon peanut or vegetable oil
> 1½ to 2 pounds boneless pork butt or shoulder, trimmed of fat
>   and cut into chunks
> ½ to ¾ teaspoon salt
> 3 to 4 garlic cloves, smashed and chopped
> 2 teaspoons fresh-grated ginger
> 6 cups chicken or pork stock
> 2 to 3 cups cabbage kimchi (store-bought or homemade),
>   divided
> 4 green onions, sliced
> Garnishes: fried ginger, fresh green peas, sliced rice cakes,
>   Korean red chili paste or sambal oelek, sliced nori, a drizzle
>   of sesame oil

Heat oil in a large Dutch oven or soup pot over medium high heat. Season pork with ½ teaspoon salt and add to pot. Let pork brown about 8 minutes. Add garlic and ginger and stir. Add stock, stir, bring to a boil; reduce heat to medium low. Skim fat as it starts to simmer and froth. Add 1 to 2 cups kimchi, stir, and let simmer about 1½ to 2 hours or until pork is fork tender. Stir in green onions and remaining kimchi (if desired). Taste and add more salt, as needed. Serve with garnishes, if desired.

XII

A TIRE D'AILES

🙥

*J*T HAS BEEN MONTHS SINCE RETURNING TO FRANCE FROM Asia, and although my lungs and throat are slowly healing, there are signs of something much more elusive, more acute, that punctures from deep inside. I keep hearing Olivier's words: *Your home is with me.* It was definitive, no questions asked, no room for discussion, as with everything he decides. Over the years, this has been both comforting and disquieting.

Because I can no longer drive long stretches without fearing an accident, I find myself breathless, pulled over on the shoulder of the road, on my way back from Flora's clinic in Marseille. I am more and more afraid of everything. My own scarred shadow. Fear of waking up with blood in my mouth where someone has cut out my tongue because I have wasted the gift of words.

The kitchen is the only place where I am not fearful, which seems fine with everyone. I buy more piles of French and American epicurean magazines, cookbooks, not that I'm able to follow the recipes, but they make me feel useful, efficient. The one book I always turn to, though, is Reboul's *La Cuisinière Provençale,* my bible to this day.

Whenever I'm in Paris, I take Saturday morning classes at Le Cordon Bleu in the fifteenth arrondissement, practice the coveted recipes on eager dinner guests. And although I'm not a chef, I have been given the power to decide the culinary fates of twenty or sometimes thirty guests in a single evening at our various dinner parties. I may fear highways and trains and tunnels, but I am fearless in the face of whole rabbits and wild boar, *cabri,* goats, that I roast with young garlic and wild herbs. I take on kilos of potatoes, slow-bake them with crème fraîche and a sauté of fragrant girolles. I think of *Omma* as I whisk up the mother sauces, experimenting with new variations on the theme.

Every once in a while, Olivier or one of our friends will request a New Orleans dish Poppy taught me to make: jambalaya, seafood gumbo, bread pudding with drunken sauce. I am secretly triumphant when every now and then Laure and her friends want American pancakes with "the maple syrup that pours out of the tin cabin" and cookies over crêpes and madeleines. They like to help stir batter or count chips so they will each have the same amount of chocolate in their individual batches. These are the times I miss my adoptive family the most, especially my grandfather. I, like Poppy, take pride in the number of strangers who show up for impromptu dinners. But it seems that I can tackle the most esoteric of recipes, the most elusive puff pastry, as long as I do not have to count the empty layers of loneliness building up inside.

Every morning that I wake up now in the azure blue of our bedroom in Provence, or the pied-à-terre tucked safely between the boulevard Raspail and the boulevard Saint-Germain, I am more acutely aware that this life of ease and comfort was not made for someone like me—a stranger, an unwanted child, a divided woman with no claim to happiness.

When I talk to my mother back in New Orleans, we are polite, never dipping below the surface: "Yes, we're going to

Corsica for the summer." "No, we'll be in for Thanksgiving, not Christmas." My mother, at first skeptical of the age difference and the fact that someone like Olivier could love someone like me, has come to adore him, especially after her visit. But even thousands of miles away, she is able to distance herself more, make me feel inadequate, useless, second-guess my happiness. She somehow always reminds me how at my age she was already a mother of two orphaned children, how she never traveled. "What do you *do* all day long?" she asks, hanging up before I can begin to answer. Writing is not a legitimate answer; neither is cooking or being the full-time companion of someone as commanding as Olivier.

To make matters more difficult, Laure has started taking my clothes and jewelry before weekends with her mother. I find my belongings in her half-zipped bags. She takes things from Lulu, too, small gifts I have given her. Laure keeps everything—she reminds me of myself—a souvenir of a time that existed. She keeps it all within touching distance. I know I will find the flowered Kenzo top and American kids' cookbooks I will give her for her upcoming tenth birthday in her bed, stuffed under the pillow. And Laure has been throwing uncontrollable tantrums, testing Olivier, asking him to choose—her or "Keem."

Despite all this, I love her, mainly because she is the daughter of the man I love, but I wonder how it is that I have become a makeshift mother, this clueless substitute. Do I have the right to discipline her? What can I possibly teach her besides the comfort of food, the gifts of the table, the importance of language, and the unique strangeness of being a foreigner?

Olivier makes more and more concessions, changing last-minute plans to accommodate Dominique, sending her money at the slightest suggestion of custody changes. Dominique keeps changing her demands, prolonging the finalization of the divorce. In France, Olivier explains to me one day, five years after the filing, it becomes automatic. He's willing to wait in order not to have to pay more or lose Laure. Then he and I can be official, legal. I don't know how much longer I can wait to be "official." My social status is currently questionable, my resident visa renewable with stipulations. Although Olivier says I have nothing to worry about, I am, once again, in between countries. And Olivier's decision to wait it out with Dominique also reminds me of other things, including the fact that Laure is his family and I am not and that my biological father never fought so much for me. All of this is proving to be too much, the reason I am sinking further, slipping away into my own deep quagmire of doubt and panic.

Olivier always knows how to solve a problem, but my panic attacks, he assures me, are not a problem. So we are on last-minute trips to Cadaqués, a weekend at the Grand Hotel de Cala Rossa on Corsica, wine shopping in Condrieu, anywhere in Italy. While eating chunks of Parmigiano-Reggiano and *frizzante* in a château in Piacenza, he tells me that we are finally going to open *my* very own bookshop.

"Where?" I ask him, a bit hesitant, savoring the salty grains of cheese. I thought he had forgotten about this project, so I never let myself hope for it.

"In Paris, of course. It's something you've always dreamed of. Or I have, for you. We even came up with a name, remember? Don't think I don't remember these things. Besides, you insist on being *so* American, having to work, have a career." I can't tell if he is making fun or not, and before I start to object, he adds, "Plus, we'll be closer to Laure during the school year." Before I say anything about the real reason he wants the shop, for the sake of Laure, he says there's property he saw on one of the two islands in the heart of the city.

"You know," he whispers between the pasta and meat courses, "you really need to have a child . . . I think it will make you feel better."

"*I need to have a child? What about you?*"

"I don't *need* to have one. I don't have that *besoin*. But I would have one with you, *for* you, because I want to, not because I need one—"

"I know, I know," I say, holding up my hand to pause him. "You did it with Dominique because *you wanted* a daughter, but you would have one with me because I *need* one, not because you want one—"

"That's not what I mean. I just think it would help you, help us. Complete the circle."

I want to say so much, that maybe I do want to have children, but only with a man who wants one, not out of duty for what he feels is best for me. But he's always got it all figured out—this life he has created for us, so comfortable and perfect.

"And then we'll have my brother build the shelves for the books," he says, referring back to the bookshop. "Just like in all the L'Occitane stores . . . I can see it already. It will be stunning, and the whole city will know this is the place to come for poetry . . ."

I hold up my glass to drink more *frizzante* and watch Olivier dissipate through the bubbles. I'm not really listening now. I wish I could be so sure about someone, much less an entire city like Paris wanting to come to my shop to buy poetry. Before I can say thank you, he tells me that after dinner maybe I should write a poem or two, write it out of my system, this slow-spreading panic. A prescription from Dr. Baussan.

"*Panna cotta* and gelato will soothe all our worries."

I nod. If cooked cream in northern Italy will make me wonder less about what I will do with the rest of my life and my patient womb, then yes, bring me bowls of it, scoops and scoops of iced hazelnut and pale green pistachio, too.

AFTER ONE OF our morning runs through the Luxembourg Garden, Olivier and I shower, dress, and ride about the city on the purple scooter. It's a sticky Indian-summer morning. The sun shines brilliantly on the market vendors at Maubert-Mutualité. We zip up the tiny rue de Bièvre and across the quay by Notre Dame. We stop at the tip of Île Saint-Louis where Olivier likes to come. It's on this island where we spent our first night together, when I was still living in Stockholm. He parks the scooter, pulls off his helmet, and starts to unstrap mine.

"What are you smiling like that for?" I ask him.

"Come." He takes my hand, walks me past the L'Occitane shop to the next block. "I want to show you something." He stops at number 81.

I shrug and peek into the window. "It's a dirty, abandoned *crêperie.*"

"Not for long. I'm going to buy it."

I peek in again. "It's small. What do you want to do with it?"

"Books, *mon amour.* Tons and tons of books. All yours."

"Mine?" I ask, a bit skeptical. "Really?"

"Yes . . . see in there"—he points—"we'll have to tear it all down, the blond stone walls are great, but everything else will have to go." He loves the promise of large-scale demolitions, wiping out the old and re-creating his version of the new.

We lunch at Le Vieux Bistro, tucked across the street from Notre Dame, watching unwitting tourists pass right by one of the best places for *bœuf bourguignon, tarte tatin* with a big chilled canister of crème fraîche. Olivier begins to draw on the back of a pad of paper. "You see here . . ." He draws furiously. "Bookshelves all along this wall, and then we'll go look at tiles for the floor, similar to the ones we have at L'Occitane but maybe just slightly different. We'll have Ariane come and color-wash the walls, and . . . it's ready to go." He bites into his slow-cooked beef, pours some sauce over the individual copper pot of boiled noodles.

"Oh, and then we'll hang one of Louis's pieces right above the desk in the entrance. The one with the three birds that you like so much, perfect for A Tire d'Ailes." In the end, the drawing resembles all the other L'Occitane shops in the city, with its iron and wood, glass and tile, hand-rubbed ocher walls.

There isn't much else to add, so Olivier, pleased with himself, suggests dessert. I think I want the *tarte tatin,* but he says I should order the profiteroles. I do love the cold ice cream against the hot bittersweet chocolate, the way they struggle and finally balance on the tongue.

NEGOTIATIONS FOR THE *crêperie* take a while, longer than Olivier would have liked, but once the papers are signed, it takes only a few months to redo the entire space—Olivier made all the final drawings and decided everything the first two days, then hired an entire work crew to tear down some walls and rip up floors—and turn it into the most exquisite shop on the island.

Since he can't get the exact flooring like L'Occitane as quickly as he wants, he lets me choose a terra-cotta tile from a shop in the Marais and which books will go on which shelves. But everything else is without dispute or discussion: He commissions an artisan to engrave "A Tire d'Ailes" into the wooden bar that will serve as the main counter. He has ordered invitations from his printer in Tuscany for the grand opening and hires

Custodia, the young woman from one of our favorite hotels on the rue Sainte Beuve, to help run the shop. She doesn't know much about poetry, but Olivier thinks she will be good, organized; she won't upstage me, he said. When I tell him I was hoping to hire a young aspiring poet, at least a bookworm, he says, "You have a mind for poetry, not for business. I can appreciate both."

THE DAY BEFORE the opening, Custodia and I spend time dusting shelves, shelving books. Aside from French and English poetry, there's poetry in Greek, Portuguese, Russian, Turkish, Korean, Lebanese, and even in the Parmesan dialect.

I arrange peonies, anemones, and roses in glass vases from Maison de Famille and Asiatides.

"Is this a new store?" a French woman calls in off the street.

"Yes," Custodia answers. "We're opening tomorrow."

"Poetry," she says, walking into the shop. "Who would ever buy so much poetry? Who's the owner?"

Custodia gestures to me. "No, dear," she says to Custodia. "I know you both work here, but *whose* shop is it?"

I answer that it's mine, but my words sound hollow, unconvincing. I'm sure she thinks me an impostor. I begin to explain that my companion opened it with me, for me. The woman smirks.

"Do you have anything by . . . Mayakovsky?"

Custodia pulls out both Russian and English editions of his poetry. The woman flips through the books, tosses them back onto the counter, and stomps out.

Custodia and I look at each other and shrug. I wonder if she was a spy for Dominique, but throughout the day many people come in and out, curious about who would open up an all-poetry bookshop, who has that much money to lose? Some comment it's noble, others affirm that it's purely frivolous, surely a rich man's caprice.

Later in the afternoon, I take a break for a quick espresso across the street. I notice a couple sitting at a window table, staring at the shop. They're both petite, in their late forties, she slightly older than the man.

"The shop is very beautiful," the man says. He nods my way, his unkempt hair falling into his thick glasses. "Are you a poet?"

"I love poetry," I answer.

"My wife," he says, gesturing for me to join them, "she is a poet. My name is Hervé. Maybe you will sell some of her books." His suggestion seems without hidden motives, purely an attempt to honor his wife's work.

She shoots him a look. "No," she says. "Don't mind him."

"I'd love to read your poetry," I say, introducing myself.

"Brigitte is very, not shy, but doesn't know how to promote herself."

"She's a poet," I say. Brigitte smiles, promising to come by with some of her books. Conversation is easy, and it feels good to establish my own relationships outside of Olivier.

"I wasn't always a poet," Brigitte says, almost apologetically. "I was an attorney, and then I did legal translations. I realized at some point that I wasn't doing what I really loved . . . so I gave it all up . . . allowed myself to choose writing, poetry, and prose, which was impossible before—"

"That's great," I say. "What made it possible?"

She and Hervé both respond, "Grignon," and then laugh. I look at them, puzzled, not familiar with the word.

"In English, you say 'shrink-wrapped,' no?" Hervé says.

I nod, smiling but not wanting to correct him. "Tell me more."

"Grignon's amazing. *Très humain. Rigoureux* . . . drives me crazy sometimes, but . . ." Brigitte hesitates. "He has helped me . . . *avec l'écriture, la vie.*"

Helped her with writing and life. I need someone like him, I think. For some reason, my eyes start to water. *"Je m'excuse,"* I say. "I think I'm coming down with something."

Brigitte looks at Hervé and then leans across the table and whispers, "I would be happy to give you his number, he only takes patients now on referral. But, I must warn you, I've sent other people there, and . . . it hasn't worked out with everyone. He works with lots of artists . . . other than that, I don't know much about him, which is the way it should be, right? He's a medical doctor as well." Brigitte scribbles down a phone number on a paper napkin, and I fold it carefully before placing it in my pocket.

"Thank you," I say. "You'll come to the opening tomorrow, yes?"

"We wouldn't miss it."

At 6:00 P.M. the following day, the shop starts to fill up. There are editors and writers I have only heard of or read about. Charlotte and Milton have flown in from Stockholm. Charlotte's first book of poetry is just being published, and she's also helped me with the selection of Swedish poets. Flora is here, too, radiant in her new Yves Saint Laurent pale violet skirt and matching suede round-toed *escarpins*.

"It's amazing what love does," she tells me. She is svelte and hasn't needed chemotherapy in months. She tries on several shades of lipstick before choosing the deep rose, which high-lights the rise of her cheekbones. Her hair has grown back fuller and thicker. She is ravishing. Jean-Marie takes her hand, kisses her neck. It has been months since we have seen him, and I am grateful for his presence.

Louis and Nelly arrive. *"Ma chérie, c'est magnifique,"* Nelly declares, introducing me to her friends as *"la femme d'Olivier Baussan."* People, tourists and locals, come in off the streets, some even buy books. There are poets who live on and around the island. Bernard Heidsieck, founder of the *poésie sonore, poésie action* movement, offers to do a reading at some point. Paolo, an Italian poet from Florence, introduces himself and congratu-lates me. He is handsome and dramatic, precious in his posture and diction, but I like him for his passion of Dante and Goethe and Rilke. He also loves Jean Rhys and Emily Dickinson.

"Yes, we will be very good friends," Paolo assures me as he and his friend Giuseppe leave after buying a pile of books.

I am pleased and thankful that Brigitte and Hervé show up. I feel in my pocket for the napkin with the doctor's name on it. Olivier hands me a glass of Champagne.

"I've decided which poet I will ask to do the first reading," I tell him.

"I've already taken care of that," he says. "There's a poet friend of Pierre Magnan's, also from Provence—"

"I was thinking about André du Bouchet. He's older and I've heard not doing too well physically, but I would love to ask him. Oh, and see that woman over there—" I gesture excitedly. "She says she's a friend of Gary Snyder's and that he would be happy to do a reading. Can you imagine . . ." I sound like a schoolgirl with a crush and start to explain to Olivier who Gary Snyder is.

"Why don't we talk about this later. I've already told Pierre that we would let his friend do the first reading."

Olivier orders Custodia to open another bottle of Champagne, a sign that this conversation is finished. He slips his arm around my waist, smiles for the photographer that Olivier's press agent has hired for the event. This is a moment to remember. Summer 1995. An island. I'm looking not at the camera, but beyond, panicked suddenly by my shameless public display of my once secret love of words.

XIII

SOME ENCHANTED LIFE

ॐ

Je est un autre.

—Rimbaud

𝒥'M LIVING AN ENCHANTED LIFE. A DESIRABLE LIFE. I HEAR it all the time. My mother, who hasn't contacted me in months, sends letters written in her tidy, perfect handwriting: "Have you found a job yet? Who do you think you *are*?" Nelly tells me the same thing, when Louis isn't listening, in her own words: *la vie privilégiée.*

"When I was your age," she always whispers, "I had my men give me the biggest jewels and entire wardrobes from Chanel, Balenciaga." Then she shows me her bare arthritic fingers with thick, grayish veins running like shriveled waterways across her hands.

Despite this privileged life everyone seems to think I am living, or because of it, panic has begun to strike more and more, like lightning. I hold my breath between bolts, counting the diminishing seconds in between. I panic on the drive to Italy via the Riviera. I've counted up to 346 tunnels so far, each one a possible collapse, like a failing lung. I gorge myself on the evening news and discover that earthquakes are possible in the South of France, a fault line not far enough from our house. Radiation from Chernobyl is still present in the crops in Provence. Tornadoes in Europe. Train derailments. Sarin gas in the Japanese underground system. Strange viruses that invade the lungs and penetrate the skin. Panic is the sound of a full jet in the bankrupt sky, flying lower and lower until I'm sure it will crash into our kitchen.

I drop hints to Olivier that I need help, but my words are too indistinct, inaudible. Instead, I fall asleep at odd hours of the day. When the maid arrives at our Paris apartment, I turn off the lights in the bedroom until she has finished. She taps softly on the door, and I pay her quickly, silently, like some underground madame. After she's left, I walk into the hallway with all the lights off and just the evening streetlights filtering through.

The rhythmic turning of the dryer and hum of the refrigerator remind me that I'm in the domestic world. I open the refrigerator, close it, open it again. Nothing smells familiar as I scan the shelves. Iranian caviar, a ripe Saint-Marcellin cheese, lamb's lettuce, *riz au lait à l'ancienne*. A spoonful of the cold thick rice pudding, one of Flora's favorite sweets, along with crème caramel, feels good gliding down my throat. I greedily devour the sweetened grains and throw away the container. Feeling guilty, I try to cook—practice a perfect beurre blanc for Olivier and bake madeleines for Laure's after-school snack. But Olivier calls to tell me there has been a change of plans, Laure is going to be with her mother this week, so he has made reservations for us at Apicius to have dinner with his best friend, Jean Lenoir, and a host of several Saudi moneymen.

My heart's no longer in it. I dump it all in the garbage, the broken eggshells and lumpy batter. I can't make anyone happy with sugar and eggs, butter and wine. Olivier can't help. He insists that he loves me too much, he needs me in excess.

"I'm going to get professional help," I announce one night in bed as he's reading the Amnesty International newsletter.

"I can help you, what do you want?"

I don't know what I want, I want to say. And not know-ing . . . "Loneliness. I'm lonely," I blurt out, not really finding the words I'm looking for, feeling ridiculous now as he contin-ues to read about the poor in Africa.

"Oh, Keem. Petite Keem." He tucks me under one arm while still reading. "I was thinking we could set up something in Mali or India." He kisses me on my cheek and eyes. "To help the women. When I was in Burkina . . ."

I drift off into a false hope of sleep, thick layers of *sommeil* to make me forget the heaviness of my limbs and organs, the pounding of my heart that resonates louder and more hollow every day. I dream there's an explosion in Gandhi's tomb. I'm summoned to investigate the site and identify the body. My father's burning incense at the mouth of the river. My mother and sister are measuring cups of water, hanging linens to dry in the wet heat of the city. My job is to read from the hot, singed map.

The next morning, while Olivier's meeting with journalists who want to interview him for French *Elle,* I pull out the Pages Jaunes. I keep checking over my shoulder, my finger shaking as I glide it up and down the columns. M for *Médecin,* P for *Psych-analyste, Psychiatre.* I don't know the difference among the three. But I want to call someone, anyone, a woman preferably in the fifth, sixth, seventh, or fourteenth arrondissement.

I open the front door, check to make sure Olivier's not near, then dial the number of a French doctor's name. By the fourth bleep, I'm about to hang up when a Françoise something-or-other answers in a nasal monotone. After a brief exchange of words, she tells me, *"Rendezvous mardi à quatorze heures."* She repeats the address slowly and then hangs up.

I arrive at her rue Raymond Losserand address the follow-ing Tuesday at exactly 2:00 p.m. A woman opens the door to a second-floor office, which actually turns out to be a two-bedroom apartment. A firm handshake and a half smile; she's wearing a sensible gray suit, pinched neatly at the waist. The color of the fabric matches her silvery hair and eyes. She doesn't say anything else, just turns and starts down the hallway. I have no choice but to follow. She leads me into a room with a king-size bed in the middle of it. She folds herself neatly into an armchair next to the door and gestures for me to sit opposite her.

"*Quel est votre problème?*" What is your problem? she asks sternly, not even looking directly at me. I can hardly hear her as I sit staring at the immense bed between us. Charcoal-colored knotted rug and a pale gray cotton bedspread with darker gray piping.

"Um . . . ," I begin. I don't really know what to say. "*Il n'y a pas de fenêtre,*" I mumble. I could have thought of something more enlightening to say than to point out there's no window. Obviously she knows there's no window. If I knew what my problem was, I wouldn't be here in the first place. It stinks of dusty sheets. I want to ask her what *her* problem is, what's up with the bed, the bedroom? But I've never done this before, and I think, Maybe this is how it is when you want someone else to help you take out something as deep as the hole inside. I start babbling, and after about ten minutes Madame Grisaille stands up and looks at me.

"*Très bien. Vous avez beaucoup de problèmes.* You are divided, and that will cost you two hundred fifty francs. Come back next Thursday same time so I can make you whole."

I somehow manage to stand up and, with the hollowness knocking in my legs, follow her back down the empty hallway. I pull out a 200-franc bill and a blue 50. She takes the multicolored money in one palm and shakes my hand hard with the other, opens and then closes the door with me on the other side. I stand for a moment with my wadded fist suspended, about to knock. I don't, of course, but there's something left unsaid. I have been summed up and dismissed, abandoned, but how can I tell that to some strange woman?

Back out on the street, day is slipping into the Seine and I make my way to La Grande Épicerie du Bon Marché. Everything in this department store food market is remarkable—the exotic fruit stand promising joy with its array of passion, carambola, crimson cactus. I want to be lost here, swallowed up whole among the endless displays of imported water in colored glass bottles—blue Ramlösa, sea green Pellegrino—among the cheeses and marble-colored olives, bread baked in their individual baskets. When I return to the apartment, Olivier's waiting, anxious.

"*Alors?*"

I shrug. I hate to admit that he was right.

He smiles, triumphant, and takes me in his arms. "When I was your age, I went through analysis, but I was a *baba cool* . . . it's what we did. Analysis," he warns me, "is the opposite of poetry. You'll lose your entire poetic sensibility."

"Did you?" I ask.

"Look," he says, ignoring my question, "we have *everything*. *Tout.* People go to see people like analysts and psychoanalysts for *happiness*. You don't need to pay a stranger to tell you that we have everything to be happy."

I walk to the kitchen and let the water pour out of the faucet full blast. I cup my hands and drink. It's cold and hurts slicing down my throat, caressing the scars from China.

"You never drink tap water—"

"Well, I just feel like it today." I sound angry and regret it instantly. Olivier walks over to me and turns the faucet handle so the water falls in slow oval drops into the drain. I lean over to stare into the water until I can't see it any longer. He bends down low to look into my eyes.

"What?" I splash water into his face, and we can't help laughing. Soon we're both wet and dripping on the kitchen floor. I make tea and stand next to Olivier, overlooking the courtyard below.

"I talked to my lawyers today. I'm going to see a notary as soon as possible."

I start shaking my head. I don't know why I must object to everything, but I do. I pour more tea and stir in some honey.

"Kimette, you never sweeten your tea."

I glare at him.

"The notary," he continues. "It's important. In case anything happens to me before . . . I want to protect you, and Laure. I don't want Dominique involved."

Right, I want to say, like she's not going to butt her way in. Am I becoming bitter? "But Dominique isn't going to let you go through with the divorce, you know it."

"Marie-Claire will be there, too, to help you through, if anything happens to me. She's been in business with me since the beginning of L'Occitane . . . since 1976 . . . I'm so old."

"Why don't you just get the divorce over with? You've been officially separated for years now."

"I don't want to jeopardize custody of Laure, you know that."

I nod patiently and let him talk about marriage even if we can't discuss it seriously until the divorce is final. And I'm terrified. Maybe it's our age difference. And how do I tell him that I don't want to be another Madame Olivier Baussan; I want to become Kim Sunée before becoming anyone else.

I'M RELIEVED THAT we're having dinner at Louis and Nelly's tonight, even though she will tell me I should have bought the *chouette* new *sac* at Yves Saint Laurent, or that my jewelry— bracelets and rings Olivier brought back from West Africa—is all wrong, except for the Cartier watch, or that we haven't spent enough money on art this year.

In some strange way, I am attached to Nelly. She can be charming and insists I am like the daughter she and Louis would have loved to adopt. Tonight is one of her dinners for the patrons, and I'm always thrilled to talk with Louis, see what he is creating. I tell him my dreams in between courses when no one is listening, and he smiles before interpreting them.

First, Olivier and I are to meet and ride with Henri Cartier-Bresson and his wife, Martine, at their rue de Rivoli apartment. Olivier is honored, and even though he has known Henri for several years, he gets excited but tries to remain nonchalant.

"What's he like?" I ask.

"A genius." He pauses and then adds, "Dominique contacted him some time back, told him about the divorce, and I've been waiting for the right moment to introduce you."

"Maybe I shouldn't go," I say, thinking that here's one more person from his past that I have to impress. What do I say to Henri Cartier-Bresson?

"Whatever you do," Olivier says, reading my mind, "don't ask him anything about photography. He doesn't want to speak of it, to anyone . . . he's drawing now."

No photography, I remind myself as Henri greets us outside and we follow him up to his apartment. He stops to greet an American woman with a delightful accent. They are old friends, he tells us nostalgically as he slowly makes his way up the several flights of stairs.

Once inside, he explains that we are waiting for Martine, his wife, as he offers to fix us a drink. There are drawings everywhere, nudes and airy figures. A photo of Matisse, landscapes, some just strewn about. I try not to stare, try to think of something smart to say. No photography questions, I remind myself.

"Olivier tells me you're a poet." Henri smiles and hands me a glass. His voice is gentle, his words deliberate. "You've opened a poetry bookshop on the island." Before I can correct him, he stands up, searches his bookshelves, and hands me a book. "My first wife, she was a poet . . ."

I am grateful for his kindness, for not letting me make a fool of myself in his presence, in front of Olivier, who admires him so.

"Please," he tells me in French, "I offer you this book of her poetry, in English."

I thank him as I flip through the pages. While Henri looks for his coat and gloves, a young woman, elegant, tall, and beautiful, suddenly appears in the doorway, holding out a scarf.

"Papa. Looking for this?" Henri introduces his daughter. She looks to be in her early twenties. I try to calculate the age difference. "How are you feeling?" she asks in French. He smiles and nods. "We're having dinner together this weekend, right? Remember? You promised."

When she leaves with her friend, Henri tells me that she was adopted as a baby. She's a grown woman now, where does the time go? Martine arrives, and we all pile into her car to go to the fifteenth arrondissement. Henri is old and tired, but there is still so much life in the way he looks at the streetlights, listens silently to the undersounds of the city. There's so much I want to ask him, learn from him, but I'm tongue-tied. I clasp the book close to me.

When we arrive, Nelly kisses me and whispers in my ear that my dress is lovely. I'm relieved, but she makes a point of saying, "*Mais, chérie,* you must have him take you to this fabulous little boutique, rue Bonaparte."

She seats me in between Louis and Henri. Olivier and I have several of his photos at the apartment—scenes from China and Mexico. He's more fragile than I imagined. Martine, quite a bit younger than Henri, a photographer as well, warns him about spices. He turns to me, unscrewing the top from the Tabasco bottle.

"*D'où viens-tu exactement?*"

I answer South Korea, more or less, but I don't know exactly where. "*Nulle part.*"

"Everyone comes from somewhere," he says sternly. "You can't be from nowhere." He shakes his head, pushes the Tabasco out of the way, and mixes some red hot *harissa* instead with his couscous grains. I stare at my reflection, upside down in the spoon. The light makes me look swollen, undefined.

In the hallway, Nelly reproaches me for not being charming and anecdotal. Sullenly, I clear dishes and help her set up the cheese tray.

"What's wrong, *chérie? Ça ne va pas avec la petite?*"

I tell her everything's fine with Laure, *la petite*. I carefully remove the damp paper from the wedge of Roquefort and busy myself with slicing Comice pears, arranging the fresh tiny rounds of Rocamadour cheese on the plate.

"You have everything," she reproaches. "I've lost it all, except Louis. He drives me crazy, but what a brilliant artist." She sighs wistfully. "I sold everything I had to support us. My jewels, *garde-robe, tout.* Sometimes I think I was foolish giving it all up, never marrying Pierre, especially before he married that other woman, and then the accident." Nelly pauses. "Money is important, and if you can have love, too, *tant mieux.* A woman must have her priorities straight. You're too young to know this now. If Pierre were alive today, I would still be his mistress. I had a rich life, not richer than yours, but . . . "

"Nel, do you know of a good . . . psychoanalyst?"

"*Pour toi?*" She starts fanning herself frantically and stuffs a slice of pear in her mouth.

I nod, the tears welling up.

"*Mais ce n'est pas possible. Pas toi.*" Her voice is shrill, and she starts screaming, out of control now, about how scandalous it is to be unhappy when I have so much.

"Please," I beg her to whisper. "I just thought you would know of someone."

"*Bien sûr,* I know. Who do you want? Moscovici? Dolto's daughter? I know many, but . . ." She pauses to lower her head and squint at me. "Does Olivier know?"

"*Laisse tomber.*" Forget it, I tell her, carrying out the cheese tray. I set it on the table, and Henri pours me a glass of *vin jaune*. I gesture for him to fill it up all the way and then take a big gulp.

Nelly's radiant at the other end of the table. Fanning herself wildly, flirting with the young Cuban dancer at her side, she keeps reminding him that she was once a *very* beautiful woman. "I don't have youth on my side, like Keem, but," she says, catching my gaze, "I have wisdom."

XIV

LE DIVAN

※

*B*ECAUSE I HAVE NO WISDOM, I'VE LANDED HERE AT 248, boulevard Raspail in the fourteenth arrondissement in the city of Paris. This is my last chance. Up the boulevard Montparnasse, past the tables at La Coupole and Le Select, a glance at Baudelaire's tombstone, past the Fondation Cartier, past the corner café with the faded green-and-white-striped awning. Today, the chalkboard promises a simple menu: the superior *andouilette AAAAA, salade verte, la tarte aux pommes maison*. I'm following the inner compass that has led me out of Seoul, out of Stockholm, but isn't indicating where it is I'm to stop. Time's running out, and the ticking inside tells me that my heart will soon implode.

Dr. Olivier Grignon has agreed to meet with me. I whisper his name as I punch in the four digits of the gate code. He said: Walk through the building, through the courtyard to the first door. There are no names, no shiny plaques of distinction, just a doorbell. I take a deep breath and then ring. A buzzer sounds, and I push open the large green door. There's no one waiting for me, not even a lipsticked receptionist. Two doors, one in front and one to the left. I go straight ahead to the one in front.

A man rushes to greet me—I've chosen the wrong door. He kindly and efficiently leads me into a small waiting room.

Suddenly, I'm paralyzed, realizing that I've failed the first test. The square window is closed, but spring squeezes through a tiny, bullet-size hole. On one wall is a series of drawings with the caption *"L'art de parler."* The book lover in me scans the shelves: *L'Album Lacan, Paris, Texas,* Godard's *L'Histoires du Cinéma. Poésie Verticale* by Juarroz, books by Pessoa, Hölderlin. Breathe. This is my first session with a real analyst. Am I dressed appropriately? How do you dress to talk to someone about your obsessions and nightmares? Do I speak French to him? Does he understand English? Korean? Swedish? What kind of name is Grignon anyway—a tree and a city both. Do we shake hands? Do I use the formal *vous* form to disclose the most intimate details of myself? Will he have me sent away?

Before I can think to bolt, the door opens and the same man from earlier welcomes me. I don't dare look straight into his face, but there's a soothing and intriguing air as he gestures for me to sit across from him. He's waiting. Waiting. We're in a back courtyard, so not even the sounds of buses or the rumbling of the underground métro will distract. I look around. If rooms were seasons, this one would certainly be fall. Underlit and smelling of sweet, warm tobacco, freshly sharpened pencils. A weathered teapot sits on the low table next to the doctor, along with newspapers, ashtrays, and small statues—Giacometti-like figures, elongated and thin, searching. The broken seat of a chair waits in the corner, and unframed lithographs lean against a wall.

I sit and wait.

He sits and waits.

"A-loooors?" he says finally, and then breathes in deeply, lowering his shoulders, settling in as he tilts his head back slightly.

Aloooors. The word lasts forever, ricochets off the walls and back into my head. How can he be so relaxed? He crosses his leg, one over the other, and I find myself doing the same. When he folds his hands in his lap, I mimic him once again. He nods. I nod. I shrug and raise my eyebrows. A tic. I have none, but if I did, this would be the perfect time for it to manifest itself.

Alors, I repeat in my head. What does he mean? Think, think. The simplest of French words.

"*Alors,*" he repeats, nods, sighs, and smiles.

"*Je ne sais pas,*" I stammer. Basic French. He thinks I'm stupid. Long pause, and then I can't stop. Words come to me, the perfect French r's and verb forms. "I don't know what's wrong, what you want me to say. I'm twenty-five . . . well, I don't really know when I was born . . ." Define yourself, I tell myself. "I can't leave. I can't stay. I can't breathe, and I can't write." What an idiot. I stop to catch my breath.

"I'm like a mother to his child, and she's not mine. Olivier loves me, and I'll never be good enough. I don't know how much longer I can stay. All my life something's been missing. I have a family back in New Orleans, but it feels like I've grown up on my own. No one ever to protect me. And there's catastrophe everywhere. Planes, earthquakes, helicopters. No one to protect us." Now I'm on a roll. "Highways that lead nowhere. Tunnels. Subways . . . Did you know in Japan, there was this gas bomb—"

"We're not in Japan." Dr. Grignon smiles reassuringly.

"But I'm Asian, at least on the outside. I'm American, and I've lived in Europe now for so long, but I'm neither here nor there . . ." I realize how ridiculous I sound and apologize for my stupidity. I stand up, ready to exit because it seems I've overstayed my welcome.

Then he speaks, says something softly I can't quite understand, but it doesn't really matter. I'll never see him again anyway. I glance up at the doctor, but he is out of focus. I clear my throat and shift from one foot to the other. "I want . . ." I hesitate, twist my hands, and shrug.

Finally, the doctor stands and waits a moment to see if I have anything else I'd like to say. I walk toward the door. He doesn't ask for money but shakes my hand and, in a voice as dim as the light, says, *"Appelez-moi, quand vous le désirez."* Call me . . . when you desire. He opens the door gently and waits for me to move toward it, smiles, and then slowly and inaudibly closes it behind me.

Appelez-moi quand vous le désirez. Call me when you desire. What a strange turn of phrase. Desire. Need. Want. I want to be in a room full of people and not feel lonely. I want to quit fighting this inner voice that tells me to pack up and keep moving. Constantly in motion so I won't have to stop and think.

Walking back to the apartment, I try to think of things I should tell Olivier. But for some reason, I don't want to share this with him. Even though Dr. Olivier Grignon is the oddest man I've ever encountered, I sense that he is my salvation, mine. And he has nothing to do with Olivier Baussan.

It starts to rain, a hard rain that blows up sheets of dust and dirt. I feel strangely solid. I feel my flesh and bones as I walk back down the boulevard Raspail, sloshing around as it fills up with water. I stop to telephone Brigitte, the poet, just to talk, tell her I finally met with her analyst, Grignon, but I'm not sure what else to say.

"I don't get it," I complain. "I ask him things, and he doesn't answer. I don't know anything about him."

"That's exactly how it's supposed to be. Trust me . . . you don't want an analyst who would tell you too much, not just yet."

I start to object, but we plan to meet for coffee soon, so maybe she can explain things to me.

After several weeks, I see Grignon a few more times. Mostly I apologize for my rambling, my ignorance of how analysis works. I am preoccupied with being the ideal patient, wanting to be clever. I answer like a student: Instead of answering with what I know, what I've lived, I always respond with something general, what others have lived.

I must learn, Grignon tells me, to see things not through the eye of history or someone else's experience. But it's difficult to talk about myself, to allow myself this luxury of asking the questions I need to understand why I am so divided, so unable to allow myself happiness, why everything seems so ephemeral and unsolid. I have been lost my whole life, no one has come to find me, so why now, I wonder, is this stranger going to help? In the beginning, it feels like a farce, a theatrical attempt; I am a complete failure. I vow never to call him again, but somewhere I sense that I will find the desire.

OLIVIER AND I spend most of our time now in Paris, go to Provence for weekends when we have Laure. She is strong-willed and feisty, smart and funny. She asks me more and more questions about Korea, being adopted. She tells me one day that she told her mother about how I was abandoned. She doesn't say much else, and after a pause, she leans into me and says that she's lucky because she has two mothers.

When Laure is with Dominique, we hop over to spend a week on Terre-de-Haut in Guadeloupe, where Olivier promises that we will focus on us, time for us. But as soon as we return, he is already promising some starving artist we will buy two more paintings, our attendance at a fund-raising dinner, my translation services for several different organizations, and that I will tag along with him to all his business meetings. I argue that I need to be at the bookstore, running things, organizing readings and signings, but to him this is secondary, not very important compared with what he has planned.

I miss Flora's wisdom and Sophie's companionship—they are the closest I have to another adopted family. Olivier thinks it's an honor to be "adopted" by so many people. I don't look at it the same way. It's just a fact of my life, as are the doubts and more frequent panic attacks.

I finally call Grignon several months later. Surprisingly, he gives me an appointment for the following afternoon.

"I don't know what's going to happen," I tell him in a rush, "but I'm ready."

He looks at me.

"To be analyzed . . . by you . . . I mean." My voice shakes, but this time I don't look away.

He nods, offering a slight shy smile of recognition. I can't read him, can't tell if he's genuinely pleased or if I've once again said something stupid.

"Oui, mais moi, il faut que je sache que je puisse être votre analyste." He has to know if he can be my analyst?

I'm appalled at first, but more than anything, I feel rejected. Aren't you a doctor? I want to scream. You don't choose the sick when they come into the emergency room with a bleeding heart or open wound, or even with something less palpable and silent like cancer or sadness. When I'm not able to say anything else, I get up and leave, furious with myself for needing him, vowing again not to call him.

But the next time I return because I've finally understood that there's an exchange, perhaps even a healing, to take place on both sides. Grignon, much to my surprise, has finally agreed to work with me. But I somehow still insist on setting the rules.

"I won't lie down on your couch, and I can't come regularly because I'm never here. We travel a lot. Olivier always plans these last-minute trips, especially when I've organized something at the bookshop."

Silence on his part, and finally he nods, a gesture that doesn't say "I agree" but rather "More, go on."

"So," I brave, "I'll just let you know when I can come. Now, how long will this take before I'm better?" I look at my wrist as if we, the doctor and I, are going to synchronize our watches to time how long happiness will take.

Happiness, of course, I learn has no notion of time, or of me, for that matter. Grignon patiently tries to lay down the fundamentals of analysis for me without being overly didactic. He discourages me from reading too much of Freud or Lacan, too much theory, at this stage. It is mainly through strong suggestion, gestures, and sounds of words I could never allow myself to speak that I learn my place, follow his lead. This is a long, slow dance, and I'm not sure I have the stamina. The only thing we agree on is three times a week to start, 300 francs a session, cash always.

In the beginning I am resistant, I can't help but censor my thoughts, trying to offer a more palatable version of myself. I often spend the first ten minutes of a session thinking of the first words I will speak, faced with fear of the blank page. But I realize little by little that I'm not a fictional character. I have the unfortunate epiphany that I am real. My life is real, my heart and my pain as well. In the beginning, I look at Grignon as the author of my life, hoping he will write me a really good ending.

"So how's it going to end?" I venture one day.

"*Ça, c'est une jolie question.*"

It takes many painful half hours to accept that this man is not going to live my life for me. Olivier, on the other hand, is more than happy to guide me from one undefined place to the next.

As Grignon and I begin to work together, I learn that this is a two-way street. I am drawn to his deep capacity for empathy and his professionalism, his poetic sensibility. Our sessions begin in French, but he encourages me to speak any words that may come in English, Korean, Swedish. But I continue in French, this language I now speak better than any other and that serves as a mask for feelings I have never been able to articulate before in any other language.

Dr. Grignon is a master of the mind, the heart, and keeps notes, reminding me of things I'd rather forget. Words flow, and he amazes me with his memory, his patience, his gentle coaxing. It is thanks to sessions with him that I can start to give shape to the pain caused by this constant need for departure. This crazy idea that I must keep running in order to survive, in order to not be loved too much or not enough. Running so I will never have to deal with someone not wanting to keep me.

I talk about my sister, about her own adoption—I do not even know if she has ever tried or wondered about her past; my adopted mother, who insinuates that I do not deserve my life, that I am just plain lucky.

"Freud a dit que nous méritons la chance." We deserve our luck, he assures me. The sessions always go back to Olivier, how he is smothering me, offering me too much, shaping my identity—both my past and my present—into something he can better understand and better control.

But Olivier, who feels powerless as I seek outside help, hints that he will forbid me to continue analysis. "It will be the end of us!" he shouts. He never shouts at me. "And did you have to pick a doctor with the same name?"

"Grignon?" I ask.

"Olivier," he says, as if about to pound on his chest.

He returns to our Paris apartment one afternoon with handwritten documents, notarized and signed by him and a witness, our good friend Jean Lenoir.

"In case something happens to me." He shows me the will. "You'll be a rich widow, shares of L'Occitane, use of the properties until . . . France has terrible inheritance laws, and the divorce . . ."

"She's not signing the divorce papers, is she?" I ask.

"It doesn't matter now," he says, shaking the will. "Plus, we're legally separated. Besides, I'm old. You're so young. I'm almost forty-five. And my father died at *fifty-two* . . . I might not have much time." He laughs.

We've been through this so many times. I'm tired of him giving in to Dominique for the sake of Laure, tired of his obsession with age, tired of hearing that he may not be around much longer. Suddenly I yearn for youth and the promise of a long, stable future, something permanent, something I have never dared want for myself. The more restless I become, the more Olivier tries to tie me down. The more he gives, the less I want.

After several months, Olivier announces that my sessions with the analyst will soon be over. "*Ça suffit.* I refuse to pay for you to talk to another man about our problems."

"I thought we didn't have any problems."

"You know what I mean. You talk about us with a perfect stranger, *un homme en plus,* and I won't have it."

"Fine," I say. "I'll get a real job. You don't want me at the bookshop anyway."

"You can't make a tenth of what I make in a month," he tells me.

I open the latest copy of *FUSAC* and flip to the classified

ads for Anglophones, circling possibilities—"English Teacher,"
"Translator." When Olivier peeks over my shoulder, I boldly
underline "Artist's Model," "Escort."

"Don't be ridiculous. You don't need to work. We won't
have the freedom to leave whenever we want, to go to wherever, Provence, the islands, be with Laure."

"What about the bookshop, then?"

"Well, that's what employees are for. That's why we hired
Custodia—"

"Why *you* hired Custodia," I correct him. "I think . . . I'm
going to go away for a few days, maybe go visit my family in
New Orleans or back to Brittany and do some writing."

"Great idea . . . we'll go tomorrow. I'll make reservations at
À la Duchesse Anne in Saint-Malo."

"I mean go away . . . by myself. Alone."

He pauses, and the look of disappointment on his face makes
me regret my words, but why must I always succumb to his
wishes? "*D'accord.* If you must. Wouldn't it be preferable to go
to Brittany . . . it's closer?" Olivier lies down next to me on the
Turkish kilim rug, stroking my shoulder. "And if you need to see
someone, fine, but can't you find a woman analyst instead?"

I shake my head, nod . . . practicing the art of gesture.

And then he whispers gently, "*J'ai envie de toi.*" He slides
his hand between my legs. As he enters, I'm suddenly a floating island, a hollow echo of myself. I want him to stay as long
as possible until I'm asleep and dreaming. When I do finally
fall into restless sleep—dreams of architecture and stone, blue-
prints of the body, clocks and an hourglass, my face fading in a
pile of sand.

XV

L'ÎLE FLOTTANTE

❧

I GIVE CUSTODIA THE WEEK OFF AND WORK IN THE BOOKSHOP, which has become a haven for American tourists waiting in endless lines for Berthillon ice cream, French poets who chat with other writers, and lots of young, sullen students of literature, mainly young men. They come in with huge book bags or oversize jackets and steal the Gallimard pocket series. I don't know why they go to all the trouble and then not take the more expensive, beautiful editions from the series La Pléiade.

One day, a young man I know only as Pierre sheepishly returns one of the stolen books. *"Je vous le rends,"* he says, handing back the book. The cover is clean.

"Merci." I can't believe I'm thanking him for the book he stole from me.

"Je ne l'ai pas aimé. Trop hermétique." He finds the poetry impenetrable and therefore pretentious, he explains. "That's why I'm returning it."

I nod. On his way out, he asks if I will read a manuscript of his. Before I can say no thank you, he opens up his bag and hands me three hundred pages of illegible handwritten poetry. "There's an ode to you in there," he says somewhat earnestly.

I tell him I don't have much time, but come back in a day or two.

I actually read some of the poems and discover mismatched lines from Verlaine and Baudelaire. The next morning, I find a box of beautifully wrapped books, all from my shelves, sitting on the threshold. Placed on top is a small mint-green-and-gold box of multiflavored *macarons* from Ladurée. Olivier says I don't know anything about business, but this seems to me to be fair trade—tart lemon curd and salted caramel cookies for illegible manuscripts and stolen books.

Olivier calls every few hours, wanting to know how it's going, when I'll be taking the train to meet him in Provence.

"In a week," I tell him, taping up a NO ICE CREAM sign in the window. "That's what we agreed on." I watch as a man stops in front of the shop, tosses out his ice-cream cone, and walks in with a cigarette and his drooling pug.

"That's too long. I wish I didn't have all these meetings. I can postpone a few and fly up there—"

"I'm fine. I need to be here."

I am finally planning the poetry reading. I have asked André du Bouchet, and after several setbacks, he is able to come. Over the next week, book publicists stop by, and editors with small independent publishing houses come in to leave artist-illustrated first editions on consignment. Brigitte and Hervé come to visit and leave some of her books as well. They are beautiful, hand-printed, some with pages still uncut. I have never seen such care taken to craft books.

I also buy poetry from various small publishers and book-shops, including La Librairie Espagnole, a Saint-Germain institution founded in the early fifties by Antonio Soriano, a Spaniard who fled Franco. Antonio's son, Antoine, who now runs the shop, leaves me books by Gamoneda, Zoë Valdez, Jimenez, Juarroz, and more. He tells me he's married to an American woman named Jan and that we should meet. I really don't have any American friends here, so I make a note to get in touch with his wife soon.

There is a lull one late afternoon, when not a single customer comes in for several hours. Just as I'm about to close the shop, a man in his late thirties walks in and introduces himself in French as Gilles du Bouchet.

"Any relation to the poet?" I ask.

He nods and smiles. His teeth are big, white, and perfectly aligned. "My father told me to come and say hello. He thought this was a jewel of a shop that I should definitely come and see." Gilles's khaki pants are frayed at the cuffs, his wool sweater and oxford shirt half tucked into his pants. He's tall and sturdy, with the good looks of an Ivy League grad student. He shakes my hand, and I notice the streaks of green and deep blue on his thick knuckles. "I've been working," he apologizes. "Paints, not words, like my father." There's an awkward shift in his eyes. "Anyway, I'm looking for some books, by Philippe Denis . . . a poet. He's a friend of mine, and I thought it would be good if you carried some of his books."

While I look up Denis on the Minitel electronic system, Gilles asks, "Would you like to maybe have tea one day, come see my work? I've set up an atelier at my father's in the sixth." He stares for a moment, as if about to say something else.

"Sure, maybe," I answer. "And maybe I'll see you at his reading?"

"Depends on when it is. I'm going to Cambodia for ten days. But I'll be back." He thanks me for looking up the books by Denis and waves good-bye. "And don't forget you promised to come and have tea."

By the time I walk back to the apartment in the evenings, I'm not really tired but satisfied with having worked full days at the shop, decided things on my own. Just as I am relishing staking out a claim on this little island in the big city of Paris, making poetry available to as many as possible, Olivier calls to remind me of several dinner engagements, a trip to somewhere we need to take soon.

"I thought I'd invite Brigitte, the lawyer-turned-poet I introduced you to at the opening, and her husband to come to Provence sometime this summer."

"*D'accord*. If they're poets, okay, even though I don't really know them."

"Hervé's an artist," I add.

"But wasn't *she* the one who gave you that analyst's number?"

I don't answer. "And I've scheduled André du Bouchet for a reading in two weeks; it's the only time he can do it. I'm so excited. His son came by, Gilles, he's an artist—"

"Have you forgotten? I promised Hamad we would meet him in Lausanne, with his financial adviser. They're really close to opening L'Occitane in Saudi Arabia."

"Do I have to go?" I venture. There's silence. "Maybe I can reschedule, but I've already ordered the invitations."

"Well, you could have asked me first. Already I let you go ahead with du Bouchet and not Pierre's friend. I didn't give you this shop so you could be away from me."

Before I can ask why he did "give me this shop," I hang up. I still can't really put my finger on why Olivier has to control everything.

The phone rings again. This time, it's my mother calling to say that Poppy has had a stroke. He's in the hospital. Is he okay? I ask, panicked. Is he in pain? He's doing fine, she assures me, but suggests I come home, quit wasting time in France. The conversation is cut short, as always. My mother, as hard as she tries not to, always finds the most inappropriate things to say, the deepest cutting words to protect herself from feeling too much.

I open the windows wide. The wind whips around the city. It's starting to rain. I wonder if I should call her back. I try calling my grandmother but realize she's probably at the hospital.

Olivier calls back to tell me that we need to talk about fitting my schedule into his plans, but I interrupt him to tell him about Poppy.

"I feel guilty for not being there," I tell Olivier. "My mother says I should get back."

"Of course," he says. And after a few words about getting me a flight, he says that I will definitely have to reschedule du Bouchet. "It's a good thing Pierre's friend is still available for the reading," he adds quickly, not letting me object. "I'll have Marie-Claire book your flight to New Orleans."

I stick my head out the window, let a few drops wash down my face, flush away any trace of tears. I look around the apartment—this house, so strange and foreign—the clean white sofa and beautiful sculptures from Mali, Cartier-Bresson's photos of men in China eating from steaming bowls. I want to be like Samantha from *Bewitched,* twitch my nose and suddenly be back in Louisiana. I want to smell a pot of red beans and rice cooking in my grandfather's kitchen, open up the lid and let the steam dampen my face and lips. I miss the way Poppy would stand at the stove for hours, cooking and anticipating the joy he knew would nourish his family well beyond the table. This is something I'm afraid I will never know again.

I start packing a suitcase, wondering if Poppy will hold out until I get there. I make a list of things to tell Custodia while I'm gone. Suddenly, I am nostalgic for a time before the bookstore, before the stroke. I miss the Olivier who used to fly to Stockholm every weekend, who didn't have to order and control everything into his idea of a perfect world. But there are many new people to know, and I remind myself of the possibility of these friendships—Jan, the American wife of the Spanish publisher, Gilles, Paolo, the Florentine poet. And Brigitte and Hervé. Why, then, I wonder, do I feel so alone?

IT'S LATE, AND no one's waiting for me when I arrive at Moisant Airport, but it feels better this way. No one in my family knows I'm here this soon. The air's thick and hot, like walking into an oven. Riding in the cab, I roll down the windows to breathe in the hot wind and the scent of jasmine and magnolia in the air.

"Can we take St. Charles Avenue down to the French Quarter? I'll stop on Governor Nicholls." I'll stop to visit my great-aunt and ride with her to see my grandfather.

"You from here, dahlin', or what?"

"In a way," I tell the cabdriver, who takes a puff of his cigarette, then flicks the ashes out the window. Some blow into the backseat, into my hair and eyes. He looks at me curiously in the rearview mirror.

I roll down my window all the way to take in the sweet olive tree, ordinary with tiny white yellow blossoms but luxuriant, shameless in its intoxicating sweetness. We stop behind St. Louis Cathedral so I can get out and break off a tiny branch of this tree. I think of the sweet olives and bubblegum trees that burst yellow every spring in my grandfather's garden, how he used to sit, before the stroke, in the coolest part of the shade, enjoying the subtropical breeze as my young cousins played hide-and-seek, trying not to scratch the poison ivy trampling up his arms.

AFTER LEAVING THE hospital, Poppy spends the week in his blue cotton bathrobe, balancing himself with one hand against the kitchen counter, teaching me certain things, mainly how to finely chop the celery and onion for his chicken salad, which spices to use for his oyster dressing. So much emphasis on recipes, but he refuses to eat. I watch him at the head of the table, pushing around morsels of colorless food over his sad plate. But for the short time I'm here, he insists I learn how to make crawfish bisque. I've watched him a million times, but he insists.

"First take the crawfish that's been cooked in that spicy crab boil. Then you pick the tail meat and clean the heads." Poppy watches as I squeeze the liquid out of the stale French bread, sauté the trinity of green bell pepper, onion, and chopped celery. After he has watched me stuff about fifty heads and once they are simmering in a spicy tomato sauce, he wants to make sure I know about the stuffed cabbage leaves and his famous artichokes bursting with garlic and herbs. He tells me this as my grandmother sets a plate of eggs sunny-side up and grits on the table for his lunch. He waves it away like a foul odor.

My mother and I argue about everything. She wants to know why I didn't bring Olivier and Laure with me this time, why Olivier would give me a shop. What did I do to deserve my very own bookshop? She doesn't understand my choices, this life I have forged for myself, why I choose to stay so far away.

Poppy interrupts to say he wants to play Spades, watch the chefs on PBS.

"Remember . . . remember . . ." He struggles with his words as he throws down a king of hearts. "Use only Binder's French bread."

One day, I tell him I will cook only if he eats, something, anything. "Come on, Pops. You have to. How about some rice or pasta?"

He shakes his head.

"Sweet potatoes? Fried potatoes with mayonnaise on French bread?" This was always one of his favorite sandwiches, sometimes dressed with shredded lettuce and sliced Creole tomatoes.

He nods and smiles and then shakes his head, pulls the bathrobe tight around his waist.

"Soup? Split pea."

He nods slowly. "Okay, a little bit of soup. Kimmy," he whispers as I'm running to the store, "I'll eat the soup . . . if you make some chocolate pudding."

He has always loved sweets. Even though he has been diagnosed with adult diabetes, just within the last year or two, he refuses to give up his Hershey's Kisses or pastry cream–filled doughnuts dipped in chocolate. Ice cold milk with crushed ice, vanilla, and sugar. My grandmother calls my sister to have her pick up some beignets from Café du Monde on her way to the house.

When my sister arrives, she stiffens as I go to hug her. She has never been good at tragedy or the mildest sadness. She keeps to herself. She is so different from the child who would wail at the top of her lungs, throw herself onto the floor to get her way. She stands close to Poppy, anticipating his every need, but doesn't say much else except that she's surprised to see me here.

When my grandfather is resting in his favorite chair and my mother and grandmother sit at the table to talk, Sue and I get up to wash dishes.

"Did I tell you my accounting professor is Korean?" she tells me suddenly, filling the sink with hot soapy water. "I asked him about Korea, showed him my adoption papers."

I turn off the faucet, wanting to hear more, so much more.

We've never talked about this before, even when I went back to Korea. "Do you want to go back to Korea one day?" I look up. She is taller than me, strong boned and pretty.

"Maybe, yeah . . . I'd like to know."

She goes on to tell me that her name was made up. Han Sun Ae. A Korean judge named her. "Dr. Jin told me it meant 'little girl,' how generic."

"But we've always been told Sunée means 'soft love.' " Suzy rolls her eyes at this signification, pulls her thick black hair into a ponytail. "I thought you wanted to be an archaeologist."

She shrugs. She is obsessed with history, excavations. She wants to go to Pompeii, she gorges herself on books about queens and kings of centuries ago. But now she studies numbers, weighs and manages risk. Her lips start to tremble.

"Are you crying?" I ask her.

"I cried for two days after talking to Dr. Jin," she assures me. "Because of my birthplace, my name. Dr. Jin said that we can tell a lot about where we're from, which region, just by our name." Her eyes tear up. "And my name just means 'little girl' . . . what kind of birthplace is that?"

I go to hug her, but she leans down to turn on the dishwasher, letting the noise drown out any words.

Later that afternoon, she sits next to me and says she wants to talk.

"I know it seems weird, after all these years, but I'm growing up, I'm an adult, and I don't want any hard feelings."

"I don't have any," I assure her.

"I do. I did. You know you were always the favorite in the family—"

"Not with Mom and Dad."

She nods but goes on to talk about my grandparents and my great-aunt. "You were older, smarter. The day you went away to college, I thought things would be better, but they just talked about you even more. 'When's Kim coming home?' everyone wanted to know. Look, this is hard for me, but I just want to be friends. It might take awhile. But I realize it's not your fault. We were little kids."

This is the most we've said to each other in years. I want to hug her, thank her, tell her how much I love her and am sorry for being so far away all these years, that I didn't mean to abandon her. But she cuts the conversation short; she is still distant—closer, but distant.

My last morning, Poppy has dressed in tan pants and a freshly ironed shirt, a white cardigan sweater. He is clean-shaven and smells of Old Spice. He walks me out to the car, carrying binoculars to watch the comet he read about in the morning paper. He kisses me good-bye and points to the sky.

"Come back soon, Kimmy. I don't know how much longer I'll be around. I'm getting old, you know."

Yes, over eighty, but my grandfather is ageless to me. I hesitate, then wrap my arms around him one last time. He tells me to go now, that he'll be fine, waving to me from up there; he manages to point to the sky again as if he can already spot his place up in the clouds.

FRENCH-FRY PO-BOY WITH
HORSERADISH CRÈME FRAÎCHE

We do not fear carbs in Louisiana. We embrace them, introduce them to other carbs whenever possible. My grandfather used to pan-fry potatoes in a skillet, slather them with mayonnaise and lots of black pepper, and serve them with warm French bread. Verti Marte, a corner grocer on Governor Nicholls in New Orleans, used to deliver a version of these fried potato sandwiches late into the night, to any French Quarter home or, better yet, local bar. With extra wow sauce (horseradish mayonnaise), it was truly a perfect after-midnight snack. Here's my version.

> *2 large russet or Yukon gold potatoes*
> *1 cup canola or olive oil*
> Fleur de sel, *or sea salt*
> *Fresh-ground black pepper*
> *½ cup crème fraîche (or thick sour cream)*
> *1 tablespoon mayonnaise*
> *1 teaspoon lemon juice*
> *1 tablespoon prepared horseradish (or fresh grated)*
> *Hot sauce (optional)*
> *1 loaf French bread*
> *Garnishes: shredded lettuce, tomato, sliced onion, Dijon*
>   *mustard*

Peel potatoes, then cut lengthwise into quarter-inch-thick sticks. Rinse potatoes in several changes of cold water. Drain in a colander, spread cut potatoes in a single layer on several paper towels, and pat very dry. (It's important to remove all moisture so potatoes won't spatter when frying.)

Heat oil in a large heavy skillet over moderate heat until it begins to shimmer (and deep-fat thermometer registers 375 degrees). Put oven rack in middle position and preheat oven to 200 degrees. Once oil is ready, fry potatoes (in 2 batches if necessary), turning occasionally, about 6 to 7 minutes per batch or until golden. Transfer fries with a slotted spoon to a baking sheet lined with several layers of dry paper towels. Sprinkle hot fries with salt and pepper. Keep fries warm in oven if frying in 2 batches. Combine crème fraîche, mayonnaise, lemon juice, and horseradish in a small bowl. Season with salt, to taste. Add a few dashes of hot sauce, if desired. Pile onto French bread and garnish, if desired.

XVI

HOME, AGAIN

৩৩

OLIVIER'S WAITING FOR ME AT THE TRAIN STATION IN MARSEILLE. If it were up to me, I would have taken the train to Avignon as I usually do, since it's shorter from Paris, but he prefers I come into Marseille because the drive to Pierrerue is easier for him.

"You've got to get over your fear of flying," he says, kissing me hello. "I thought you were over that after I sent you to the fear of flying seminars at Air France, you know, with the simulator and all."

"I was, but it comes back . . . I can't explain it." I'm still jet-lagged even though I stopped in Paris for a few days to check on the bookstore and see Grignon before taking the train to meet Olivier.

"It would be so much easier for you to fly back and forth rather than take the train. That's what the classes were for," he insists, taking my bags and loading them into the car. "That's how you solve the problem."

"Well, it didn't work. Obviously the fear is much deeper. It can't be resolved in five hours in a simulator. Besides, I like the TGV. And I was already on such a long flight from New Orleans."

"It doesn't matter anymore."

It doesn't to him, because he has meetings in Provence and has strongly requested, practically ordered, me not to stay in Paris anymore without him. I won't be flying alone again anytime soon. He doesn't understand how I could be away from him, how I'm able to do anything without him.

But now, just for an instant despite his orders, home actually feels as if it's here, even though I don't tell him this or how good it is to be in his arms.

"*Tu ne pars plus sans moi,*" he whispers into the top of my head, hugging me. No more leaving without him.

My eyes burn from lack of sleep. I nod, squeeze his hand. If I speak, the words will come crashing out.

"*Tu es avec moi, maintenant.*" You're with me now.

I feel weightless in Olivier's arms, and he grasps me tighter, feeling, I hope, my wish to be anchored, my need to be moored.

I whisper that Poppy's not going to make it much longer. His heart is swelling with liquid; the doctors explained the risk of congestive heart failure. The stroke is just the beginning, and his diabetes doesn't help.

We stop for bottles of water and gas, and when we get back in the car, Olivier tells me that he's going to go ahead with the launch of the new company involving olive oils. The bottle I gave him was just the beginning. "We need to find a name . . . something that works in French and English. *Oliviers,* olive tree."

"How about Oliviers and Co.?" I suggest, tired and not making any sense. "You know, with the ampersand symbol."

He repeats after me, first in English and then in French. He nods. "Of course, Oliviers & Co., *c'est génial.* It works in both languages. Yes, I'll call it that. When we get to Provence, I want to show you the prototype for the first bottles."

I'm surprised he actually liked my suggestion. For a moment, I allow myself to be absorbed back into Midas's world.

XVI

૪૭

The drive down to Provence is lovely, with signs of spring everywhere. Luminous golden fields of rapeseed, fragrant lavender blooms on the horizon. The air smells of rosemary and fresh thyme blossoms. Another chance at a new life. I search for my favorite flowers, but there are fewer and fewer fields of bright red poppy.

Olivier sings along with Léo Ferré on the radio, mouthing the words and holding my hand so tightly that it's starting to sweat. I doze on and off, feeling floaty with the time difference. He asks me if I want to stop along the way or continue driving.

"Whatever you want," I answer, meaning what I say.

"*Vraiment?*" he asks, surprised. I will agree to anything as long as he doesn't disappear.

IT'S DUSK WHEN we arrive at the house. I have souvenirs for the kids and toys for the dogs. Sophie stands in the dimly lit kitchen trying to decipher my crumpled, handwritten recipe for Poppy's shrimp Creole. I wave at her through the glass-and-iron door while Olivier unpacks the car. She doesn't see me at first, but when she looks up, I hardly recognize her face, drawn with deep circles under her eyes.

"It smells strange in here . . . something's burning," I say, rushing into the kitchen. "Sophie, are you okay?" I forget the custom of kissing hello and go to touch the bruises on her shoulders and arms, but she pulls away from me and cowers into herself, continuing to peel raw shrimp as garlic and onions burn on the stovetop. I shut off the gas.

"I didn't even hear you come in." She lifts her arm and with the back of her wrist tries to move long strands of hair over her eyes. "I fell again." She smiles. "I'm such a klutz."

She tells me this before I've even asked, and she won't look at me now. I brush her hand away to reveal a green-and-blue mark the size of a small plum just under her hairline.

"Where is he?"

"Keem. Come back."

I'm already down the hill, screaming for Serge. I run into him near the fig trees between their house and ours, and we're both shocked to see each other so suddenly.

"*Salut, Keem.* Welcome back." He leans in to kiss me hello, and I resist the urge to shake him.

"Serge, listen—"

"You listen . . . I have some bad news."

"Really?" I ask, one hand on my hip, ready to forbid him from touching Sophie again.

"Flora's back in the hospital," he says, his voice thick and resigned, his eyes moist. "She's lost sight in one eye. Spots all over her lungs. CAT scan tomorrow. Where's Olivier?" I point to the driveway, covering my mouth with both hands before the cries can be heard.

Sophie runs to me. "Did you say anything?"

I shake my head. "It's Flora."

She takes my hand and walks with me back to our part of the property. "You didn't give me a chance to tell you. We all know that this is her last chance. The doctors have always said it. They don't know how she resists, but her body can't hold out anymore."

Sophie and I pack our bags and plan to drive to Marseille while Olivier and Serge contact doctors in Paris and Switzerland. The phone rings.

"*Chérie,* you're back. How's your family, your grandfather?"

"Okay . . . not really. Nelly . . . I can't talk . . . Flora's in the hospital."

"*Mon Dieu.* It never stops. I told her to call my doctor in

Eygalières, he's the best . . . why doesn't anyone ever listen
to me—"

"Sophie and I are driving to the clinic first thing in the morning," I say dryly.

"Will Olivier be at the house? Louis and I are about to drive
through Avignon. We're coming tonight. Did you forget?"

"I'm so sorry, Nel, with my trip back home and now Flora—
I haven't slept in . . . I don't know how long . . ."

"*Très bien.* We can stay here, but it will be difficult to find
a room and so expensive. *Non, Louis,*" she whispers, "we've
already driven seven hundred kilometers, and we can't afford
to stay anywhere else."

"Just come. We'll work it out. Olivier will be here." I hang
up the phone, exhausted.

I stretch out on the daybed in one of the upstairs rooms and
fall into a half sleep, thinking of Poppy, Grignon, Suzy's tears
over her birth name, Sophie's bruised face. *Que reste-t-il de ceux
qui sont absents?* What remains of those who have disappeared?
What kinds of marks do they leave? *Que laissent-ils comme dépôt,
comme trace, comme marque? Ou même comme cicatrice?* My last session with Grignon just an hour before I got on the train was
about sickness and health. The ways in which we touch others,
the marks we leave behind. His last words were *"Cicatrice signifie
guérison, n'est-ce pas?"* Scars indicate healing, *n'est-ce pas?*

THERE IS NOT much healing going on at the Clinique la Timone,
in the third-floor room where Flora lies in bed, silent, staring
through a tiny window that faces out to the Mediterranean too
far away. Her body is bandaged after the surgery, and her face is
swollen with chemicals.

"*Il est là, Jean-Marie?*" She tries to raise herself up on the bed, searching for signs of her lover in the dark. I sit close to her, tell her to relax. "Keem? It's you." She's out of breath and grasps my hand, holding it close to her cheek, hot and damp with fever.

"Are you in pain?" Sophie asks, distractedly rubbing her thumb over her bruised forehead. "Shall I call the nurse?"

Flora shakes her head. "Kimette, did you call him? When's he coming?"

I can't decide if I should lie or not. Flora senses everything. She makes a sound I've never heard before, soft muffled cries, until her body is shaking, casting wild shadows on the bare walls of the sterile room. Sophie and I sit silently and wait, let her cry it out.

"He loves you so much," Sophie says, stroking her arm.

"I know that. It's difficult for him. But I just want to see Jean-Marie one more time." She allows herself a few tears, and when the nurse comes to give her painkillers, she throws a pillow at her and yells for her to leave.

Sophie and I take turns monitoring her. Finally, I fall asleep on the foldout cot. Every time I turn, the thick plastic-covered mattress crunches beneath me. I drift in and out of sleep, dreaming of Flora high up on a hill, her eyes closed, arms open to the wind. People are there, with erased faces, but I know that they're watching, ready to tell us things we've been wanting to know, things we've been afraid to ask, because we already know the answer. Poppy's on a ship, whispering something important, but the wind eats his words, water fills his face, rust corrodes his heart. I know he will soon be one of the disappeared, another one of the missing.

DR. ESKANDARI HAS decided that Flora will be better off with friends or family than in a hospital bed. The home care nurse will have to come every day to administer medicine. I want to take her home with us, care for her as long as possible. Olivier agrees, and he and Serge set up the main downstairs room for her. When we arrive, Flora limping, grasping my arm, the children greet us with joy. Laure hugs me and kisses me madly.

"Lulu and I blew up ten whole balloons and taped big drawings for Flora all over her room." I whisper that she's an angel. Her smile turns quickly into a frown when she asks, "*Tu restes ici maintenant?*"

I reassure her no more hospitals, that we're all here to stay. We're the living, not the dead.

Over the next few weeks, Flora seems to be doing better, although she is constantly cold. She spends days sitting out by the pool, wrapped in layers of blankets, watching the kids play tag and Marco Polo. Even though she doesn't have much of an appetite, she helps me crush garlic with olive oil for aioli, peel and rinse the slime off salsify that I wrap in ham and bake into a rich gratin. She likes the Mornay sauce. She kneads pizza dough for the kids and helps arrange flowers in tiny glass vases to place all over the house. In the afternoons, I read her stories by Márquez and Borges, then Tolstoy and Chekhov. Librettos of *Tosca, Carmen, La Bohème.* She wants to hear all the stories of tragic heroines.

"*Toutes folles. Mon Dieu,* when will they wake up?"

"That's enough tragedy for the day," Sophie announces, just back from the market one morning, as she spreads out the goods on the table on the back veranda. An array of fresh beans, cheeses, tiny fennel-infused sausages, and breads.

Flora sits in the hot sun, her thick legs sticking out under a bright blue sari, a hunter green stole wrapped around her shoulders. She motions for me to give her the basket, she wants to help shell the peas.

"Jean-Marie is never coming back," she tells me, plucking a pod, inhaling the sharp green scent. "Gloria will never let him go . . . all those televisions out the window finally paid off." She makes a crashing noise with her mouth and cheeks. It knocks the wind out of her. "If you're going to get me to work, I'll need some Champagne," she says, trying to wink at Laure.

"Me too," Laure says, then turns to me and asks if it's any good, Champagne.

Without the smallest bit of commentary, I go to the cellar and bring out a bottle of vintage Dom Ruinart and a tray of our most expensive flutes. Laure and Lulu gather at the table.

"What are we celebrating?" Lulu asks, licking her lips as the bubbles dance up to the rim of the glass and tickle her nose.

"*La vie,*" Flora answers. "*Toujours la vie, la vie toujours.*"

FLORA'S DAYS ARE spent in a state of drowsiness and constant pain. She can hardly speak because the tumors are crouching in her throat, crowding out her words. They fill up her brain and lungs, closing in on the regions closest to the heart. She holds on until the last moment, waiting for Jean-Marie—he saved her once. But it has been too many months since he has called or tried to see her. Flora's fired the home care nurse and has me come to her room every morning now. I bring her her medicine, and she makes me sit on the bed, tell her how Olivier and I met. She wants every detail, how it felt to be apart. She wants to feel the cold of Stockholm, taste the salt of the herring and the wicked wind from the Baltic Sea. Everything we shared in our early months together.

"He loves you so much," she mouths. I nod, tears filling my throat. "And love is what keeps us in the world of the living." She says this every day, and I wipe her face with a clean towel dipped in lavender essence and springwater, press my lips gently to her forehead.

"*À demain,*" she always whispers, about tomorrow, and then tilts her head in place of a wink. "When does Olivier return?"

Olivier's in Dubai for three days. I didn't want him to go, but he didn't want me to continue taking care of Flora this way, with all my heart and time invested. "Let her family take care of her, let her brother come from Normandy," he said. I am her family, I told him.

I sleep on the seagrass daybed in Flora's room. Sophie wants to take turns, says I need sleep, but I can't leave. I don't want her to disappear without me. I want to see her go. I want proof. We're here to help one another live and die in a more gentle manner.

Flora's not afraid anymore. But she still waits every day for Jean-Marie to call. I try to reach him several times. Once, when he answered, he asked how she was and then hung up when I asked him to come to her.

Olivier calls every few hours. I take his calls sitting out on the back veranda overlooking the barren fields. Sometimes I watch the hunters until they disappear into the valley. Beyond are the Italian Alps. Olivier's talking about Hamad and the Bedouins.

"I'll be back tomorrow," he says.

"Tomorrow may be too late." I hang up the phone and walk barefoot to the edge of the property and close my eyes. There's a slight evening breeze. I want to flap my arms and be lifted up. But instead I go to make tea for Flora, slice some bread and cheese for myself, feeling almost nothing, empty, no tears. I spread crushed olives on the bread. Anchovies. I'm not hungry, but I want salt. I crave it so much these days.

Sophie and I sit with Flora, cursing Jean-Marie, as if he could save her. Later, when she is finally asleep, we sit out on the terrace. Sophie lights a cigarette, pours me a glass of wine.

"I've been meaning to ask you . . ." She hesitates. "What's

going on with you and Olivier? I know it's not my place, but . . . things don't seem right."

I try to explain something, try to speak, but can only shake my head instead. Sophie takes my hand. "I know," she says, tears in her eyes. "It's different with Serge, but it's the same."

<hr/>

GRATIN DE SALSIFY

This is a twist on a Belgian dish of endives wrapped in ham and baked with cheese. Try plump white asparagus instead of salsify or endives. Salsify gets sticky when peeling and oxidizes quickly, like a peeled apple, hence the lemon juice in the cooking liquid. Substitute good-quality deli ham, such as Rosemary or other Italian ham, for the prosciutto. If ham is very salty, reduce amount of salt in cooking liquid and in the Mornay sauce.

> 4 to 5 stalks salsify, trimmed, peeled, and rinsed (about
>   ¾ pound)
> 2 to 3 lemon slices
> 2 to 3 bay leaves
> ¼ to ½ teaspooon salt
> 6 to 8 cups low-sodium chicken broth or water
> 1½ to 2 cups Mornay sauce (see page 40)
> 12 slices prosciutto or good-quality cooked ham
> Fresh white or fresh-ground black pepper, to taste
> Garnish: grated Gruyère or Comté, and chopped fresh parsley
>   or fresh chervil

Preheat oven to 350 degrees. Cut salsify into 4-inch pieces. Combine salsify and next 3 ingredients in a large pot. Add enough chicken broth or water to cover. Bring to a boil and let cook about 8 minutes or until salsify is tender but not mushy. Gently remove salsify with a slotted spoon and let cool.

Spoon a third of the Mornay sauce in bottom of a baking dish. Wrap each salsify with a ham slice and place seam-side down on top of sauce in baking dish. Cover with remaining Mornay sauce. Top with grated cheese and a crack of fresh white or black pepper. Bake for 25 to 30 minutes or until top is golden and bubbly. Garnish, if desired. *Serves 4 to 6.*

XVII

LE REPAS MAIGRE

✆

THE BITTER WINTER WIND WHIPS IN FROM THE HIGH ALPS. It's the season to be jolly. December 1996, my fourth Christmas here in Provence. Serge started hitting Sophie again. Olivier told me not to get involved, but then he gave Serge an ultimatum: Quit drinking or pack up and leave. I know this was hard for Olivier, mainly because it is an admission of defeat.

Serge left for two weeks, just enough time for Sophie's wounds to soften and for her to start missing him again, and then he returned from Morocco one late afternoon with musk oil and bracelets for Sophie, a rusted bicycle for Lulu, a pocket-watch for Olivier, and a Berber wool coat for me.

"Noël is in three days, not today, Papa," Lulu exclaimed, tugging on his hand, not letting go. Her lip quivered and the way she mimicked Sophie by keeping her head down, the only way to know that at seven she was ashamed of loving a man so much even though he had already broken her heart.

We were in the upstairs living room, feeding the fire. Sophie looked at Olivier, whispered that she wanted Serge to come home for Christmas, for the kids.

"He'll be back," I told Sophie, not sure of anything at all.

"They don't leave for good unless there's another woman

involved, or death," Flora had said just before Serge showed up, grinning and full of promises from Tangiers. Flora adjusted the patch she now has to wear over her left eye. The tumor has grown so that it impairs her vision. "Otherwise they stay forever."

We decide not to go away for the holidays in order to be closer to Sophie and Serge as they work things out and to be here for Flora. But while taking care to make sure everyone is happy and comfortable, and planning menus for Christmas, something comes over me, a longing I can't explain, a desire for a home that is on the other side of the world, a place I once knew but where nothing is familiar and where I am not welcome.

Asia appears in smudges of black-and-white images in my dreams at night. During my waking hours, I search for the shapes and flavors of this foreign place, at the market in Forcalquier, in the drawer of my refrigerator here in Provence.

One afternoon, we make lists and menus, and when Olivier raises his glass in a toast, I know that, once again, every detail has been decided.

Lulu rides her bike around and around the billiards table. "I'm hungry," she finally says, smiling at her father. She and Laure have decided they want tiny *ravioles de Royan* for dinner with lots of Gruyère cheese. Everyone seems to have found their appetite, except for me, since Serge's return.

"We'll have a traditional Provençal Christmas this year," Olivier announces. Two years ago—luckily before the stroke— my grandparents finally came for a visit. We had pasta with truffles and cream, a stuffed goose, Poppy's oyster dressing, baked sweet potato casserole, *salade verte,* and cheese. Poppy, Olivier, and his mother, Giselle, and I sat at the table for hours after everyone had gone to bed, talking, Poppy and Giselle going over war stories and drinking lots of red wine.

Olivier chooses some preliminary wines while I pull out my stained and tattered copy of *La Cuisinière Provençale*. We decide that for the traditional *repas maigre*, there will be salt cod steeped in milk for three days, as well as *anchoïade*—a garlic-rich anchovy sauce to eat with celery and cauliflower—boiled cardoons baked in béchamel sauce, and a few wayward offerings: *terrine de foie gras d'oie,* Iranian caviar, and smoked Scottish salmon. Olivier's sister and mother will take care of the *treize desserts.* Thirteen traditional sweets to represent Christ and the twelve apostles: *la pompe,* black-and-white nougat, dried figs, raisins, almonds, and hazelnuts. Walnuts, prunes, mandarins, apples, pears, *calissons d'Aix,* and quince paste.

"Tomorrow when you go shopping, don't forget to buy milk, we need it for the *brandade,*" Olivier reminds me.

"I'm going with you to the market," Flora reminds me. I start shaking my head, but before anyone can speak, she raises her hand and, coughing, says, "It's my life, what's left of it, and I want to participate in Christmas one last time." Breathless, she pulls the blanket up to her neck and adjusts her head on the sofa pillow.

"*D'accord,*" I concede.

The next morning, Sophie and I buckle up Flora in the backseat of my Saab. It's icy on the streets, the air like sickles in our throats.

"Are you sure you want to come?"

"Keem, of all people you should understand—"

"I do, I do," I say, shaking my head.

"*On y va.* Lobsters and goose livers are waiting for us." Flora wants to go to the Hypermarché in Manosque or the largest Casino supermarket around. She wants the vast array of things. She hobbles into the store, holding on to the cart as I roll it slowly up and down the aisles. It's too cold for her to go in the refrigerated section, so she sends me with a list: two capons, two whole fresh goose livers, milk and butter, cream and eggs. She wants oysters and smoked trout with apples, celery root, and black truffles fresh from our backyard.

"Can you make oysters *en Sabayon* and bread-stuffed truffles?" she asks me.

I nod, of course, whatever she wants.

"*C'est bien, ma petite.*" She pats my head in a maternal gesture. I hold on to her elbow, gently guiding her down the spice aisle. She touches everything, holds a bottle or bunch, considering the weight of each item.

When the baskets have been piled high with more than enough, we stand in line with all the other shoppers. Sophie and I wait in one line, Flora in another, longer one. I watch as she leans against the edge of the checkout counter, weary yet determined to wait her turn.

PREPARING CHRISTMAS DINNER is a disaster. My heart's not really in it, and Olivier senses this. When I burn the baked cardoon gratin, he throws the whole smoking dish into the garbage and decides to take over. I stand behind him as he does the final rinse of the salt cod in the sink and peels potatoes for the *brandade*.

Pascale and Giselle spread out their confections on the dessert table I've set up with the traditional three white tablecloths for the occasion.

"My mother used to do it this way. She'd spend days preparing the quince and confectioning the nougat." Giselle hands me a piece of the soft white candy filled with almonds and pistachios. "*Et ta mère?*"

My mother really was never a good cook, although she

tried her best. When she did attempt anything in the kitchen, it was always fast, spaghetti sauce from a jar stirred into thawed ground meats. White bread that stayed soft for weeks at a time, toasted and topped with creamed tuna. Luckily, Poppy was in full charge of holiday meals: a table laden with baked sweet potatoes topped with butter, brown sugar, and pecans, pineapple-crowned roasted ham, creamed green beans with artichoke dressing, turkey and giblet gravy, oyster dressing, soft shiny Hawaiian rolls. We'd finish with bread pudding and hard sauce, my grandmother's ambrosia, Nani's rum cake, and my uncle Eldred's brownie pie with whipped cream.

Olivier pulls me aside. "What's wrong? You don't care about Christmas dinner. Everyone will take it personally."

"I'm just thinking about Flora, and we always spend Christmas here, we never go to the States."

"You know it's complicated with Laure . . . Dominique insists having her one of the two days."

"I know. I just miss my family sometimes, and there are lots of things I've tried talking to you about . . . I'm just not . . ."

"Sure? Happy? Are we going to talk about *that* again?" He pours in too much olive oil. *"Merde."*

"Just add more potatoes."

"I know how to make *brandade.* I've known since before you were even born."

I start to walk away, but then he holds out a forkful for me to taste. The potatoes are undercooked and the cod still too salty. I shrug. "Not bad, it's . . . good," I lie.

Olivier takes a bite and spits it out into the sink. *"J'en ai marre."* I've had enough, he shouts, and dumps it all in the garbage on top of the scorched cardoons. "You're not helping." He stares at me, waiting. "So I'm just going to call Allo Couscous, and voilà, we'll have a terrible North African dinner delivered.

For Christmas in Provence." He washes his hands and shakes them dry, splattering me with the cold water.

"Papa? Kimette, are you crying?" Laure comes into the kitchen, takes my hand in hers, and pats it gently. She's got green and gold stars stuck to her chin and hands. "I was wrapping your gift." She smiles. "It's a big surprise."

"Show me," I tell her. I hug Olivier and follow Laure upstairs to the tree. Lulu is down on her stomach, shaking the brightly wrapped boxes to her ear.

"Lulu, you have to wait."

"*Je sais.*" She gets up and sits next to me on the sofa, Laure already on my lap.

"What are you going to get Papa?" she wants to know, spreading out my hands to play pattycake.

I haven't the slightest idea. What he wants from me is nothing I can give him. "I haven't decided yet, but something he'll *really* like."

She seems relieved and hands me ribbon and tape, colored pens, and I get on the floor with the kids and forget for a moment that I'm not one of them.

Later, Pascale and Annie, Olivier's sister-in-law, knock on my office door, come in before I answer.

"*Ça va pas?*" Pascale asks. "Annie and I are worried about you."

"*Non, non, tout va bien,*" I lie, not wanting to ruin anyone's holiday.

"*Allez,*" Annie says, sitting in a chair next to mine. "Olivier's not easy, we all know that. But he loves you so much."

"I know."

"It's the divorce, isn't it," Pascale says. "It's taking too long. We told him not to let Dominique—" I shake my head, denying anything's wrong, to them and to myself. "He's my brother, and I know he has his reasons, but sometimes he forgets that he's not the only one who knows how to make decisions."

"Just hang on," Annie advises, clasping my hand in hers. "He can be too much sometimes, but you love each other . . . he needs you."

"It's not just the divorce," I offer as an explanation. "The holidays, something's missing . . . I can't explain it—"

"You miss your family," Pascale finishes my sentence. "You know, Olivier says we are your family. American and Korean . . . we're everything you'll ever need."

Annie kisses the top of my head as she and Pascale leave my office. "Whatever you do . . ." She pauses. "Don't leave."

I look up at her, frightened. Who talked about leaving? Can they look into my heart and read my deepest thoughts?

While the others continue wrapping gifts, I boil a pot of water and stir in some white rice, drain it, and mix in salted butter. *"Nabi,"* I whisper. It's one of the few words I remember from my Korean lessons. Papillon, I translate to myself as I take a deep breath to calm the butterflies in my stomach. I sit on the floor by the tree, amid all the gifts, and balance the warm bowl on my knees. I pick at some of the grains, roll them around my tongue. I close my eyes and with each swallow wish for a taste of home.

XVIII

EVERYTHING, NOT YOU

ॐ

*B*ACK IN PARIS, THERE ARE STILL SIGNS OF FLORA EVERYWHERE
from when she and Jean-Marie stayed with us during the
opening of A Tire d'Ailes. I find an earring she must have forgotten and a handwritten note, a message jotted down in her
big loopy handwriting about various PR people who called. I
think of all these things and the holidays, how they celebrate in
other countries, as I'm lying down again at Grignon's.

The tip of the pencil makes soft scratches on the paper. I
have no idea what he's writing, if anything at all, but he won't
stop.

"I don't have anything to say today."

Silence.

"Did you hear me?" I ask.

Dites. Speak, he encourages.

"What could you possibly be writing when I'm not even
talking?" Long silence. I hate myself for needing to be here. I
hate these games where we outwait each other. I want all the
answers right away. Is that why I'm here? "What about hypno-
sis?" I finally suggest. "To remember things about the past."

"The past?"

It seems I've gotten his attention. "Korea. The language, at least."

"The painful part is not remembering."

"Or maybe discovering that I wasn't loved."

"Choosing to leave or to leave behind is also an act of love."

"It's always about love," I answer, "the beginnings and endings—what about the deep, dark middle of it all?"

More soft scratches on the paper.

"You said that asking the right question will also give me the answer. But there are some things, no matter what questions I ask . . . that I'll just never know."

"And sometimes not knowing is the best answer of all."

No matter how frustrating it is to not understand immediately, I follow his lead, remain respectful and gentle as I pay him and leave, confident finally that the answers will come to me one day.

I STILL CAN'T say the words—am I leaving Olivier or running from myself? I have no choice but to choose this separation. If I leave, I convince myself, it will only be temporary, time enough to shake things up, let Olivier know I'm serious, allow space for me to grow into a whole person. I want him to understand it this way, but Olivier refuses to accept my pain, my lack of roots, my division, that he could be the source of anything but happiness. I have convinced myself that I don't deserve this life he wants so much to give me, this identity that doesn't belong to me because I am so divided, so unsure of who I am.

I schedule extra sessions with Grignon, listening for the subtlest objection to my leaving Olivier, but he doesn't give any indication. I ask him for medicine, "some kind of painkiller or antidepressant, whatever you doctors dole out these days." I am feeling irreverent, restless, and frustrated. He tells me if I feel I need medicine, he will give me a doctor's name, but he won't prescribe them for me.

Merde. "What can I hope for in a man? To be understood?"

"Neither desirable nor possible."

"Communication?"

"No real communication possible, pure communication, anyway."

"Then what? Is it just one big misunderstanding, then?"

"*Il n'y a pas de malentendus, que des malentendants.*" There are no misunderstandings, just misunderstanders.

I am tired of these word games. "All I want is to be loved, simply, for what I am and not for what he thinks I should be. What is the price I have to pay—solitude?" He doesn't answer, so I push harder. "I don't want to be a part of it, I'm retreating from the world."

"No, you must live in the world. It's not a question of isolating yourself, but to know what is tolerable for you . . . when to say yes and when to say no. Or no and yes . . . like coming and going . . . they're one and the same."

OLIVIER AND I go through the motions, like deep underwater divers without a map or meters. We sink into late night slumbers, breathing in each other's dreams, gasping for air; then we awaken to spend the day packing boxes, drinking wine; we fight and argue, embrace again.

When the morning comes, just before the movers arrive, Olivier stands there facing me, unable to speak. Neither of us believes this is real. I look through the cartons of packed books and photos. I try to give him back the Leica, but he shakes his head. I place it on the mantel, next to a photo of us in Stock-holm, so close up, so blurred. I don't want to take anything with me, really, just the bare necessities from this life.

"Kimette." He sits on the white sofa, knees pulled close to his chest. "I'm begging you not to leave."

"I have to go, Olivier." Please don't let me go. Like Laure when she was younger, I want him to take me in his arms while I'm still kicking and screaming on the inside.

"I didn't know how to keep you, and I'll never forgive myself . . ."

And I'll never forgive myself for not knowing what I want, why I don't want what he wants to give me—love and a place in the world I don't have to fight for, an identity that isn't mine.

The movers, like magical elves, arrive promptly, quickly busy themselves with the task of carrying things out, bringing nothing in. At the sight of this, Olivier jumps from the sofa.

"I'm going to wake up Laure."

"No," I whisper. "Please don't wake her up."

Olivier ignores me, screaming that I should know better than to disappear without a word. I convince myself that this is only temporary. Olivier doesn't believe it's real—how could anyone leave him, rupture the life he has manufactured so carefully, this small empire of the heart he has spent years fortifying?

"No, don't, please."

"So you're not leaving?"

I shake my head no, nod yes. "But I don't want it to be more unbearable than it is."

"Do you think she'd rather wake up and discover that you've just disappeared? That you didn't even say good-bye?" Olivier starts down the hallway, his body tense and purposeful now.

"No!" I scream, running after him. I grab at his shoulder and he turns around, half angry, half sad.

"You don't get it, do you? Laure loves you like a mother. And you're abandoning us. Do you know what that means?" he demands. "You know how you've suffered. Your own mother who left like a thief in the night." As the words spill out of him, Olivier reaches in the air as if he could take them back. But he can't stop now. "You've always said, 'If only she had said good-bye . . .'"

"I'm sure she did say good-bye, I just can't remember."

"A proper good-bye before leaving you at the market, on the bench, in the dark."

I want to punch him, but I start hitting the air instead. The tears finally well up, and I let them pour out of me, the years of unreported tears. Every time Olivier tries to calm me down, I push him away as hard as I can, harder each time, until I'm down on the floor, sobbing. I don't recognize myself. He straddles my stomach and presses me to the floor, pinning down my arms. I can feel his heart thumping, and his body starts to shake with mine.

"I'm terrified," I whisper. He repeats my words, and we sit for a moment, holding one another, letting the sound of our voices resonate. I'm terrified of choosing this separation. He is frightened of being alone, faced with what failed, what was missing in order for this to work for both of us.

The bedroom door at the end of the hall opens and Laure appears, morning sun illuminating her like an angel fresh from a dream. She yawns and smiles at us, rubbing sleep out of her eyes. "What are you two doing?"

One of the movers asks, "This goes, too?"

Olivier gestures for him to leave immediately, and just then Laure realizes we've both been crying. She runs to us, tears streaming down her face, as she pushes Olivier off me and straddles my stomach.

"*Ne pars pas, Kimette. Ne nous quitte pas.*" Don't go. Don't leave us. Laure's cry echoes through my heart. "Pa-pa! Do something."

I sit up and carry Laure into the living room. As we sit, she clasps on to me, anticipating my letting go. I hold her tight and bury my head in her hair. She smells like sleep and sweat, such sweetness of the night. The three of us sit huddled together, and for a moment I'm convinced that this isn't real, that if I will it, Olivier will turn to me any moment now, caress my cheek, and slowly coax me out of the dream. But something made me go this far; I can't turn back now.

He's staring, hand suspended, unsure of his next gesture, his next move. Olivier, who owns his world, looks lonelier than I've ever seen him. Lonely because he's touched me. King Midas has touched and turned me into a speechless, precious metal.

I'm on the bench waiting for Omma to come back. My knuckles are hard and blue from the cold, my fist clenched around the morsel of food, waiting, waiting, waiting. I am so tired of the anticipation. Shipwrecked. I drift ashore, searching for the coastline of a warm body, a place that feels like home.

XIX

ROOM OF MY OWN

🕉

I DEFIANTLY RENT A TINY ONE-BEDROOM APARTMENT ON THE Left Bank with a small balcony that looks out onto the Eiffel Tower. It's small, about the size of our steam-room and shower area back in Provence. But I convince myself that this is all I need as I begin to fill the 450-square-foot space. I build shelves out of wine crates and drape Indian cotton throws over the bed. The walls are newly painted white, a clean slate.

Olivier would say it looked like a souk in here, with its labyrinth of empty boxes and mismatched fabrics. If I'm honest, if I take a moment to sit and really look at it, I would agree with him. I miss the grand spaces and empty hallways, the open fields of Provence with its fields of poppy and sunflower. But I stop myself from missing it too much. I have made a choice, and whether or not it proves to be the best choice, it's mine.

Olivier calls and says he wants to come for dinner. Every night he asks and I refuse. He has sold our place on rue de Luynes and moved to the rue du Bac, renting Nelly's friend Gianna's apartment. "It's not like our space, but not bad." My space is definitely not like rue de Luynes, but it's what I can afford. I make my own bread, it's both therapeutic and inexpensive, and eat lots of vegetable curries with rice. I've lost five kilos, and most of my clothes don't fit the way they used to.

I finally agree to meet Olivier for lunch one day. He has me come to the new apartment first. When I recognize our sheets and blankets, our curtains and table, it's comforting, strange, and sad. He asks me to get in bed with him, just one last time.

I find the familiar places of his body that I liked, inhale his scent one last time. It is familiar but awkward, all too fast and desperate. He cries openly when it's over, but I turn away to wipe my tears. After, he insists on a late lunch at a place not too far. At Les Ministères, Olivier pours too much wine, orders a thick bloody steak, and I pick at my fish, watching the lumps harden in the cold, thick béarnaise sauce.

A week later, Olivier sends me a check for 10,000 francs for no apparent reason. I hold it up to the light, balance it in the palm of my hand as if to weigh it, wondering what he wants in return. I stuff it in the bottom of a drawer, beneath some photos.

Olivier calls, screaming every day, "I should have never let you go!" or, "I didn't know how to keep you!" The words are unbearable. Why didn't he think about this before—why didn't I?

Several days later, he invites me to lunch again, but I know now it is better to refuse. My refusals infuriate him, but I can't stop hurting him, hurting myself. Olivier is the man who knows how to turn everything into gold, but with all his power and money, he is incapable of inventing the formula to make me stay, to ground me, something I wish for so desperately. Part of me did not want to leave, but I did. I repeated my own abandonment, preempting another absence—the fear of being left again, this time by someone I have grown so attached to, a real family. I left to prove that I could be a person, independent of his needs and wishes and idea of what I should be, to find my own place. So if I know this, then why is it that I have never felt so alone and disillusioned by my own desires?

ONE EARLY MORNING, he calls, and I can barely pull myself out of the nightmare. "Kimette? Are you awake?"

My heart races. He hasn't called me Kimette in weeks. "It's Flora, isn't it."

"I'm sorry, *oui, elle est morte.*" She died in her sleep, back at her house in Forcalquier, he goes on to explain.

I blink several times. It's 6:00 a.m. "I'm coming down, when's the service? I can leave today—"

"No," he tells me sharply. "Her family hasn't decided yet . . . they're coming in from Normandy, and . . . listen . . . I've thought about it, and . . . you can't come."

"You can't decide everything. I have to be there. Tell me."

"How would that make me look? Like such a fool in front of all our friends, who just don't understand how you could have left me . . . and then you show up for this."

"For *this*? You mean Flora's funeral? Is that all you care about? How you'll *look* to everyone?"

"She's dead. She knows you loved her. I know you took care of her. Her family wasn't around, but you don't have to be there anymore." He says these last words slowly, sharply. "It's better, I advise you strongly not to come."

FOR DAYS, OLIVIER leaves messages, apologizing, but I don't return his calls. I want to be there, but he's made it very clear that I would not be welcome. Instead, the day of the service, I walk the several kilometers to Notre Dame and light two candles, one for Flora, one for Poppy to get better.

When I return, I fast-forward through the messages, catching just the last bit of Olivier's final message: "I wrote an homage to Flora . . . in fact-you should have been there."

He sends another check for 25,000 francs, money, he says, for me to return to the States. *"La France est trop petite pour tous les deux,"* he claims. France isn't big enough for the two of us. Another 25,000 will come my way once I am back in the States. "Go back to the States, maybe go to New York. Be a writer." I don't want his money, but a week later, I need to deposit it to pay back taxes from the bookstore, pay off publishers for their books left on consignment.

He calls late in the night to tell me that he is planning on opening L'Occitane in SoHo and one in New Orleans, which street do I think is the best? Oliviers & Co. will open in the States as well. He is like the grand conquerors of past eras. Olivier the Great. First he buys Île Saint-Louis, then rue de Buci. Grand Central Station, Prince Street, Royal Street. He is a champion at this sentimental Monopoly, rolling snake eyes, always passing go, choosing from the treasure chest. I wait for Chance and am forever negotiating bankruptcy. But despite the large sums that appear magically in my account, I stay in Paris, stubborn and more determined to make a life of my own.

He finally tells me that if the bookstore doesn't start to make money, we will have to sell it. He knows this is how to hurt me, punish me, and I am powerless.

"But, it's poetry . . . you've always said it's not here to make money . . . it exists because it *is* poetry."

"That was then. When we were together. I can't support it now."

*   ⋆   ⋆   ⋆*

I BEGIN BY quietly telling my best customers that I am taking a loss, putting everything up for a bargain, even some of the furnishings. They buy up all the signed editions from poets who have come to do readings—Gary Snyder, Bei Dao, Tomaz Salamun, Octavio Paz from his visit during the Marché de la Poésie—and then armloads of the cheaper pocket editions. A local poet and musician offers to do a fund-raising concert to save the shop. I sit dazed at the counter, sad that this is what my life has become—a vendor of someone else's words on an island in Paris; my last hope to be saved by a French musician playing Tibetan bowls.

Poets come and read as they try to help sell more books. I offer a discount to my loyal customers, and then soon it is a blown-out clearance sale.

I try to find Custodia a job with a small publisher in central France, but she tells me she has decided to move back to Portugal. She's in love, for the first time in her life. She is radiant as she tells me this. She reminds me of Flora, in the good days with Jean-Marie. "Love . . . it's better than poetry. I'll take sex over all the rhymes anytime," Custodia declares.

"Oh, and there's a message from Madame Inès Frenier, editor at one of the major French publishing houses." Custodia explains that Inès heard about the closing of the shop and wants to have a book signing with one of her best-known poets, Jean-Pierre Clemenceau, before it's all over. I find this odd since usually the writer or the publicist will contact me, unless it is a small independent house.

Inès shows up the next afternoon at the bookstore, almost empty except for a few young university students. Her pale blue Chanel suit and matching kitten heels make her look like a washed-out doll. But she's swift, and her eyes never leave mine.

"Kim," she says, "it is a pleasure meeting you. I'm so sorry to hear about the bookshop. I can't stay long, I have a rendezvous. . . . You must meet Jean-Pierre before the final reading. He's a good contact to have in the literary world, and for me, he sells quite well, considering it's poetry . . . but you know . . ." Her eyes drift off momentarily. "I must, how do you say . . . balance his ego."

Inès leaves some books for me and disappears almost immediately.

A few days later, as I am reading through Clemenceau's books, a man in his early forties appears at the shop. "I'm Jean-Pierre Clemenceau?" he introduces himself as though it's a question, as if maybe I'm supposed to know who he is.

He's tall, with curly dark hair, graying at the temples. I can't shake hands because of the book I'm holding. He smells of warm fire and strong cologne, Fahrenheit or Egoïste.

"I was in the neighborhood and thought I'd come and introduce myself before the book signing. I'm sorry to hear that you are closing the shop—"

"Well, not right away . . . if I can help it." I close the book gently, and he smiles at having caught me reading his book.

"I'm off to a meeting, but I'd like to invite you for a café sometime . . . soon." And he is off, just like Inès and all the others who stop by to see me on the island to do business before leaving for more important rendezvous.

★   ★   ★

JUST WHEN I am about to close up for the day, a young woman, petite with long dark hair, walks into the bookshop.

"Hi," she says, "I'm Jan. The American . . . you know Antoine, he owns the Spanish-language bookstore. I'm here to pick up any of our books that didn't sell. I heard you were closing. I'm sorry—"

"Don't be sorry. It's a long story."

"You're American, too?" she asks, sitting on one of the chairs, thumbing through the most recent Paris *Where*. "I'm from Ohio." She's very matter-of-fact and smiles easily, a friendly North American smile with a refreshing lack of Parisian pouting and complaining. "I've been here a long time."

"With Antoine, your husband, right?"

She nods, tilts her head, a bit distracted or worried at the mention of Antoine. "Maybe I should go ahead and get the check from you, too."

I quickly gather the books her husband left on consignment and pay her for the ones sold. We make a promise to have lunch sometime.

Jean-Pierre and Inès have decided that the big event for Jean-Pierre's book needs to be postponed. Which is fine because we are losing money every day, and since no one is eager to buy the shop, Olivier has decided to do something else with it—open the first Oliviers & Co. olive oil store in this space. He will help me renew my work papers, he promises, so I can stay if I insist, "but the shop has got to make money."

Jan comes to help me sell the rest of the books and slowly move things out—a handmade kite from Thibault, some chairs and books, and signed first editions.

Soon the bookshelves are stripped of any trace of poetry but are filled with olive oil jugs, bottles, and tall branches of the ancient peace tree placed throughout the store, signs of Olivier, our travels through the Mediterranean. Because the transformation is so fast, I find it difficult to walk by 81, rue Saint-Louis-en-l'Île. I won't let myself miss the bookshop, miss Olivier, even if I sometimes wonder if I made the right decision. I wonder, just for a second, if it's time for us to get back together. And then I remember my desire for independence.

So, I am determined not to be defeated. I buy a baguette and slather it with butter and cheese, drink lots of coffee, as I concentrate on reading employment ads, following up on old contacts, and sending out my CV. Later, I will go to the market and buy beef, red wine, fresh herbs for a daube I haven't made since leaving the heart of Provence. I am determined to stay.

❧❧❧❧❧❧❧❧❧❧❧❧

LA DAUBE PROVENÇALE

There are many variations of this dish of beef stewed in red wine. Traditionally, the meat is protected from the heat by a layer of lard and cooked in a *daubière*. Use a heavy-bottom casserole dish, preferably enameled cast-iron. I like to thicken my daube with tapenade for added flavor. This is best made one day in advance.

> 3 pounds beef chuck, trimmed of fat and cubed
> 3 medium yellow onions, quartered, divided
> 3 to 4 carrots, cut lengthwise and cut into thirds
> Bouquet garni
> 3 cups dry red wine

2 tablespoons balsamic vinegar

2 slices thick-cut smoked bacon, diced

⅓ cup all-purpose flour

1 teaspoon fleur de sel, or sea salt (plus more for flour)

¼ teaspoon fresh-ground pepper (plus more for flour)

3 to 4 garlic cloves, smashed and coarsely chopped

1 orange

1½ to 2 cups beef stock

2 to 3 tablespoons black olive tapenade

Garnishes: black olives (such as Niçoise), fresh parsley

Combine beef and 2 of the onions and next 3 ingredients in a large nonreactive bowl. Let marinate 5 to 6 hours. (You can let marinate overnight, but note that the wine flavor will be much stronger.)

Heat bacon on medium high in a large heavy-bottom pot or Dutch oven until fat begins to render, about 5 minutes. Place flour in a shallow bowl or plate; season with a pinch of salt and a crack of pepper. Remove beef with a slotted spoon and drain well. Lightly dredge beef chunks in flour, adding a little more flour, as needed. Add beef to pot and let brown, turning occasionally, about 8 minutes. Add remaining onion and let cook about 5 minutes. Add salt, pepper, garlic and a strip of orange rind, and stir. Add reserved wine marinade (reserve onions, carrots, and bouquet garni). Bring to a boil, reduce heat to medium high and let wine reduce, skimming fat, about 15 minutes. Add 1½ to 2 cups beef stock or water (just to cover meat), stir, and add reserved onion, carrot, and bouquet garni. Stir and cover pot and let cook on low heat on stovetop about 3½ to 4 hours (or bake at 325 degrees for same amount of time), or until meat is tender. Remove any fat with a spoon. Remove orange rind and bouquet garni and discard. Zest remaining orange and add to pot. Squeeze juice from the orange, add to pot and stir. Let cool, cover and refrigerate overnight.

To Serve: Skim fat from surface of stew. Heat on medium until warm. Stir tapenade into sauce. Taste and add more salt and pepper, if needed. Garnish, if desired, with black olives and fresh chopped parsley. Serve with large pasta shells or polenta. *Serves 6.*

XX

ISLE OF MISFITS

☙

*J*HAVE MY FIRST JOB INTERVIEW WITH YVES BORREL, THE
CEO of a financial firm that invests in IPOs and other small
businesses on the French stock market. After speaking with me
a few minutes, Yves tells me that I will get paid 14,000 francs
a month net, plus benefits, to be their in-house translator. As
we shake hands good-bye, he leans in close to me. Despite very
blue eyes that make him almost attractive in an odd way, he has
repulsive breath, with hints of cold, wet tobacco mixed with
garlic.

"*Et, Keem,*" he says before I leave. "I must improve my
English. One to one." He raises his eyebrows and makes some
strange sound.

"I'll be busy enough with translating—"

"I pay you three hundred francs a lesson, nothing to do with
your salary as translator." He's not much taller than I am, so I
can see the large wet pores on his chin and nose. But 300 francs
an hour for the lessons . . . 300 francs will pay one session with
Grignon. I accept.

"*Très bien, on commence demain.*"

★　★　★

ONE MORNING, WHEN Yves shows up late for his lesson, he announces that he's had a restless night of sleep and has forgotten his homework so we'll have breakfast instead before his meeting in the first arrondissement. We walk to a café along the rue de Rivoli. I'm hungry, so I'm glad that I don't have to go over the present progressive and conditionals on an empty stomach.

"*Deux petits déjeuners complets,*" Yves orders. He takes my hand in his and starts kissing my fingers. I pull away. "*Non, Keem.* You do not understand. I cannot stand it anymore, cramped in zee little room with you pronouncing English words, and zee way you look at me with your black eyes and—"

"Yves, I'm your English teacher."

"Not anymore. I fire you. So now you can be my mistress." He slides his chair to my side of the table, puts his hand on my thigh. "*Allez,* don't be so *américaine,* my little Asian flower."

The waiter arrives with a beautiful platter of steaming coffee and a basket of croissants, *pain aux raisins,* toasted brioche, jewel-colored jams, and sweetened butter.

"You eat and zen we go to my offeece and lock zee door."

"Yves . . ." I laugh nervously, pushing his flushed face out of mine. This is like the worst scenario from a French movie. Any minute now, the director will show up in his beret and, crushing his mustache into the mouth of the megaphone, order: *Arrêtez, arrêtez. She's not the girl for this scene.* I will be fired and whisked off the set, fade to black, then back to my old self, back in my old skin, with Olivier and the house in Provence, roasting pheasants, reading stories to Laure and Lulu, lying in a hammock listening to the mistral whip in and out of the poppy fields . . .

Yves's lip is dripping red. "*Keeeem!*" he yells. "*Je saigne, arrêt.*"

I meant to bite his cold tongue that he slipped inside my mouth but caught only the lip instead.

"*Merde,* you bite me."

"I *bit* you," I correct him, gathering my books and tapes. "Bite, bit, bitten." I take one last look at the basket of pastries, regretting the buttery dough, then rush out of the café, my heart pounding, past the place de la Concorde, past the golden Jeanne d'Arc, through the métro entrance, down, down, down deep into the rumbling stomach of the city.

AFTER THE EPISODE with Yves, I am more cautious about job offers, not to mention men. I realize, too, that meeting them is easy, especially when you're not looking. They're everywhere, although I'm not ready for any of them. Most are semiavailable, and all of them are perfectly and wholly destructive. They are my illusory attempts at freedom and independence.

Because I never go back to Yves and his company, I respond to an ad in the paper for an English teacher. I teach three times a week in various companies—mostly ad agencies with young French executives and small businesses. The rest of the time I spend doing freelance translations for a lawyer and a literary magazine editor. I'm far from rich but am making enough to survive comfortably. Mostly I keep to myself, reading in cafés and escaping in movie theaters. I try to stay away from the phone. Olivier calls several times a day.

Paolo, the Italian poet I met at the opening of the book-shop and head of an Italian theater troupe in Paris, invites me to a concert and dinner after at his favorite trattoria hidden away near the Buttes-Chaumont. I like getting out of the neighborhood.

Paolo's friend Giuseppe is standing in the middle of the small dining room, his hair wild like that of an underpaid musician, juggling plates of antipasti, handing a glass of this to one woman, blowing kisses to another, and turning up the volume of "La donna è mobile."

"*Ciao, bella.*" He kisses me, then Paolo, lingering on his cheek.

"*Signorina.*" He bows ceremoniously, then fingers the fabric of my skirt. "*Bellissimo,* but," he asks, looking at Paolo, "your friend, does she know how to eat?" He puts his hands around my waistline, squinching his nose, deciding how much he should fatten me up.

Giuseppe makes another grand gesture, and an enthusiastic Italian leads us to a round table in the front of the room. Immediately, waiters bring us bottles of San Pellegrino, glasses of *frizzante,* and tiny round pizzas with herbs that burst like the sun in the mouth. When things have calmed down, Giuseppe glides over to our table carrying a huge bowl of steaming pasta.

"*All'arrabbiata. Des pâtés enragées.* Kim, you look like you like spicy food, yes?"

I nod. Paolo pours us red wine and serves a heaping pile of the angry pasta into my bowl. The steam is fragrant and spicy. He watches as I fork the penne. It's perfectly al dente, with a little sweetness from the tomatoes and salt from the olives, then fire just on the back of my tongue. I close my eyes.

"I like you." He nods to me. Then his eyebrows brighten up, following a tall young man walking to the back of the room. "I like him, too. *Che bello.*"

After pasta, Paolo comes back from the kitchen with a plate of cheese. "From Parma, my country." The Parmigiano-Reggiano is grainy, with just the right amount of salt. I close my eyes and remember Tuscany. Olivier and me in Arezzo. The restoration of Fra Angelico's frescoes, the Duomo in Parma, with Correggio's swirling figures being sucked into the sky. One black point of light. The immense wheels of cheese kept in the banks in Parma. Siena and the tower, the racing of the horses.

"Kim, you are far away. In Italy, I hope."

I nod. One of the waiters pours us each a shot of grappa, and we toast.

"Tonight, it is on the house," Giuseppe announces, sitting close to Paolo. When we try to object, Giuseppe adds, "Friends are more important. Keem, you come next week or whenever, even without Paolo. I make you my *zia's* hot *arancini*—the best way to eat leftover rice."

THE MONEY I earn teaching and translating covers my rent and most of my bills, but no more than one session a week with Grignon. It does not cover shopping sprees at Issey Miyake and Kenzo, stacks of poetry from La Hune. I miss my own books, dinners at my favorite bistros, last-minute trips to a summer coastline. I've given up so much, I wonder then why Grignon won't at least have the courtesy to tell me what to do with my life. Couldn't he just wave his magic wand and bestow some semblance of happiness on me? I want to ask him.

On the way home from an evening session, I buy a baguette, some Camembert, and a container of grated carrot salad. I have 30 francs left over for a cheap bottle of Beaujolais. It's freezing, and my stomach is hollow. I could take the métro to the trattoria; Paolo and Giuseppe would feed me.

Instead, I walk past La Coupole, where well-dressed men and women are lingering over steaks, dipping *pommes frites* into warm béarnaise, a large platter of shellfish. I stop and peer in. For an instant, I tell myself that I must hurry; I have to get home, where the kitchen will be warm and Olivier and Laure will be waiting for me. I'll open the door and Laure will wrap her arms around my neck. Then she'll lead me to the table where she's got her homework spread out and Olivier next to her, deciphering English phrases from her *Hello, How Are You?* textbook.

"*Comment dire 'demain' en anglais?*" Laure will ask.

Demain means tomorrow.

Tomorrow, tomorrow, *toujours demain.*

Someone spills a bottle of wine on the table. The crash of the glass takes me out of the reverie and into the reality of having just missed the bus.

When I get home, the house is empty. I flick the light switch, but the electricity won't come on. It has been cut off. "*Merde,*" I curse as I search for candles in the dark. I forgot to mail the check. I've never learned to balance a checkbook. In the dimly lit room, I search for the ringing phone. It's Olivier calling from Singapore. I light a match and watch it burn down to my fingertips before blowing it out.

"It sounds like you're just next door," I say to the darkness.

"I'm not," he says wistfully. Then he tells me he saw some silk dresses that he thought I'd look good in, and he was reading Whitman on the plane and wondered if I was happy.

"You know better than to ask me that." The sky has started raining again. "It's June," I complain, "and I'm cold."

"I'm going to call the new L'Occitane perfume Feuilles d'Herbe, after Whitman, you know the book . . . from Stockholm . . ."

I nod as we hang up. The phone rings again. It's my sister calling, wanting to know if I'm ever coming home.

"I am home."

"But you left Olivier. You can't be in France if he is."

"This isn't Monopoly. You sound just like him. How's Poppy?"

"He has good and bad days. This week, mostly good."

I open the windows and look up into the night; I wonder if Poppy is pointing to his place in the sky. The city spreads out like an old map, illegible and worn at the creases. My Paris has never been just the Paris of American tour books with their miniature Eiffel Towers and one-day excursions to Monet's garden in Giverny. But since I've left Olivier, it has become dimmer. My Paris is now the Tomb of the Unknown Soldier and the Canal St. Martin, the *bateaux lavoirs*, Père Lachaise. It's gray and colder with every day nearing the solstice.

I go through the mail, stacks of unopened bills, unread books. France Télécom wants money to facilitate my *communication*, EDF wants money to light my house. I live in one of the darkest cities in the world. A city of economy, coins, and savings. A big fat piggy bank of a city. Courgettes for 5 francs a kilo at the Sunday market, and if I want to splurge, perhaps half a Camembert *au lait cru* and cornmeal bread for 15 francs from the Portuguese stand. It lasts a week and can be sliced thin and toasted until the very last crumb.

I close the window, carefully open a letter from Laure. She sends me messages with drawings of jets and stars and lots of little lips for kisses. She fills the margins with hundreds of tiny hearts painstakingly drawn with a blue Marks-A-Lot. Laure ends her letter with different versions of her signature: LB, LBaussan. Laure, *tout simplement*. Which one do I like best? she wants to know.

The phone rings again, and I let the answering machine pick up. If Olivier's not in Spain or Singapore, he phones from Taiwan. "I bought you a very high-grade oolong, from Formosa," he announces proudly. "Very broad leaves. It smells like the sea. Better than what we used to buy at Mariage Frères." Olivier sighs, and for a moment I'm back at the Marais teahouse where tea guides in fitted white linen suits offer harvests according to mood, color of the sky, or what you plan on eating. Exquisite tea *gelées* with citron and vanilla from the Bourbon islands, all too expensive now for my modest income.

But I've never been good with money or directions, and sometimes I find myself back on the rue Bonaparte, rue de Grenelle, or Place Vendôme at the *soldes,* not resisting a Jean-Paul Gaultier skirt at a bargain price of 2,000 francs—the cost, I calculate quickly, of 6.6 sessions with Grignon.

Sometimes I meet Louis for dinner when Nelly is out of town having her colon cleansed or her body rehydrated in Vichy or visiting some count in Venice. Neither of us has much money, but we splurge on *terrine de foie gras* with sweet onion compote and glasses of chilled Sauternes. We feel sinful and decadent, like little kids behind Nelly's and Olivier's backs.

"How is Olivier?" he asks, lowering his voice, hunched over into his plate of jiggling *blanc-manger.* Louis has always had a sweet tooth.

"He only yells at me every other day now." I try to laugh, swallowing a section of my grilled grapefruit, crunch one of the fried basil leaves. "Have you seen him? Is Nelly still mad at me? You know she wrote me a devastating letter, telling me I'd never be happy with a man, that I didn't deserve it, and . . ." I wipe my eyes with the back of my hand. "I'm sorry, Louis." I catch my breath. "Have you been able to work much?"

He pulls at his arthritic fingers. "I'm no spring chicken, but I have to take advantage of the time while Nelly's not here. And no, I haven't seen much of Olivier. He's not seeing any of his friends right now." He pours the rest of the bottle of Cheval Blanc into our glasses.

"To absence," I propose.

"To the Banque de France and overdraft protection," Louis toasts, pulling out his debit card to pay the check.

I SHOW UP to a session one day and hesitate to go toward the couch. "I can't pay you today," I tell Grignon, head bowed.

"Well, you can just pay me next time—"

"I won't be able to then, either."

"Hmm," he says, and stops to think. "Will you be able to pay me one day?"

"Yes." I nod and lift my head.

He ushers me in, and somehow we end up talking of debts, what I owe my parents who didn't leave me behind, what I owe Olivier, what I will owe Grignon. I leave the session understanding that it's not about owing *money,* it's about respect, not only of my family and those around me, but respect for myself, *my* life.

SUMMER IN PARIS is an echo—hollow sun beats down on empty streets. Everything is closed. Parisians have packed up their cars and filled their trunks with goods, off to the coast or the islands for the month. Even Grignon is leaving me. I panicked during my most recent session when he said he would be leaving for the summer, most of July and into August. I sat paralyzed on the divan as he stood after our time was up.

Unexpectedly, he quietly wrote down his address on a piece of paper, told me I could write him in his absence. Then he made sure to give me an appointment the week of his return. I was grateful but also wondered about my own state of emotional health, why he would give me his address if he didn't think I might need to contact him in case of some emergency. I looked down at the piece of paper—an address in Switzerland and one in the South of France, the only clues that he has a real life.

Jan, the wife of the Spanish publisher and the only American I know here, and I meet at Odéon to walk together to the thirteenth arrondissement to swim at the outdoor municipal pool. It's been a few weeks since we last saw each other. She's been having problems with Antoine, details about the bookshop and marital strains that she's not quite ready to discuss, but soon, she promises.

It's miserably hot, and the leftover summer people all cram next to one another, the men ogling the women. I close my eyes and remember the pool in Provence, overlooking the hills. Olivier hasn't called in three days, and he won't answer any of my calls. I leave messages, send him notes.

I distract myself by reading the headlines of *Libération, Le Monde*. The Dutroux affair captures headlines in all the papers— a horrifying story of a Belgian man and his wife, owners of a day school, accused of abusing the children. Just as I'm about to speak, Jan looks over and, spreading out her towel, says softly, "I have to tell you something."

I fold up the newspaper.

"I've asked Antoine for a divorce."

I look at her, not surprised, really, but still not quite understanding. I try to think of the last time I saw him, them together . . . it's been months. Antoine roasted red peppers and eggplant, showed me the latest manuscript of a Guatemalan writer he was going to publish.

"I know you were just at the house. We put on a good front. I'm taking his lead, acting like nothing's wrong."

I try to think of what to say. Maybe they just need some time apart, something to spice up the routine.

"You can't possibly begin to imagine." She stares at me and takes a deep breath. She puts on her sunglasses, rubs in some lotion to protect her skin. "I haven't told you anything about the trial—"

"The trial? What trial?" I immediately think it's about the bookstore, maybe a legal matter with a writer. "Do you have a good attorney?"

Her lip starts to quiver, and then she buries her face in the towel. "I think he's going to have to do some time." Finally, after a long pause, she takes the newspaper from me, folds it over and over again, while telling me about Antoine's past relationship with a woman from Spain. "Antoine and this woman had a common bond. Their parents had fought against the regime of Franco, and they, Antoine and Juana, I guess they thought they were fighting their own revolution. For socialism or communism."

"So it's political," I answer, trying to make sense of it all.

She nods, then shakes her head. "When we met, I thought it was romantic. I was a young American from Ohio . . . what did I know about revolutions and political oppression? We grew up on cheese balls and buckeyes." She laughs, revealing the smart, self-deprecating sense of self I treasure about her. "Antoine grew up on anti-Fascist brochures and *tortillas espagnoles*. His mother makes one with chorizo and peppers that I've finally learned to make. It's soo good." Her voice drifts off.

I offer her a bottle of water. She swallows, and I stretch out on my towel.

"I'm confused about it all myself," she finally says. "He hasn't been very clear, but what I understand is that he's done something and I'm not sure he's innocent. I don't understand any of it, actually . . ." She hesitates, not sure if she knows me well enough. "We had already discussed divorce, back when all this came to light, when he realized how serious it was, about a year ago. Maybe I was in denial. . . . There's no evidence, none . . . but . . ." She leans back, lifts her rib cage high in the air, gulping for breath. "The marriage hasn't been working, and it won't get better if he has to do time. I can't talk about it anymore. I need to sort things out for myself. I'm going to take a plunge," she says.

"Yes," I whisper as she stands at the edge of the pool. I watch her dive into the deep end. I realize she will tell me more if and when she is ready. For now, I must be the buoy, my friendship the flotation device.

A FEW WEEKS later, Antoine writes me from La Santé prison in the fourteenth arrondissement, mainly to repeat that he's innocent and to request that I take care of Jan, treat her like a sister, like a relative, care for her well-being and her future as if she were my own blood. So I arrive at her Montfaucon apartment with my books and bags. I get up early to shop at the open-air markets, buy food, cook, do laundry, make sure she opens the shutters every day and doesn't forget to breathe.

After her weekly prison visits, I meet her at a café for tiny cups of coffee. Sometimes Brigitte, the poet, joins us and distracts us with galleys of her new books. She is writing a play that will be produced at a theater in the Marais. Sometimes Jan and I get into bed with piles of cookbooks and magazines. We read French *Saveurs* and *Côté Sud, Cuisines du Bout du Monde,* out loud, showing each other the beautifully photographed terrines and delicate *tartes sucrées* we want to emulate, the port city cuisines of Marseille, San Sebastián, Bordeaux. We memorize the secrets to perfect layers of rich pastry and tender roasted meats trussed with kitchen string. We drift off to sleep, she dreaming of distant bars and cages, I of wanting to be tied down.

We dream of comfort food, sometimes of American things, just because we can't get them here. Nachos and cheese with pickled jalapeños, peanut-butter-and-jelly sandwiches on soft white bread.

"Remember Wonder Bread?" Jan swoons one early morning, drifting in and out of sleep.

"Bunny Bread," I whisper.

Jan's mother sends a cookbook from the States, one of those Junior League publications from a town in Ohio. We laugh hysterically as we flip through the plastic wire-bound collection, reading off the recipes to each other.

"Here's one for holiday ham balls." She says it with a midwestern twang that makes my heart ache with longing.

"Cheese balls, whiskey weeeners," I read. "And how about those odd-colored congealed salads with canned fruit and marshmallows?" We both jiggle in disgust.

For our next dinner party, we end up pooling our money to buy pumpkins and fresh langoustines, instead, whole pheasant to roast with dried pears and apricots, cheeses and glazed chestnuts. Our group of friends—Erik, a Canadian expat I met at a poetry workshop at the British Institute; Eric-Marie, an expelled Franciscan monk who used to come to the bookshop—and a handful of others—Alain, a handsome French actor; a rotund Polish gourmand—arrive at Jan's impromptu, often between 7:00 and 8:00 p.m., *à l'heure de l'apéritif.* When Gilles isn't painting he comes, too. Along with Paolo and Giuseppe, when he can get away from the restaurant. They know that we'll be cooking and arrive offering wine, some market flowers, a tattered book or two. They sit at the table as Jan and I serve up comfort—creamy pumpkin or black bean soup, cheese polenta, veal stews, and soft baked custards.

There's always a moment of shared silence as we eat, each swallowing his or her own sorrows. We gather to refurbish the soul in a *pot au feu,* or Indian curry, Jan's lamb tagine with prunes and nuts. They particularly like the dishes from New Orleans, my grandfather's recipes for gumbo and red beans and rice. I make huge pots of osso bucco and a fresh farm chicken stewed in cream and wine from the Jura. Sometimes we make spicy pasta dishes late at night, just for the two of us, with garlic and anchovies or onions and cream, or long-simmered soups of pumpkin and chestnut.

But in reality, we're nothing but a group of misfits, *marginaux,* who have chosen not to take the easy way to our heart's desires. We're enthusiastic and naively hopeful; we talk of projects, ideas that won't change the world but may help us help one another. We attend Gilles's gallery openings, Brigitte's readings, celebrate when Erik publishes an article on the Roma Gypsies for the UN, when Alain lands a well-paying role in a film to be shot in New Orleans, of all places. We drink cheap bottles of red while concocting prison escape plans for Antoine. We scoop out roasted bone marrow while someone reads an article about a loving wife who had a helicopter swoop into the courtyard of La Santé and extract her murderer husband out of the prison courtyard.

Antoine stays in prison while Jan slowly takes herself out of it. I continue to long for Olivier and try to busy myself with teaching, writing, friends in general, and men in particular. Aside from dinners with Jan & Co., I have an odd schedule of men for a while.

Some Monday mornings, a translator of Portuguese poetry rides through the dusky streets on an orange bicycle, the basket filled with hot puffed croissants and a chilled bottle of Deutz Champagne. He seduces me first with breakfast and then with lines from his favorite books by Pessoa, always hoping for something less melancholy. Sometimes it works, but for me it's more about the immediate intimacy and not his whispered promises afterward of a long, stable relationship. On Wednesdays, I meet a French American artist for lunch, listen to him talk of his relationships with various French actresses. Sometimes I ride back with him to his studio on the outskirts of the city in Montreuil, let him paint my face on a canvas using hideous bright colors before trying to get me into bed. An Indian book editor I meet at a café invites me for drinks at his Saint-Michel nest and offers to take me to Goa for the holidays. Of course, I won't go, I remind myself. I hardly know him, but I like his energy, especially because I have none these days, and more than anything, I am lonely and tired and forever hungry. I am blasé with these men who are not Olivier. I am not sufficiently needy. Sometimes yes, often no. I have become the worst cliché of the Latin lover. I have no time to think about any of these men. They are just filling a space, temporary and insatiable. I want to be weighted down; I am shameless in my longing for gravity and wholeness—ashamed of my old ragged heart.

PAOLO CALLS AT 7:00 a.m. from Giuseppe's restaurant one morning and says he'll be by to see me in a few minutes. And he does: He shows up at my door, dressed in linen and sandals. I can barely get out of bed on this hot summer morning.

"Come, we go to the sea," Paolo says, a little too brightly for such an early hour, a Panama hat on his head. "Giuseppe and I close the *ristorante* for two weeks. Business has been very good at the trattoria. It's amazing how much pasta tiny Parisian women can wolf down when the men are not looking. So Giuseppe is off to Bologna to see his mama, and I invite you, my very good friend, to the coast for a weekend. It is not Sicily or Capri, but it is the sea," Paolo announces.

I don't care if it's not Sicily or Corsica or Venice, at least it's not Paris or Provence. I jump out of bed, grab a straw market basket, and load it up with bathing suit, sundresses, and sandals. A big floppy hat. My camera and film, and we're off. We climb into Paolo's rented Twingo and drive the three hours to the Gold Coast. The windows rolled down and the heat blowing in distract me.

We get to Cancale just in time for lunch. Cold raw oysters from the bay—delicious, although milkier this time of year— and Riesling, a bitter green salad, Camembert de Normandie and *tarte à la fraise* for dessert. Driving up the coast in a tipsy breeze, we arrive at the walled-in city of Saint-Malo. There's still enough sunlight to highlight the fortress. The air's salty and nourishing, the coastline rugged. There are signs everywhere advertising *moules frites* and buckwheat crêpes filled with andouille or onions and cream. We stop for a sweet Breton pastry and a glass of hard farmhouse cider before checking into the Hôtel Chateaubriand.

Later, dining at the restaurant À la Duchesse Anne, I tell Paolo distractedly, "Olivier and I used to love to come here. That's how I knew about the hotel. We like the one in Cancale, too, but this one is so close to the water."

"Are you going to get back together?" Paolo asks suddenly.

I've never really allowed myself to admit that maybe yes, I would like to. We've flirted with the idea over the phone, but one of us always retreats.

Paolo waits for me, anticipating whether I will cry or not. When he sees that I am not going to, he orders chilled langoustines and mayonnaise. Whole turbot grilled and served with a divine beurre blanc. "Why does he have to be gay?" I wonder aloud. Somehow we manage profiteroles with dark chocolate sauce that the waiter spoons at the table. After, we take a late-night stroll along the beach. I feel restored, whole for just a brief moment.

Paolo and I share a room at the hotel. Our twin beds over-look Chateaubriand's tomb. *"Romantico,"* Paolo whispers. We fall asleep with the windows open and a light sea breeze salting our lips and face. In the middle of the night, I feel a hand sliding up my leg. I turn over and Paolo is staring at me.

"Paolo, arrête avec tes conneries." I slap his hand away. *"Je veux dormir."*

"Kim, let me touch your body."

I prop my head up on one elbow. The lighthouse from nearby Dinan shines every few seconds on his face. "What are you doing in my bed?"

"I want to be with a . . . woman. I love you, *mi amore.*"

I blink several times. His eyes are so black, I can't tell if he's asleep or drunk.

"We can have beautiful *bambini* together. Little almonds for the eyes, *frizzante* for the hair. *Bellissimo.*" He pulls down the covers and starts rubbing up against me. I'm surprised to feel how hard he actually is.

"Paolo!" I can't help myself and start to laugh. At first he's angry, rubbing his crotch, and then he sees that behind the laughter I'm actually a bit scared.

He apologizes, then sits up. "It is impossible for me to, you know, with a woman, anyway, but I just thought, maybe." He starts laughing, too, at the absurdity of it.

We lie still in bed, imagine how goofy our children would look with his curly mop and my slanted eyes. We giggle like two kids, kicking each other gently with our toes, pulling the covers off each other, telling jokes until sleep creeps in bed with us. I dream of babies, tons of them. Newborns who speak several languages, who pull at me like the tides. I lose them one by one, in the sea, on land, in the air, floating like kites up into the sky.

The next morning, after large bowls of *café crème* and buttered *tartines,* we walk along the ramparts. In the distance, we notice a tall man and a little boy attached to strings. I recognize one of them. He waves and limps over to us. It's Thibault. I introduce him to Paolo.

"I've heard a lot about you," Paolo says, shaking his hand.

"What are you doing here?" I ask Thibault, taking in his pungent odor mixed with the salt air. We walk together, Paolo falling in step behind us.

"You look . . . so . . . *mon Dieu . . . si belle.* How long has it been?"

I shrug. I want to ask him so many questions—about Olivier, about Flora's funeral . . . I want to explain about my not being there, how Olivier forbade me—but we walk silently.

"Olivier and I aren't friends . . . I just want you to know," he says, almost reading my mind. I say nothing, waiting for more. "And we all know that he told you you couldn't come to Flora's funeral. I know you were there for her."

I start to explain, but he raises his hand to silence me. "It's the anniversary of my sister's death. My brother and I came to get away. That's his son." He points to the little boy, holding the kite. "I'm doing okay. And you?"

"I'm alive." I smile.

Paolo and Thibault's nephew start trying to get the kite up in the air. "Flora was born not far from here," I remind Thibault. He takes my hand, leads me to the edge of the water. It's cold. We walk a bit more, not needing to say anything at all,

understanding there is so much in silence that can keep people afloat.

∽෧ᏹ∼෧ᏹ∽෧ᏹ∽෧ᏹ∽෧ᏹ∽෧ᏹ∽෧ᏹ∽෧ᏹ∽෧ᏹ∽෧ᏹ∽

CHICKEN IN *VIN JAUNE* WITH MORELS AND CRÈME FRAÎCHE

𝒯his golden wine of the Jura region of France, also known for its superb cheeses, offers a delicate, nutty richness. If you must, substitute a dry sherry such as fino or amontillado.

> *2 cups dried morel mushrooms (or dried cèpes)*
> *1 (3- to 4-pound) chicken, cut into 8 pieces*
> *Sea salt and fresh-ground black or white pepper, to taste*
> *Fresh-grated nutmeg, to taste*
> *1 tablespoon butter*
> *2 tablespoons olive oil*
> *2 to 3 shallots, sliced*
> *2 cups of* vin jaune *from the Jura (or dry sherry)*
> *8 ounces crème fraîche or heavy cream*

Rinse morels in cold water, then place in a bowl and pour hot water over. Let soak and plump, about 15 minutes.

Season chicken pieces evenly with salt, pepper, and a grate of fresh nutmeg. Heat butter and oil in a large heavy-bottom pot on medium high heat. Add chicken and let brown, turning once, about 10 minutes. Remove chicken to a plate and reserve. Add shallots to pan and cook 1 minute. Add wine and bring to a boil. Reduce heat to medium-high and let cook, uncovered, scraping bottom of pan with a spoon, about 10 minutes or until liquid is reduced by half.

Remove morels from liquid, being careful to leave behind any grit. Add morels to pot, stir in crème fraîche, and add reserved chicken. Cover and let cook another 20 minutes. Spoon sauce over chicken, cover and let cook another 5 minutes or until chicken is cooked through. Taste sauce and add more salt and pepper, as needed. Serve warm over rice or with roasted potatoes and accompany with *vin jaune* or an oaky Chardonnay. *Serves 4 to 6.*

∽∾∾∽∾∽∾∽∾∽∾∽∾∽∾∽∾∽∾∽

CREAM OF CHESTNUT SOUP

When fresh chestnuts are in season, roast and peel them first. Make sure to use the best quality chicken broth—if you don't have homemade, buy a high-quality free-range, organic broth and note that the amount of salt you add will vary depending on the level of sodium in your broth. The *crème de marrons* adds just a hint of sweet richness to the soup.

> 1 teaspoon olive oil (or bacon fat)
> 2 shallots (or 1 small baby leek, whites only), chopped
> 1 sweet-tart apple (or pear), peeled, cored, and chopped
> 14 ounces roasted whole chestnuts (about 2½ cups)
> ½ teaspoon salt (plus more to taste)
> ¼ teaspoon pepper (plus more to taste)
> 3 to 4 sprigs fresh thyme
> 1 quart good quality chicken broth
> ¼ cup heavy cream
> 1 to 2 teaspoons crème de marrons (chestnut spread)
>   (optional)

Garnishes: crème fraîche, fresh celery leaves, foie gras, ginger-bread croutons, sautéed wild mushrooms, crispy bacon, or a drizzle of walnut or almond oil

Heat olive oil in large soup pot over medium high heat. Add shallots and apple and cook, stirring occasionally, about 5 minutes. Add chestnuts, salt, pepper, and thyme. Stir and let cook about 1 minute. Add broth and bring to a boil, skimming fat as it rises. Reduce heat to medium low and let cook about 25 minutes or until chestnut and apple are tender. Remove from heat. Remove thyme sprigs and discard. Using a slotted spoon, transfer chestnut, apple, and shallot to blender and puree until smooth. (If pureeing while hot, do not cover tightly with lid; instead, hold a dish towel over small feed tube before blending.) Add a little broth if too thick. Pour back into soup pot. Heat to low. Stir in cream. Stir in *crème de marrons,* if desired. Serve warm with a drizzle of crème fraîche and garnish, if desired. *Serves 4.*

XXI

TRAIL OF MEN

ॐ

*B*ACK IN PARIS, THE RATP IS ON STRIKE AGAIN, SO THE whole city is back on its well-heeled feet. I miss the coastal breezes of Brittany already. The air here is stagnant, and I can't wait for autumn. Grignon has finally returned from his summer vacation, and I've just walked the ten blocks from a session with him back to my place in the unbearable heat. I pour myself a glass of sparkling water, stir in *sirop d'orgeat*, sweet almond syrup that reminds me of summers elsewhere. Jan calls to invite me to a conference at the Maison des Écrivains. *Poésie et le Corps*. Poetry and the Body, with Jean-Pierre Clemenceau. I'm exhausted, I tell her.

"But it's *the* Jean-Pierre Clemenceau," she exclaims over the phone. "Have you read any of his work? He's *so* melancholic," she swoons. "Juan-Carlos can't stand him. He finds him pretentious."

Juan-Carlos is the new man in Jan's life. "He's the dancer," she whispered when she introduced us last week. A handsome Peruvian with long black hair and strong legs. I don't trust him, but Jan is taken by him. He's a good distraction.

It's still over ninety degrees at 8:00 p.m., so I put on a black linen dress and gold strappy sandals. I don't really know who I'm dressing for, but I want to impress Inès if she's there. Or maybe it's Clemenceau I'm thinking of. He has called twice since we met just before the closing of the bookstore. I call Louis and invite him to come along.

After the conference, we're gathered, Jan and Louis (minus Nelly) and I, around the bar in the courtyard.

"Henri Michaux he's not," Louis says. "But very interesting *quand même.*" Before I realize it, Jan has Jean-Pierre Clemenceau, the poet, pouring her a glass of Champagne, staring at her. His laughter is deep and hearty. Nothing serious or poetic about it, and that puts me oddly at ease.

"This is Kim. She's American, but speaks French fluently."

The writer takes my hand and tells me he's *enchanté.* "We've met," he says. Jan turns to me, and I shrug. "Inès is my editor; she arranged the reading at her bookshop, months ago," he explains. "We met, but . . . never really got to talk."

I step outside to hail a cab for Louis. "Are you sure you won't join us for dinner?" I ask him one last time.

"No, you go on. I have my tin of beans in the studio. I'm an old bird, you know. Nelly's in Brittany recovering for the week."

We kiss good night, and when I get back to the lobby, Jan and the writer are chatting about René Char and Verlaine. When they see me, Jean-Pierre hands me a glass of Champagne.

Jan whispers, "Juan-Carlos is furious with me. I've got to go. Call me tomorrow."

"What about dinner?"

"Jean-Pierre, I'm sure, will be happy to join you," she says, rushing out.

I can feel him, the writer, staring. "Do you like cuisine from the Jura?" he asks, taking my arm and leading me out to the street.

It's too hot for mountain cuisine. "In a different time," I answer, "any other season, but I'll be happy to accompany you."

"I'm from the region. Right up this street." He points. "There's this wonderful bistro that serves specialties from Montbéliard."

I don't really know where his region is, and we never quite make it to the bistro. Instead, we walk along the Seine, talking of homes and leaving homes, animated by our common need for anchors and buoys. Jean-Pierre rambles on about voyages and lack of roots in such a way that it's as if he has been eavesdropping on my life. At an outdoor café, we linger over smoky Scotch, but suddenly everything seems urgent, this brief moment I have with the poet.

"You're married," I say after my first empty glass. This is not really a question, but he answers anyway.

"Yes. Technically, but not really. Separated. My wife lives in the suburbs, and I have a studio on the Left Bank. It's an arrangement . . . while we discuss . . . divorce."

"Oh, I'm sorry." I sound so provincial.

"We've lived like this for years. She waits for me to come back. Sometimes I do. Then I always leave. It's my *état*. And you? You must have men circling around you, *non*?"

"Not the one I want," I say, surprising myself. Is Olivier the one I've wanted all along? I wonder. Could he have been the one person to make me happy? Or am I just lonely? I look out into the street, wanting silence as we take in the sounds of the river lapping up against the two islands of Paris. There are so many bridges in this city, so many paths to cross.

"People are lonely here," Jean-Pierre says, finishing my thought, but not really talking to me. The wind blows, and the sound of a tugboat bleats ahead of us.

"It's getting late. I think I should get home." Before he can say anything, I stop an Alpha taxi and open the car door.

Jean-Pierre kisses my cheek quickly and clumsily. "I'll call you," he says. The rain starts, and from the window he's blurred. I can't quite see if he's looking at me or already beyond.

When I get back to the apartment, there's a message for me to call Paolo. I agree to go to the Italian film festival with him next Sunday. Dinner even, anything to not think about the writer.

We watch a Pasolini film and a Fellini cycle at the rue Saint-André-des-Arts cinema. Paolo breaks his pasta-every-day rule and takes me to the Korean restaurant across the street from the Korean embassy in the seventeenth arrondissement. The *salade de méduse* is cold and silky on my tongue, the grilled stuffed tripe surprisingly delicious and perfect with the rosé from Bandol.

"You are so far away, *bella Keem*. In Korea, I hope."

I nod gratefully and dip my steamed dumpling into the thick, garlicky red sauce, trying not to think of the poet; but nothing helps. Jean-Pierre pulls at me like the evening tide. He writes what I wish I had written. Words to give life and capture the restlessness inside.

"You are thinking of that horrible writer. Jan told me you met with him."

I look down at my plate.

"Kim, he came to the trattoria, Giuseppe saw—"

"Paolo, I don't want to know."

"He is famous in some circles and a *very* infamously married man"—he raises his hand to my objection—"even if he says he is getting divorced."

"You've been with married men," I point out to him. "And you even believed them when they said they were divorcing."

Paolo nods touché as he knocks the green onion out of my chopstick playfully. "I'm just saying I do not trust him. He is no *bene* for you."

"*Mangia!*" I order. I know he's right, but I refuse to admit it to him. Paolo's jealousy is sweet, protective, but I am drawn to Jean-Pierre, his drifting ways. Maybe he is just a continuation, as Flora told me long ago. But he is nothing like Olivier, except for his age. And I can't figure out the knotted relations with his estranged wife. I avoid bookshops because they carry J-P's books, literary centers planning lectures by him, but I'm still captivated by him.

ONE EVENING, LATE November, coming out of the library at the Centre Pompidou, I see Jean-Pierre at the Café Beaubourg, writing furiously in a green notebook, smoking a cigarette. I slip into the flow of people to go the opposite way, but he recognizes me and gestures for me to come and join him.

"*Bonsoir.*" He looks happy to see me. "I've tried calling you several times, but you never answer." As I sit next to him, his knees brush against my leg. "*Café ou apéritif?*"

It's almost 6:00 p.m., so I order a porto.

"I wrote you a poem," he says softly, so quietly that I'm not sure I've heard him. He blushes like a young student. I don't say anything but am smiling inside as I swallow the plum-colored liquid. "Do you know Italy?"

I nod, not daring to spill out everything I love about the country, my many road trips with Olivier to Alba, Lugano, Venice, Tuscany . . . the gas stations filled with wheels of cheese and aged vinegars.

"I'm giving a conference in Aoste next month, on Malraux."

"Sadness?" I ask in English, leaning forward.

"*Malraux.* Not *malheureux.*"

"Hmmm . . ." I lean back. "I don't really know Aoste."

"Why don't you join me. I will be happy to get you a ticket."

He says this so casually. He orders another round for us. We drink almost in silence, as if we have been together for years. There's a heaviness I feel in his presence, a deep, necessary weight about him that reminds me of my own searching ways. "Shall we have dinner this time? There's a great little bistro next to my place."

I don't know why I'm here, but when he leans close to me, his warmth and darkness mixed together keep me adrift. I want to ask him what state he's currently in, single or suburban. But I know better than that and order a third porto before going with him out into the city.

We dine at Le Mâchon and afterward walk for hours along the quays of the Seine, talking, whispering promises. We drift in and out of cafés. People recognize him and nod or tell him how much they enjoyed his latest book or a recent lecture. We run into women he knows, young, stunning women, students of his who seem to blossom in his presence. I don't feel I'm with him or not, but he holds my hand as if I were his, as if we belonged to each other, and for the time I tell myself it might be true.

Olivier and my father are on a bus in Seoul. They're searching for Charlie, a young Asian soldier who has kidnapped my sister. My mother is driving the bus. We pass through brightly lit streets, windows filled with prostitutes dressed in blue. Mother covers my eyes. The police stop us and tell us we have to change routes and go through North Korea. Suzy and I are forced off the bus.

Then we're back on the bus, and Olivier has to urinate. He does, profusely, flooding everything and the streets of Seoul. Helicopters above. He can't stop urinating. Then we're in a castle with a group of retired German tourists. The queen is lounging on a red velvet divan, crushed velvet cushions in purples and golds.

"What time is it?" I ask her. She's fat and hates me.

"I will burn the bus," she says, and cackles loudly, "in exactly twenty-three hours."

It smells like smoke, and the windows are open with the street-lights and rain pouring in. I hear a man's voice rise out of the dark.

"Non, je ne reviens pas ce soir." Not tonight. *"Tu n'es pas malade."* You're not sick. The voice has a body. Jean-Pierre's standing naked with the hall light illuminating him from behind. He looks like a ghost with the smoke swirling around him.

"Tu veux de l'eau?"

Yes. Water would be good. "Did someone call?" I realize we're back at my place and can't remember if I dreamed him on the phone.

"I just called Claire to tell her I'd be in the city this week-end." He gets back in bed with me.

"What time is it?"

"Two in the morning. Are you okay?"

"I thought I dreamed—" He takes me in his arms and whispers that dreams don't mean anything if we don't want them to. It feels good to have him in my bed. Safe. I start to doze off.

"Claire thinks she has pneumonia." He rolls over and strokes my back. "But last time I left, years ago, she broke her hip."

"And the time before that, you said she had cancer of the uterus—"

"False alarm."

"How did she get my number, anyway?"

"I called her while you were asleep. She left me a message."

"Look, maybe you should leave," I tell him, wanting him to and not.

"I'm staying." He sits up and looks at me. "I feel good here, Kim. It's been a long time since I've felt good with a woman."

"Since the last," I say skeptically. My heart's pounding so hard, I can feel it in my ears.

"I've seen a lawyer about the divorce." He says this like a present he's been waiting to give me. I hold my breath and start shaking my head. "I should have done it years ago . . . but . . . I can't tell her now."

"Jean-Pierre, it really is time for you to go."

And to my surprise, he does. He climbs out of bed and pulls on his clothes and goes out into the 2:00 a.m. streets. After he's slammed the door, I crack it open quietly so I can hear his footsteps all the way to the end. I want to listen for the very last step.

JAN AND I are sitting at the bar of the Havana Café on the boulevard Saint-Germain, making lists, something we've promised not to do anymore. "Okay," she says, and reads out loud, pencil in the air. "No ex-cons, *pas d'hommes* who 'freelance.'" She laughs. "How do you say that *en français?*"

We have our own strange language, Jan and I, a combination of French and English with some Louisiana and Ohio, a bit of Spanish thrown in for good measure. We don't even realize it until someone else, like Brigitte or Paolo, reminds us that we're not making any sense.

It's girls' night out. She's wearing dark chocolate pants and a mint-colored silk sweater. She's pulled her long hair up into a thick chignon, which renders her big brown eyes more relevant. I'm in black, already mourning Jean-Pierre's disappearance—tonight he is dining with his wife to discuss the divorce proceedings. Jan's own divorce is finalized. The judges didn't hesitate owing to Antoine's trial.

"And no men in relationships with other women," I say emphatically.

"Or in relationships with other men."

"No men who eat congealed salads," I add, sipping the last sugary mouthful of a fresh mint mojito. *"Plus d'écrivains."* No more writers.

"Has he called?" she asks, ordering two special rum cocktails from Ernesto, the bartender.

I wish I smoked cigars. I need one now, but I shake my head instead, rolling and unrolling the damp paper napkin. Ernesto flashes a big, bright Cuban-exile-in-Paris bartender smile. He has a crush on Jan.

"Well, you'll find out everything when he gets back later." Jan turns to look at me. *"Tu le vois,* you're seeing J-P later?"

"He's staying over there tonight. In the suburbs."

"Kim—"

"It'll be easier for him to meet with his parents tomorrow morning, he won't have to drive out there again."

I take a sip of my drink, feel the sting of soda on my tongue. Maybe I should go sit in the humidor and chill out. "Please don't say anything. I trust him," I whisper halfheartedly. "He's always come back to the city, and just this once, *je comprends."*

Jan scribbles something on our list, and I wonder if I'm convincing myself or just her.

WHEN JEAN-PIERRE HASN'T called the next morning, I panic and start emptying out the refrigerator and pantry—throwing out everything furiously, wilted mâche lettuce and two-week-old yellow Portuguese bread from the market, rounds of cheese that have taken on a pale blue tint and matching fuzz. I won't call, I've promised myself. He's having lunch with his parents, I remind myself. I start alphabetizing books, leaving out the C's in poetry. But I flip through some of his books and remember what it is about him that caught my attention in the beginning. He writes about what's missing, left behind, and searching always for the one love you'll never have. At twenty-seven, am I still so naive to imagine that I could be the one love he wants, that anyone wants? This is what he's told me and made me believe. I stack the books together and slide them to the bottom shelf. At 4:00 p.m., the phone finally rings.

"*Salut, toi.*"

"Oh, hi. It's you," I answer. "No offense."

"He hasn't called?" Jan asks. "I'll be right over."

About fifteen minutes later, I open the door, unable to speak.

"*Pauvre petite.*" Jan hugs me, taking the cigarette from me and crushing it in the ashtray. "His cigarettes, *en plus.* You don't even smoke. I've brought food, Paolo's stopping over. And Gilles is coming after he drops some paintings off at the gallery for his new exhibit."

The phone rings, and we both jump. "Don't answer. Let him suffer." It rings two more times, and then the answering machine clicks on. I hear my voice, too high and cheerful for the occasion, asking the caller to leave a message. Two beeps and nothing.

Finally, I call him. J-P answers right away. I was just about to call, he lies. It's 7:00 p.m., aren't we having dinner? I ask. Then he tells me that Claire is sick and he's going to stay another night. I hang up and hate myself for it.

Jan starts sweating onions and carrots and celery, tosses in ground veal and lamb. "I can't cook in the state I'm in," I whine. She ignores me and starts washing herbs. Gilles slices a baguette for crostini. Paolo's brought baby violet artichokes and a whole *jambon de San Daniele* from Giuseppe's restaurant. Gilles is tender and has sensed the missteps of the writer, but he is kind and nonjudgmental.

At the table, Gilles tells Paolo and Jan how we met at the bookshop. "I didn't make it to my father's reading, but Kim did come to see my work at the atelier, we had tea . . . she actually liked it. My work, I mean."

I nod, a bit sullen.

"Besides, you don't want to be with a writer," he jokes. "They're all screwed up, a poet no less. I should know . . . my mother married two of them."

"Who was the second?" Paolo asks.

"Char. My mother left André to live with Char." Gilles doesn't offer much more than this, but Paolo is excited to be sitting with the stepson of such a passionate poet. There is a certain volatile aspect to Gilles's nature, and to have his mother leave his father for another raging poet was always a great source of pain. "Now artists, on the other hand . . . We're much less complicated." Gilles winks.

By the time we've finished two bottles of red, I'm almost ready to forget J-P. I excuse myself to go in the other room and lie down. My head is spinning, Jean-Pierre and Claire's broken bones, her bloated uterus. I call his apartment to leave a message. After two rings he answers. I drop the phone.

"Are you okay, Kim?" Jan sits on the bed next to me, scowling at the receiver as she hangs it up.

"He's there. He's not in the suburbs with Claire. He's in Paris, and I—"

"Are you sure?"

"*Bonjour,*" I offer.

"*Bonjour,*" she says distractedly, pointing to the manuscript. "What is it?"

"You don't know what it is? I'll tell you. A story that includes *une Américaine* living in Paris. A relationship"—she hesitates, focusing her big brown eyes on me—"that goes nowhere. Sound familiar?"

"Is it that bad, Inès? Why are you so upset about an unpublished novel? There're tons of them." I gesture to the piles stacked in the office.

"This is *not* fiction. This is Jean-Pierre Clemenceau *à nu.* Remember, I'm the one who told you about him in the first place." She slides the manuscript closer to me, then on second thought flips through it and closes it again. I can't tell if she's mad or trying to warn me.

I had no idea he was writing this; he said he was writing a book of prose poetry. I don't tell her this, but before leaving, I manage the courage to tell Inès that I really don't want her to publish my name in the book.

"Any woman would be honored," she responds, narrowing her smoky eyes. She pauses a moment and then says, "I'm going to publish it."

GILLES, THE ARTIST, calls one evening and asks me to go away with him. I haven't seen him since I left him and Paolo at my place as Jan and I ran out to Jean-Pierre's in the middle of the night.

"I'm sorry about running out like that," I say, a bit embarrassed.

"That's not important." Our friendship has blossomed despite all the ambiguities of two restless single people in Paris. "I just need you to come."

"I don't know if it's a good idea . . . I'm taking a break from—"

"It's not what you think," he says, his voice tired and worn. "Tina's dying."

I've never met his mother. I just know Tina's American, and Gilles loves her immensely. Gilles is an honest *revolté,* someone who takes every day as a serious affront to the struggles of the artist's vision, his place in the world. He frightens me at times. Even when we first met that day he came into the shop, I saw something that I longed to be—pure and truly passionate even about the smallest things I could never change about the world. "Do you want to come over now?"

"I'm at her house . . . in the Drome. There's a train this afternoon."

He knows I love traveling by train and that his friendship is important to me. On the way down, I think about Gilles. Timing is everything, and instead of each of us spending time trying to disentangle ourselves from other half relationships, we'd meet for thick veal chops and wild mushrooms, cheap red wine. We'd often meet for coffee on some Left Bank terrace before heading to see a Godard film. We'd return to his atelier to cook and feed some unresolved hunger. Gilles cooked the way southerners do, dump cooking. Throwing in a little bit of this and some of yesterday's that into a big seasoned skillet. We talked about his art, our missed opportunities, loves like half-moons waiting for fullness and clarity. He is like Thibault to me, a tall, misplaced brother of sorts.

When I arrive at the train station, Gilles kisses me sloppily on both cheeks. I've forgotten how massive he is, a solid block. He apologizes for not having been to the market, for the day-old bread and almost empty bottle of wine he has back at the house.

"It's Monday," I respond, trying to make him feel better. "Almost everything's closed, especially in a village this tiny."

We find a small shop that's still open. We choose dried sausage, baguette, and a bottle of *vin de table*. The store owner tells us that she has some tomatoes in her garden across the street. We follow her, and she also pulls up some perpetual celery and butter lettuce.

"How's your mother?" she asks Gilles, handing him the vegetables. "I knew her," she tells me. "A beautiful woman, tall and golden, like her son . . . with a grand need to love."

When Gilles is not at the hospital, we take long walks in the woods, through the arid hills of the region. He talks about his stepfather, Char, and his father, André. He shows me photos of his mother. Mostly, though, he talks about trees, the names and colors of their leaves, the forms in all their splendor. Have I ever really *looked* at a tree? he wants to know. Have I ever tried to understand its secret underground system of growth? Truly appreciated its branches and the fruit they bear? His voice trembles with a newfound fear.

I remember then his capacity to frighten me. His rage pierces the forest, and I secretly wish I hadn't come, wish selfishly that I had stayed in Paris, dining on some terrace bistro instead. But then I realize how unbearable it must be for him to notice such things of the living world when his mother is passing on to the world of the dead.

On what ends up being Tina's last day, I wait for Gilles in his dented gray Volvo, at the foot of the village. It's late afternoon, and in silence we drive around to nowhere in particular, Gilles telling me he will find a way to resolve certain things with his father before he dies, which he will, soon. In a sudden need for escape, he suggests crossing the ocean to the States, in a naive wish for anonymity, to New York City, where he could get lost in the vast new world.

I drive his car, listen to his rage silently. I roll down the windows to catch the last light and air of the evening and stop the car alongside an apricot orchard, drawn in by the overpowering fragrance, heady with the last days of summer.

"Are you still with that writer?" he asks.

I shrug my shoulder, leaning out the window.

"I don't know what you see in him. He's a poet, pretty good even, I get that, but the rest . . . he treats you like shit."

"He reminds me of what's missing. He's lost, too, in his own way. It's over, anyway," I tell him, not sure if I'm ready to let go.

"Why are you attracted to him being 'lost'?" Gilles shakes his head. "Look, I won't let him break your heart."

It's already broken, I want to say, so what do I have to lose? But I get out of the car instead. Gilles follows me into the orchard. We gorge ourselves on the golden fruit, tossing the pits, leaving a small trail behind as we venture deeper in.

We find a cool patch of earth and lie there on our backs, our arms and mouths open, waiting for a gift of fallen fruit. Quiet as Hansel and Gretel, we listen as the wind picks up strength and the sky darkens above us. When I start to worry that we may not find our way back out, the branches shift in the breeze, opening up points of light along the path.

Gilles turns on his side, props his head in one hand, and in the half-light, I see tears form on his cheeks, slip into his mouth. It's all right, he nods. I turn to avert my eyes so he can wipe dry his cheeks, and I take in the air, deep gulps of it, fragrant with the scent of ripe fruit and the promise of finding our way back.

XXII

TUNISIA, AMNESIA

༄

*I*T'S BEEN FIVE WEEKS SINCE I'VE SWORN OFF JEAN-PIERRE, but when he calls and we meet again at his Paris studio, I'm drawn in like draining water. Moving piles of student papers and manuscripts off the bed, he whispers that this takes time, he can't just leave his wife of twenty years.

"I've never asked you to," I tell him, slipping on one of his T-shirts and a pair of his jogging pants. They feel soft and warm against my skin, still tingling. "You're the one who said from the beginning that you were separated, divorcing."

"She's lonely. I just have to call her once in a while and let her know that I'm not far."

I shake my head, partly at him but mostly at myself. He lights candles and whistles softly, stopping to kiss me on the cheek before asking me to cook something for dinner. I like the distraction and start making jambalaya with leftover roast chicken and a flimsy green bell pepper and some garlic I find in the bottom drawer of his refrigerator.

"I'm hungry, but nothing too spicy . . . my stomach's a little upset, nervous."

"Hmm . . . I wonder why," I say, shredding the chicken.

"I know we've been through this . . . I told you we were

separated and she wants a divorce as much as I do . . . if I continue to be so distant, though, it'll be more difficult."

I want to tell him to quit justifying his behavior, but he's already in the other room, opening a bottle of wine. I add another pinch of cayenne, a few extra dashes of hot sauce, to the dish.

TWO DAYS LATER, Jean-Pierre tells me that Inès is planning on publishing his book in the fall. He starts to tell me about the manuscript. I don't tell him that Inès has already told me about it. It's on the table when we get to his place. There's also a message from Claire. *"Ça va mieux depuis ta dernière visite. Beaucoup mieux. J'accepte de te voir un peu de temps en temps. Même si on se rend malheureux. Je t'attendrai."* I'll wait for you. It's better since your last visit. He plays Claire's voice twice with me sitting right next to him. He likes me to hear it. He wants me to suffer, too.

I want to leave, but J-P reproaches me for being so childlike, so provincial, so American and puritanical. "When we met, you told me you were getting a divorce, that you had been separated for months."

He stands above me, pulls back his shoulders, rendering himself taller than he already is, and says, *"J'ai le devoir devant Dieu et la loi de faire l'amour avec ma femme."* He claims it is his duty before God and the law to make love to his wife.

"Va-t'en!" I scream. "Leave. Go fulfill your duty." Liar, I want to scream, but he would only like the drama. I realize then that I'm the one who's supposed to leave. I gather my few belongings—towels and sandals, candles, some magazines and books—stuff them into a shopping bag, and storm out of the apartment. I hail a cab back to my place.

When I arrive, J-P has already left me two messages. I erase them both without listening. About twenty minutes later, he shows up at the door, smoking furiously, with a big blue suitcase and a pith helmet on his head.

"What are you doing here?"

He storms in and starts packing up a suitcase for me. "It's four-thirty. If we take a cab to Orly, we can get the next flight out to . . . wherever."

"Are you nuts?" I ask, following his lead, making piles of shoes and cotton sundresses, shampoo, and creams on the bed for him to throw into a carry-on. I want to hate him, but actually I hate myself more because this gives me such a rush, this dashing off to nowhere in particular. I have convinced myself that I am living someone else's life, and this is simply what this someone else does.

At Orly, Terminal Sud, J-P and I stand side by side, studying the flashing screen of imminent departures. The last flights out today are for Casablanca, Ile Maurice, and Tunis. We confer: The flight to Casablanca is full, and we don't have our vaccination cards, so our only option is to go to Tunisia. Neither of us has ever been.

"North Africa will be good for us," Jean-Pierre assures me, squeezing my hand as the plane finally takes off. "It's just far enough."

I'm exhausted, tired of fighting with him, against him, and fighting myself. This is our last chance. We're running away. I'm running away again. I should have left him months ago, but he claims to love me. And that's all I really want. Love, Flora told me so many times, is what keeps us with the living. And that's where I want to be, not among the dead. And if all we are is just a continuation, as she assured me, then let it go on.

I'm not making any sense, I tell myself as I press my cheek against his shoulder, trying to remember Olivier's scent, longing for the simplicity and wholeness of his love. Jean-Pierre strokes my damp hair and forehead. I concentrate on the moment, try to push away the deep realization that I am punishing myself for leaving Olivier by being with such a destructive person.

"Sleep," Jean-Pierre whispers. "I told Claire we were leaving." I pretend not to hear the last part and fall into the deepest sleep, thick and hot in my bones.

"TUNISIA, AMNESIA," JEAN-PIERRE whispers to me at the Café des Nattes in Sidi Bou Said, a village painted in blues and white perched high above the Bay of Tunis. He can't help smiling at his clever rhyme in both French and English. Months ago, I would have smiled, too, but I can't pretend anymore. Instead I take another puff from the long twisted pipe of the narghile, a type of hookah. The water bubbles, and every once in a while a dark-skinned boy with smooth hands mounds charcoal mixed with apple or rose-scented chips onto the top of the pipe. The aftertaste is like burnt barbecue, but for the moment it seems so much more palatable than arguing with Jean-Pierre, who sits across from me, an exact mirror image of my cross-legged self. I lean back ever so slightly and exhale, slowly letting the smoke cloud up the space between us.

Jean-Pierre Clemenceau, who looks no longer like the swarthy hero from a vintage spy movie, but rather like the faded poster version, pulls out a large Kraft paper envelope from his worn leather backpack. His rhythm and gestures are precise and dramatic from years of teaching in the most prestigious European institutions. J-P—the James Bond of letters—flashes his perfect smile as he rubs the envelope enticingly between his hands. He loves this suspense, and I can't help thinking how much Olivier would dislike him. J-P waves the envelope again to catch my attention.

"Do you have no interest in a story about *you?*" he asks me in English, shifting positions subtly so we are no longer alike. I let the smoke fill the air again before taking the envelope from him.

"Me? Or a story disguised about you?" I answer in French. He won't look at me now. Instead, he pretends to be writing something in his green leather notebook, orders a pot of mint tea, anything to avoid me.

"Here," he finally says. I notice that his hands are trembling slightly, so I wait a second more before taking it from him. From the weight of the envelope, I know that inside is the story. The paper is thick and gritty like dried salt or sand. I smell it, the sharp citrus scent of his cologne, Chanel's Platinum Egoïste. I've been smelling everything since we've arrived—the warm flat rounds of bread, our torn bus tickets, the hazy water served in tiny glasses that automatically accompanies the strong coffee. It drives Jean-Pierre crazy—"zis sniffing like a dog for police"— and I think that's partly why I can't help myself. I want to make him crazy, I want him to suffer in any way possible.

On the first page of the manuscript is a charcoal sketch of me. Jean-Pierre has caricatured what attracts and disturbs him the most, my "impenetrable black eyes and slightly dented round-shaped face." And the title: *L'Histoire d'Elle. The Story of Her,* crossed out with a big red X.

"What is it?" I ask, scratching my left shoulder, which I notice now is no longer smooth and tan, but peeling from too much Tunisian sun. J-P reaches over to press his thumb hard on the roundest part, fascinated as the white print pulses away.

"I can't mark you anymore," he says tauntingly.

"So what is it?" I know exactly what it is, what it's worth.

"*Tu le sais.* Inès is ready to publish it when we are, when we return to Paris."

"Now you and *I* are we?" I correct him. "What happened to you and your ailing wife?" He winces. I relish this rare and fleeting moment of power over him. Before, I could never have said the words *your wife*. "I wonder what ailment *ta femme* will come up with during this trip. Pneumonia, MS?"

J-P clears his throat. "Claire's decided she's willing to share. Weekends with her and the rest of the time—"

"What are you now, *a pie*?" I ask, scanning the margins, which I now realize are littered with perfectly horizontal letters, small curves like half-bloomed flowers. I stop at the words *pas assez* written carefully in French on the third page. Not enough? "Who wrote these?" Silence. "You let *her* edit the manuscript?"

I want to be absolute, like the heroine in one of the spy movies, toss his latest oeuvre over the cliff into the Mediterranean. But even though I'm stronger than months ago, I'm still not convincing in the outbursts of passion J-P considers quintessentially feminine and what he ultimately thrives on. Instead, I place it gently on the *table basse*.

He nods, shrugs, blows more smoke between us. "She likes it, but wants more sex, graphic details." He says this as if he's told me that the bus leaves at 5:00 p.m. or that we're having couscous royale instead of fish tagine and not that his estranged wife wants more details of our affair in black and white. "And she wants me to use your real name. Kim." He says "Kim" like an afterthought, as if he'd almost forgotten.

"I told you I don't want you to publish this." I think of Olivier staring at the window display of his neighborhood bookstore.

"But it will be a bestsail*or*," he assures me. "And when it is all over, it is important to have proof."

"Poetry never makes it to the bestsail*or* list, not even in prose." Not even yours, I want to add. Instead, I focus on a young man as he brings over a tray of pastries and a metal pot of steaming tea. He fills two green-and-gold glasses, nods, and walks away. "What do you mean by proof?"

"That we, you and I, existed, *non?*"

"No." I shake my head, handing the manuscript back to him and accidentally knocking over the plate of pastries. An orange swirled one lands on my sandaled feet. "I don't even know why we're here," I lie, raising my voice. My hands are starting to shake. I take a deep breath, concentrating on scraping the sugar from between my toes with a corner of the envelope. "I'm still leaving if you stay, and I'm staying if you leave."

Jean-Pierre knows I'm not making any sense and probably thinks I'm going to cry now, but I'm not. Teary-eyed women always makes him nervous, along with the sexy La Perla underwear ads in the Paris métro, improper use of the subjunctive, and uneven exchange rates.

"Kim, you can't stay here. *Mon Dieu.* It's North Africa. You think you can just come into people's lives and, how do you say, be part of their lives until you are ready to leave again? Besides, my editor said any woman would be honored."

I stretch my arms and torso so that my chest is high and visible and I'm sitting eye level with him. "If you've forgotten," I say, deepening my voice, "your editor is a woman." I stand up and, towering above him, continue. "Who knows, you probably slept with her, too."

This is neither a question nor a statement, just a cheap shot, but J-P is already trying to get someone's attention so he can pay what he owes and forget this whole conversation. But then he continues.

"You're jealous. Not of her, but because you know you'll never be like me. You just play with words, write a few lines now and then. I'm a poet. I'm the published one."

I turn my back on him and stride over to the balcony perched high above the sea. I bite my lip and the inside of my cheek. Yes, he's the published one. He's much older as well, I try to justify. But how is it that whole books come so easily to him while I struggle, rewriting constantly to find *le mot juste,* to give shape and definition to the emptiness inside? Jean-Pierre somehow lets go much easier; I was hoping maybe to learn to be so cavalier.

I can feel him behind me now, and any minute he'll apologize or mutter something only he will find charming, something to mask that he's not what he's always said he was and that no matter what, I will always remember.

No matter what, tonight is our last night together. We will take the bus from Tabarka back to Tunis. When we arrive, the souks will slowly be quieting down with a blanket of burnt musk. At the outdoor cafés, where there are only men, we'll sit at a table near them, and I'll wonder where all the women are. I've spotted them along the seawall. They dance among themselves, gyrating their hips to a *hallah, hallah* rhythm. I want to lose myself among them, their sheaths and clothes, hypnotizing scent, lose Jean-Pierre, but he is solid and steady, guiding us through the labyrinth of our last sleepless night together.

BACK IN MY apartment, as I begin to unpack, everything reminds me of J-P—greasy waxed paper from sticky pastries, dented tubes of *harissa,* and hotel flyers. At the bottom of my carry-on is the envelope. He must have slipped the manuscript inside before leaving Tunis. I open it up. Paper-clipped to the manuscript is a note: *"I'm not a pie. If you won't share, Claire will always take me back."*

The phone rings, and I answer quickly, suddenly hoping it's Olivier.

"*C'est moi.*" The voice on the end of the line is hollow and smoky, as if rising from a burning tunnel.

"*Pardon? Qui?*"

"Jean-Pierre. Have you forgotten already?"

"Tunisia, amnesia," I reply, instantly regretting repeating his words. "Why are you calling me?"

"I want to see you."

"Is Claire no longer playing the saint? Has she suddenly come to her senses after all these years?"

"*Elle ne joue pas.* She *is* a saint. And I'm killing her being with you."

"You're not with me, J-P. Let's make this clear. I'm alone and you're not. You're the poet. I'm not. You're—"

"After all that, *fini?* You are many things Claire is not."

"Don't waste your breath. Yes. And I'm happy that she's so many things I'll never be."

"You. You want everything. Claire's patient, understanding, willing—"

"I know, willing to share. I'm not."

I hang up the phone. It feels good. I pick up the receiver and bang it down again and again. How could I have been so broken to think he was going to love me? To think he could take away the loneliness? He was a distraction from writing, from missing Olivier. A glimpse of a successful writer, something he told me I could never be. I realize that I have to free myself. I skip around the room barefoot with all the lights on and the windows open. I catch a glimpse of myself in the hall mirror. My face is flushed. If Jean-Pierre wants to be in prison, he doesn't have to lock me with him.

In the bedroom, I open all the drawers and closets, emptying them of anything of Jean-Pierre's—one of his favorite shirts, a pair of socks, a notebook. No, not the notebook. A pack of

Camels and a baby blue sweater. I gather them up and shove everything into a plastic Champion grocery bag. I slip on my sandals and walk down to the métro entrance. I stop in front of a Paris Propre trash can but can't bring myself to throw it all away. The light flickers from the gas station across the street. An SDF, a homeless man, is at the door counting his change. *"T'as une petite pièce pour moi?"* Anything for me? he asks.

"It's really not the best time," I tell him, feeling ridiculous.

"Okay, how 'bout next Monday?" he jokes.

I hand him the bag. *"Ça, alors."*

He looks in and pulls out the Manrico cashmere sweater that I paid too much money for, the color of J-P's eyes. "A little out of season, *non?"*

I shrug, and we both laugh.

"You are not from here. *Merci."*

I walk into the station market, shaking my head. I buy a slice of lemon tart and a bottle of water, go out and sit on the bench at the bus stop, trying to remember the last time I felt so freed.

When I get back to the apartment, I listen to a message Olivier has left. A message that he would like to meet tomorrow afternoon or sometime soon. I play it over and over again. I can't sleep, haven't slept since I got off the plane from Tunis. I pace back and forth, thinking of all the things I will tell Olivier tomorrow if we do meet. I step into a hot shower, and the steam rises off me. I smell like musk and cardamom, North African dust. Later, I toss and turn, dream of Olivier over and over again.

ONCE AGAIN, THE city is dead. Jan and Juan-Carlos are in Spain. Paolo is touring with his theater troupe in Italy. I make myself sit down and write, go through mail, and pay bills. I find a letter from Sophie, a brief note that she's forgiven me for leaving and is now worried that we'll never see each other again. I've spoken to her only once since I left, and she cried on the phone, saying she wished we could have spent more time together before I left. In the letter, she explains that she has finally left Serge. When I call her, she says she was inspired by my own leaving. "I had on that pearl gray sweater you gave me and thought of you as I waved good-bye to Serge. I felt empowered. I figured if you could do it—leave, I mean—I could do it."

I am embarrassed to be the inspiration behind her separation, but she says that she and Lulu are living in a town not far from Forcalquier, struggling but free of Serge's violence and dominance. When I try to say something about how sorry I am, how much I miss her and Lulu, our time in Provence, she cuts me off.

"It's difficult," she says. "But I want to look to the future, not the past. That's all I really want."

When Paolo returns from Lucca, he calls to tell me he wants me to go to all the hot clubs with him and meet a nice single, straight man with no baggage. Instead, I go with Gilles to the annual Bergman film festival, something I usually enjoy going to alone every summer.

The singsong sounds of Swedish come back to me. I find myself bobbing along with Bibi Andersson, and I'm reconciled with the language, my father's family's cadences. Bergman brings back the world. We sit through *Wild Strawberries* two sessions in a row and whisper the lines with the actresses from *Persona*. *Jag vill ocksa att någon ska tåla med mig. Jag vet att levet är inte sa kult och sa fint.* I too want someone to talk to me. I want to count in someone's life, and I want that someone to be Olivier, but he has cut me off.

We hung up on each other simultaneously last night. It wasn't the call I was expecting after his message that he wanted to talk. He called at 2:00 a.m. from his cell phone to tell me he had met a *real* woman. I could hear the traffic and the sound of the river down on the quay. With every word, he kicked an invisible stone into the Seine. Every word a beat of my pulse. *"Putain! Merde! On ne quitte pas un homme comme moi!"*

"What kind of man does one leave, then?"

"Not one like me."

I bit my lip, concentrating on the sounds of the tugboats and the crashing of the river, Olivier's pride echoing off the quays.

"WHAT'S A REAL woman?" I ask Grignon at the next session. He doesn't answer. Somehow I knew he wouldn't. He waits patiently for me to answer my own questions. I sigh excessively, stretch my limbs, wiggle a little on the couch, count the number of books on the shelf across the room from me.

"He's found a lover, not an *amante,* but he loves her, he says. And it's my fault. I forced him into it."

"Quand un homme se trouve dans le lit d'une femme, il y est pour quelque chose." When a man is with a woman, he has something to do with it.

"So, it's not my fault. But will she really count, mean as much as I did, if she's just a lover?" Maybe I am talking about myself.

"Avez-vous oublié la boîte?" Have I forgotten the box?

I ask Grignon which one, but I know exactly what he's talking about. It was another dream from weeks back about a beautiful Korean box made of dark beautiful polished wood. Inside are scratches and dents in the grain. There are photos—tiny,

tiny faces of people I know, some I don't remember. Olivier and I are at the Bon Marché. A woman shows us the box but says we never knew how to count, never understood what really counted. In the end I know, *ils ont tous compté pour moi.* Yes, we all count in one way or another.

XXIII

BELOW SEA LEVEL

*M*Y MOTHER CALLS TO SAY THAT POPPY IS NOT GOING TO GET any better. Before I can respond, she asks if Olivier and I are doing all right, why he never answers the phone at the new number I've given her. I make up an excuse because I can't bear to tell her that I've left him. Can't bear to hear her accusations that I've ruined my life, or worse, to hear her confirm that maybe I didn't deserve it—that I have spit in the face of luck.

I buy a ticket back to New Orleans to visit my family. I spend the first few nights at my grandparents' house. Poppy has taken a turn for the worse; he's eighty-five years old, but he is aware that I am near him. I decide to sleep on the couch across the living room from his chair where he sleeps now sitting up.

It's late when I finally convince my grandmother to go to bed. "Don't forget to give him his medicine," she tells me. "And if you can't help him when he needs to get up and go to the bathroom . . . make sure you wake me up."

I assure her that I'll be fine. That I can get him water. Late into the night, I tell Poppy stories about France, and he asks me too many questions: How's Laure? Is Olivier doing okay? He doesn't go so far as to ask me why I left him—he knows without my having to tell him. In his drug-induced state (medicine for his congestive heart failure), he tells me how much he liked Olivier, even if he understands the sadness that seemed to weigh heavily on me the last few times I was home.

"I just want you to be happy. I've had a good life, and that's all I want for my kids and grandkids. Happiness. How do you say that in French?" he asks.

Poppy finally dozes off, but the heavy wheezing keeps him from sleeping soundly. Every hour, I raise my head and open my eyes, trying to focus in on something familiar. I forget where I am, and then I make out my grandfather's shape in his chair, wait to make sure he's breathing, and then fall back asleep.

It's strange being back, and I try to make up for lost time with my family, so I make the rounds, visit my great-aunt in the French Quarter, other aunts and uncles scattered throughout the city and beyond. And when my mother's sister asks me to fly to Arkansas to house-sit and take care of my two teenage cousins, I don't hesitate, even though I want to be by Poppy as much as possible.

It's early evening when I arrive in Little Rock, so my aunt and uncle have already packed and are dressed, ready to go to my uncle's medical fund-raising event. So they kiss me hello and good-bye and tell me the boys have eaten and are finishing home-work. I take a tour of the grand house, a rambling five-thousand-plus-square-foot home at the end of Foxcroft Road. The guest bedroom has huge floor-to-ceiling windows that face the bed, so in the morning you wake to the trees pressed to the glass and the sound of the river just beyond. Wishing for a more intimate space, I go into the kitchen and make myself a sandwich, call my grandmother, who says Poppy's asleep, not to worry.

Late in the evening, I take out my laptop and sit at the kitchen table and start writing, first a few lines of a poem and then lon-ger paragraphs about Korea and Provence, recent conversations with Olivier. Pages and pages come to me. I write it all down, trying to make sense of some of it.

Before going to bed, I double-check all the locks, go upstairs and make sure the boys are in their beds, turn off the lights in my aunt and uncle's bedroom. I have never slept well alone in new homes, even in familiar ones. I get a glass of water to take with me and see myself in the kitchen window, rippled from the reflection of the outdoor pool. I look exhausted. I check the locks again and lead Ben, the big Akita, to sleep on the floor next to my bed. I climb in and turn off the lights and wait for my eyes to adjust to the darkness.

Somewhere between a dream of Olivier's voice and the memory of South Korea, the phone rings. I answer in French, *"Allo, oui?"*

"Kim Sunée? It's Aunt Kim." Her voice is calm and determined. She is my mother's second youngest sister and my godmother.

"What time is it?" I ask.

"It's one in the morning. I need the hotel where Aunt Patty is." I know what she's going to say, but my silence and hesitation make her speak. "Poppy died a few hours ago. In his sleep."

I start to ask her a million questions: Are you sure? Where's Grammy? Was he in pain? Where is everyone? But she wants me to concentrate on finding the hotel info so she can contact my other aunt.

After I give her the information and hang up, I am suddenly terrified of the silence and strangeness of my surroundings. I wrap the covers tightly around my body to keep myself grounded, but it seems that I am floating, suspended. I imagine my grandfather watching over me, and I see myself, alone in a strange bed in a city I don't belong in, but mainly alone.

I want to talk to Olivier. I want to be in the safety of his world, where everything is planned and taken care of efficiently, the world effortlessly at his beck and call. Naively, I imagine that maybe he could have changed this moment, somehow helped my grandfather stay with us a bit longer. I get up and turn on all the lights, Ben following me as I go upstairs and make sure the boys are safe. I sit outside their bedroom door and, listening to the soft breathing, drift off to sleep in the hallway until morning comes.

THE EIGHT-HOUR DRIVE from Little Rock to New Orleans with my aunt and uncle and cousins is mostly veiled in silence. We stop for a roadside lunch of meat loaf and mashed potatoes, but no one really wants to eat. I think of the time I visited Poppy, right after his stroke, and what I remember most is this: his untended garden and, later, his lost appetite. It should have been a clue, a sure sign that he was giving up.

At the funeral home, my sister seems confused at our arriving so soon, but she hugs me a little longer than usual. She looks professional in her black skirt and jacket, slim bare legs. She's even taller in wedge heels, and her acute way of summing things up, adding and subtracting with such precision, still makes me feel inadequate and frivolous in her presence. Suddenly, I wish I had worn something less expensive, pulled my hair back into a tight neat ponytail.

My mother takes me in her arms. She's pale and red-eyed. But as if realizing who I am again, she quickly disentangles herself from me, crosses her arms tightly across her chest, and looks through me with a gaze that's older, weary. I spot my grandmother at the altar. She's thin and pale, and her hair is dyed a terrific shade of gray violet.

"Oh, Grams," I say with my hand clasped over my mouth

before any other words slip out. I take her in my arms. She tries to smile, but two invisible strings tug down the corners of her lips.

"You must be tired." She pushes me away but takes my hand firmly in hers. She seems disoriented as she tilts her head as if to make sure the words have come from her and not someone else. She leads me closer to the coffin, and there he is, her husband of fifty years, my grandfather of half that time, dressed in a blue suit with too much makeup on, lying peacefully in a box.

I had no idea this would be open casket. This is the first dead body I've ever seen. My grandmother keeps touching Poppy's hand, arranging his tie, expecting him to respond. But he doesn't, and I tell her that this is not my grandfather, it's just a shell of his body. She pats his head, looks at him as if he is responding, telling her something only she can hear.

Family and friends take turns to pay their respects. People from my childhood. My mother nods at them, then twists her hands nervously. After several hours, we go back to my grandmother's house, then to my parents' home on the north shore of Lake Pontchartrain. My mother and sister and I gather on the big porch with the ceiling fan on high.

"Did you see him in the casket?" Suzy repeats over and over, taking my hand unexpectedly.

I want to talk about him, our Poppy. "I can't believe he's gone," I blurt out.

"I know it's hard, but you really weren't here during most of the time he was sick," my mother says. "If you had been, this wouldn't be such a shock."

"I know, but it's still—"

It feels as though I've never left. I scoot down low in my chair, fan myself with the Living section of the *Times*. It's so easy to be accused. So much easier than explaining things we don't know how to articulate.

"Your grandmother was here, your sister . . . your father . . . I was here," she continues, taking the paper from me and folding it precisely. "I've always been here." She sounds as if she's underwater now, her voice coming in thick waves.

My sister gets up, shaking her head. My mother starts sobbing, silently at first. I go to her, but she's afraid to let me touch her, to take me in her arms. I'm so sorry for all of it, sorry for her father's death, my grandfather. I'm sorry for Grammy, for not coming home sooner, for always being too much, and never enough.

THE NEXT DAY, my aunts and uncles and all of us gather together, and somehow we've managed to make food, a seafood mirliton casserole and a baking sheet of custard-thick bread pudding for my grandmother and visitors. The kitchen is filled with stale loaves of French bread, platters of dried-out finger sandwiches. I toss out the remaining crab shells, knowing this would break my grandfather's heart.

"Oh, Kim Sunée," Grammy says, and sighs, scooping out some pudding. She hugs me tightly, rocks me in her arms as if I were five again. "My little Kim. You were always older than your years." I love my grandmother's embrace, but my mother asks me to help out, so I go to pour glasses of wine, fruit punch for the younger cousins; I want to be useful.

All the familiar faces I haven't seen in years make me dizzy with sadness. My grandmother's friends asking if I'm engaged, why I haven't been home in so long. They look at me as if I'm guilty, an impostor. I panic, regretting for an instant having left Olivier, the security of his world. I want him here, alive, touching me, guiding me gently through the questions. Proof that

I have a life, a good life. I call him but get only the answering machine.

When all the guests have left, I find my mother and grandmother among the candles burnt to the wick, dried-out bread crusts, and a mass of arranged flowers. They're sitting in the dark, at the kitchen table. My mother is drinking coffee from a doll set that Suzy and I used to play with. But the pieces are chipped and her thumb and forefinger too big. All around her are boxes, photos, and papers. Worn slippers, a broken music box, a tiny multistriped Korean kimono.

She pours me a cup of coffee. It's tepid and bitter.

"There are some things you might want. Photos of your grandfather, some of your drawings, clothes, books. I'm getting rid of everything that weighs me down."

I pick up a few pictures. There's a photo dated 1975.

I'm sitting on my mother's lap as Poppy scrutinizes my foot. He's got a strange look on his face, tweezers in his hand. He keeps trying to take out the pieces, metal, glass, and needles. Everyone is staring at the foot except me. I'm staring straight at the camera, beyond, watching as they all look for something they can't see. Do they want me to speak? Strange creature. They won't ask me any more questions for now. "Just bootiful," I always answer. And they smile, waiting anxiously for Poppy to dig it out—something tangible, proof, some sort of clue as to who I am.

I set it all down, the papers and folders, sweaters, and old dresses. My grandmother pulls out a stack of photos from when my grandparents came to visit me in France. "Here's your grandfather toasting with Giselle; he loved Olivier's mother," she jokes.

"And here we are at Notre Dame."

It was December in Paris, and my grandmother and great-aunt were shopping on the other bank. Poppy and I were on Île Saint-Louis, sitting behind Notre Dame, watching the river float away from us, commenting on the passersby.

My grandfather turned to me and said in all earnestness, "People are dying who have never died before. And," he continued, looking at his crusty banded watch still set on a distant time zone, "all this time we've been sitting here and only two pregnant women." He hoisted himself up from the bench, shaking his head. He held on to my arm as we crossed the bridge to the other island. "All this movement, all this life. I need something sweet."

We walked a bit more and stopped at a *confiserie,* my grandfather tipping his hat as he crossed the threshold. *"Bonjour, señor."*

We bought a box of dark chocolates, and with each bite of bitter sweetness, I knew this would be the last trip my grandfather would make to visit me across the ocean. The last time we'd take a high-speed train to the High Alps, where he'd wake up early in the Provençal morning and pick fresh figs, enjoying the coolness of the large stone house, waiting for the rest of us to wrest ourselves from sleep and dreams. It was the last time we'd walk together, laughing and crossing foreign streets, watching people, all the life that made him so hungry.

MY SISTER OFFERS to drive my grandmother home. We want her to stay with us, but she's tired, she says, and needs some time alone.

I take a moment to call Olivier again.

"Are you all right? I've been waiting for you to call back. Are you at your mother's? I don't have her number anymore."

"No, yes."

"I'm so sorry. Laure sends her best, too."

"Is she there? Can I talk to her?"

"She's at her mother's, but I talked to her earlier." He hesitates. He has told me that Laure has good memories of me, and one day maybe we can see each other again, but not now. Not for a long time. "What can I do?"

Take me home, I want to say. Take me back. But I don't. I bite my lip instead.

"Let's talk when you get back. Call me or I'll call you . . ."

"Maybe we could try to . . . I don't know." The tears come softly and fill up my mouth and throat. My mother's not standing far, so I tell Olivier I'll call him back.

"Yes, maybe we could . . . ," I hear him say back. *Je t'embrasse.*"

My mother blinks as if trying to focus. She pours more coffee, and I sit down and wait, mimic her gestures as we drink from china-doll cups, so fragile, in this quiet kitchen of the night. I need air, so I suggest that we go outside, sit on the back porch.

"There's a nice breeze." She nods, following me out. I pull up a rocking chair for her and sit on the swing.

"They're evil," she says, slapping her legs. "The mosquitoes this time of year." She hums a tune that I vaguely remember from when we were children. And then she sets down her cup, leans urgently toward me. There's something she's thinking but hesitates to share.

"Kim, are you happy? So far away, from us, from me?" She sits back in her chair, a bit breathless. She closes her mouth, and I notice her skin falling in soft folds around her chin and cheeks. I nod. She smoothes her hand along her neck and face. "You'll never have wrinkles like me. Asian skin doesn't age like ours."

I want to tell her so much, about leaving Olivier, my life in France, how difficult it is, that I'm not sure I made the right decision. I want to tell her about Flora and my friends Paolo and Gilles, Jan. Even about the unexpected desire I have to fall in love with someone my age, maybe think about a more stable future, words that I think she would want me to say. I want to reassure her, maybe reassure myself. But I don't know where to start, if she can hear me.

"I worry," she says timidly. "You may not believe it, but I do."

"You don't have to worry about me."

There is a long silence, and then she asks, "Why don't you and I go to counseling together?"

I try to explain to her about my sessions with Grignon, but she uses the words *therapy* and *counseling* as though they're over-the-counter remedies for headache, muscle pain.

"You were so poised and calm," she continues as if I weren't even there. "When your father and I first saw you, we didn't know we were going to take you with us. But you smiled and climbed in our laps, every day for a week." My mother turns away, and I can see her body starting to shake, years and years of unsaid words, of unshed tears. "I just want to be friends," she manages to whisper.

I shake my head. "Mom . . ."

She scoots down low in the rocker. She looks so small and frightened, I am suddenly filled with pity. The Spanish moss tosses in the breeze, and I remember that it's a natural disease, the moss spreading in silence. I tell her this for no reason at all.

"I'm leaving tomorrow," I tell her when she doesn't answer. "And I don't want to fly back across the ocean with hard feelings between us—"

She rocks back and forth abruptly, her face wet, flushed with sorrow. I want to go to her, take her in my arms, but she's stiff and silent now except for the muffled tears.

"You should go now. It's getting late," she whispers, walking to the edge of the darkened porch. She lets me hug her. She's brittle in my arms. I want to invite her to come and visit again, tell her something reassuring. "Your grandfather was happy you came home," she whispers.

She is not really looking at me, but to the wind. I try to focus in on what she sees, eucalyptus and sycamore trees, Spanish moss bending gently in the breeze.

"It *is* a disease, you know . . . that Spanish moss," she confirms. She reaches out for me after all these years, and I squeeze her trembling arm.

Yes, I nod, not knowing what else to say.

"Good-bye," she says, talking no longer to me, but to the night, her hand reaching out as if she were losing sight, as if only the dark and intangible parts of the world could help us now.

For an instant, I realize how in some ways I do resemble her. I turn my face to the wind, try to see what she sees. Trees bending graciously in the breeze. Fractured light casting strange shadows on our hands and bodies. There are no more words for now, just little leaves inside of us, these good-bye branches.

ON THE FLIGHT back from New Orleans, all I can think of is how I wish I had spent more time with Poppy. I think of Flora and those I've left behind. Olivier. I want to see him, ask for forgiveness for leaving him. More than anything, I'm ready to find a place to call home. I want so much to talk to Olivier, to see him again.

The phone rings before I've even unlocked the door.

"Keem?"

"I was just about to call you. I have so much I want to talk to you about."

"Me too. This is really important." There's a moment of hesitation, so unlike Olivier. "Have you been running?"

"Just got in from the airport."

"How's your family? Your grandmother? How are you?"

"Okay. Not really. I guess we're as well as we can be. Poppy talked a lot about you right before . . . Listen, Olivier, can we meet? Soon?" Long pause.

"Of course. You need me right now, I know, but things are different."

"I'm okay. I just need to see you . . . When I was in New Orleans, you said maybe . . . we could . . . try to see if maybe we could work things out. Remember?" There is silence. "Remember?"

"*Écoute.* You left," he says, raising his voice. "I gave you everything I thought you wanted, and now—"

"That *you* wanted," I correct him, and regret it instantly. It seems later than it is. Six p.m. or a.m., I don't know which, and my stomach is empty. I'm thirsty, too. I slip off my sandals and stretch my feet along the cold hardwood floor. "Let's not have this same conversation. I want to start over, Olivier. You know I've always loved you. I didn't know how to—"

"Keem, you just don't live in this world, do you."

"I hate when you tell me that—"

"Poetry. Images. Frozen forever. That's what I love about you, even if . . ."

"It doesn't matter. We've been separated long enough. If we still love—"

"I've met someone." He pauses again. I don't believe him. "A simple, sweet woman who's not a threat to my heart."

I hold the phone away from my ear.

"She's an art teacher from Strasbourg." He pauses, waiting for me to object, but I want to hear it all. "She knows everything," he continues. "About how we met, how much I loved you, how much you hurt me, your need to leave . . . she accepts it all—"

"Olivier, stop it."

"She's my age. She understands what that means. Doesn't want kids." He pauses. "She's not complicated. She knows where she comes from. I'm just asking that you free me." I shake my head and cover my mouth to silence the tears. "So I can love someone else, just a little bit. Just a fraction of how much I loved you. Because you always said I loved you too much."

"I can't. During the whole flight back, I was thinking about how we'd get back—"

"She just wants to be happy—"

"Does she sleep in our bed, Olivier?" I really don't want to know, but I'm suddenly angry and can't help myself. "In *our* bed?"

"*Merde.*"

I know this is our last chance. "Olivier, I just want to see you, in person. I've never asked you for anything."

"That's the problem. No, she never stays over here. I always meet her in Strasbourg . . . or elsewhere. *Ça ne te regarde pas.*" It's none of your business.

"Please. Let's meet tomorrow. Just this once."

"It's late. I've got to go now."

"Will you call me later?"

"I can't. I have a dinner."

"With *her*?"

"I'll try to call you from the mobile . . . to see when we can meet."

"Tomorrow. Let's say tomorrow. It's important."

"Okay. We'll see. *D'accord.*"

★　★　★

I GO TO Jan's to tell her the news that Olivier and I are going to see each other, maybe work things out. I try to sound hopeful and not desperate, even though I'm a bit of both and, more than anything, exhausted, disoriented.

"You haven't slept, and you've just buried your grandfather; maybe you should just take some time . . . to take it all in." She pours boiling water into a pot of daisylike blossoms of chamomile and leads me into the living room. She sets out two bowls and a pot of honey and motions for me to sit.

"I don't have time," I answer, not able to sit. "I've wasted so much of it already. I wish you could have met Olivier. You will . . . soon."

She doesn't say it. She doesn't have to, but I know she doesn't think it's a good idea, this running over to meet him. But I have an adrenaline rush like never before. I pace around her apartment, trying not to think of Poppy, my family. Keep moving, I tell myself, keep moving, don't stop, and maybe the world won't come crashing down.

"I think you should get a good night's sleep. I'll make us some pasta. We'll go for a swim in the morning, get back into this time zone before making any rash decisions."

I want to tell her that maybe I should go back to my place, but the last thing I can bear is being alone.

AT 8:30 a.m. Paris time, I'm still at Jan's and it has been at least twenty-four hours since I've slept or eaten, even though Jan tried to tempt me with her homemade pumpkin soup. I'm shaky with jet lag and the excitement of reconciling with Olivier.

"Maybe you should wait to talk to Olivier again until you've slept," Jan suggests.

"I have to go. He told me last night he'd meet with me."

"He told you he'd call to set up a time," she reminds me. "Let's have some tea and baguette and think this through."

But I'm already at the door, twisting my hands, running a brush through my hair one last time. "Wish me luck."

I walk the twelve blocks or so from Mabillon to 40, rue du Bac. I spot the purple scooter immediately in the courtyard, and my heart fills, so happy to see that he's home, just as he said he would be. I recognize the heavy linen curtains from our old apartment hanging from the third-floor windows. He's home, alone, as promised. I let out a sigh. I am here to ask his forgiveness.

Since I forgot to bring the door code with me, I can't enter the building. I wait: 8:45, 9:00, 9:15. The clock in the entrance clicks away. Finally, a woman comes out of the building, and I enter. I find the initials *OB* and ring. I hear a bell sound several floors up, followed by a dog bark. I ring again. Barking. Ring, bark, ring, bark. Could it be coming from his place? Our dogs are in Provence.

There's a second door that leads into the building, so I must wait. I wait. Suddenly I wish I had slept, but this rush of adrenaline keeps me going. Twenty minutes pass, and a woman finally exits. I slip in. My heart races. I feel like a bank robber, a jewel thief. I am filled with anticipation. I can't remember now if he's on the third floor, French, or fourth floor. I've been here only twice, and all the doors are the same.

I knock softly on the first door, and a small, toothless man opens, wearing a golden Hermès bathrobe. I excuse myself and knock on the door across the way. For some reason, I hold my palm over the keyhole. Why? In case that woman from Strasbourg or, worse, some one-night stand appears? No woman comes. Olivier flings open the door, furious. I have never seen such rage in his eyes. His hair is sticking up, and his face is puffy with sleep. He's wearing a pair of navy Gap shorts and a New Orleans Jazz Fest T-shirt. I know immediately that he's not alone. I try to force my way in. He grabs a cocker spaniel that barks at me.

"Whose dog is that?" I ask.

He grabs it and shoves it back into the apartment. He slams the door and starts making his way down the stairs, forcing me to go down backward.

"You lied!" I scream. "You lied! I knew it. You said she never sleeps here. I knew you weren't alone. I only came to find out the truth!"

All I want is for him to hold me. We stand there staring at each other.

"You have no right to come here, no matter what I tell you . . . no right."

"But you said we could see each other today, talk, maybe . . . maybe get back together," I whisper.

"I said that last night. But you have no right."

"Liar!" I scream. I can't help but shout, then a sound I don't recognize comes from deep inside, as if someone is gutting me.

He grabs my shoulders and shoves me hard toward the entrance, surprised by his own force. "You haven't slept, have you," he says, stopping for a moment, about to caress my head. He leans so close, I think he's going to take me in his arms. "And I know you miss your Poppy. You're not in a good state right now." Then, just in case I might have misunderstood these words or his gestures for anything else, he adds, "You really need to leave."

"I'm gone," I tell him. "You'll never see me again."

"Vas-y!" he screams back, gesturing with his hands as if pushing me away. "I'll never have to think about you again. *Plus jamais."*

I try to touch him, go for his heart. I want to puncture it. He grabs my wrists, squeezes them as hard as he can. He looks down at his hands. "What am I doing?"

We have lost control of everything. Someone rushes past us and up into the stairway, reprimanding us in French. Olivier throws us out into the first building and stands there sobbing, shaking his head. The dog barks in the distance. I want to kill the dog, kill myself. I pound the glass as he rushes to the stairs and disappears into the dark stairwell.

I don't really know where I am. I try to see what time it is. The vintage Cartier watch Olivier gave me years ago is dangling off my wrist, he ripped the band, and this makes me smile for some stupid reason. We have just battled it out, and I am the loser. What if Poppy could see me? Is this the happiness he wished for his kids and grandchildren? I start laughing, then sobbing so hard that my body begins to shake.

I start to walk, slowly, trying to figure out what time it is. My watch reads 2:20 a.m. What time is it in Tunisia, New Orleans, six feet under? I don't remember the last time I ate or slept. I stumble into a café and ask for napkins and some change. My wrists are scratched and bleeding. I go down by the toilettes and dial Grignon's phone number. The instant I hear his voice, I start crying again. I start to hyperventilate.

"You're twenty minutes late for your session."

This makes me cry even harder, and he tells me to come at 2:00 in the afternoon.

I order some coffee and ask the time again, but every answer seems like a lie. I'm exhausted, hungry, but I can't eat. I keep touching my arms and wrists, the exact places where Olivier touched me, amazed at the bruises and wounds already beginning to form.

At 1:55 p.m. when I arrive at Grignon's office, I've been walking around the city for five hours with swollen eyes, crying on and off. What will I tell him? I don't think I'm depressed—nothing matters when you're depressed. I am immeasurably sad; and in sadness, everything seems to matter.

"I don't want to lie down on the couch," I tell him when I arrive. "I'm scared." But I can't face Grignon, so I lie down. It feels good to stretch out. I close my eyes. I hold my breath, knowing that if I were to die, this would be the best thing, the best place, the best time. I don't know how many minutes pass. Three or fifteen or two hours. I start to breathe normally, realize I'm alive, and slowly begin to cry again.

"Tell me," he says softly.

I can't catch my breath, and every time I try to speak, only sobs. I can't stop myself. "I—I went to see him," I say finally. "He told me we could see each other this afternoon, and I went early. I know I shouldn't have. And he was enraged, came flying down the steps like a madman . . . he was furious. But he lied. He said she never stayed there." I recount the whole bloody scene, the vulgar names he called me, and the fury . . . the moment we almost embraced, but how he grabbed my wrists instead. I lift my arms above my head so he can see the bruises.

"Why did you go?" Grignon asks.

I shake my head, and tears stream down my cheeks. "The men. I've made such a fool of myself. *Je suis ridicule.*"

"*Est-ce que vous vous êtes respectée?*" The question is, did you respect yourself?

I shake my head. *Bien sûr que non.* Self-respect has not been on my agenda lately.

★   ★   ★

I MAKE ANOTHER hasty decision to no longer see Grignon, because unjustly, secretly, I want to blame him for letting me leave Olivier, stumble into relationships with men like Jean-Pierre, for not telling me how to live my life, for not giving me the secret ingredient for happiness.

But one day I wake up, panicked. I pull on yoga pants, running shoes, and an oversize sweater, and pull my hair into a sloppy ponytail. I call Grignon, not knowing what time or day it is.

"I need to see you," I tell him. His voice is slow and soft, so I know he's in a session. "It's urgent," I say, wanting to shake him out of the trance.

"*Très bien, venez à neuf heures.*"

At 8:44 a.m., I'm standing at 248, boulevard Raspail, counting down the minutes before my time.

When Grignon opens the door, he makes a point to look down at my shoes, up at my hair. I nod, as if to say "I know I never go out looking like this." I pace back and forth a couple of times before making my way toward the divan, but Grignon gestures for me to sit across from him. It's the first time we will sit face-to-face.

"*Dites. Racontez-moi.*" Tell me, he says gently.

It has been years, and here I am face-to-face with myself, this voice that won't give me the simple recipe to a nice life, write me the happy ending. I'm breathless. I stand up again, ready to bolt.

"*Mais où allez-vous?*" he asks, wanting to know where I'm going. I go toward him and throw 300 francs in his lap, ready to storm out. Any other time, he would have let me, but he stops me, repeating softly, "*Mais où allez-vous?*"

I turn around. "Why don't you tell me. Tell me where it is I'm going."

He gestures for me to sit again. I stand for a moment, looking down at my tightly laced running shoes. A standstill. Why am I so stubborn? Where *do* I think I'm going? I look up, and he is standing now, still, arms by his side, a smile, not mocking or laughing, just the gentlest look in his eyes to tell me everything's going to be okay.

I realize I have no idea where it is I think I'm running to, not now, not all these years. My voice is crowded out with tears, years and years of tears that have built up. I hate myself for this weakness, this indulgence, but it feels good, primal. Grignon gestures to a box of Kleenex, and I take a handful, thankful and obedient.

I am grateful that he knows, unlike other men in my life, that I want to be stopped from leaving. Even though I am always ready for a fight, so stubborn that I will shoot myself in the foot, my pride will make me go away to nowhere in particular just to make a statement—to say that I'm strong, independent. In another language, these words would mean something else, convey what I truly am: a loner, lonesome, and irreversibly heartbroken.

"I'll see you on Wednesday," Grignon says slowly, cheerfully, making sure I hear him. "Wednesday."

I nod, whisper, *"Mercredi,"* and, *"Merci,"* before I rush out into the street, back into the world. I will be back, but it is only a matter of time before I am ready to leave France, leave behind ten years in a country where I have mastered another language of survival.

XXIV

THEN, AGAIN

*HIBAULT SENDS ME A LARGE SQUARE ENVELOPE FROM Provence. Inside, I find a small kite to assemble. Chiseled bamboo sticks and thin sheets of violet-streaked paper the color of Indonesia sky in the spring, he describes. Included is a note written in his indecipherable handwriting—like plucked feathers: "I made this for Flora, but never had a chance to give it to her." I turn it over for more, but there's nothing.

A week later, Jan and I go to the Café Charbon in Ménilmontant in the eleventh arrondissement. It's the place everyone's talking about. Outside, September fills the sky with its rich colors of pink and gray. As we descend deep into the underground, I recall my first autumn in Provence years ago. Soon it will be Laure's birthday. Another year without seeing her. Olivier thinks we need more time. I make a note on my ticket stub before exiting to send her a card, a CD, some flowers, any sign that I haven't forgotten her.

At the long wooden counter of the café, a man sits next to me, waiting. Months before, I would have made myself available, smiled, cocked my head in that certain Parisienne way. But random men, no matter how intelligent or beautiful, no longer excite me as potential lovers. The closer this one scoots to my side, the more I am repulsed by his overgrown hair and very smooth voice.

"*Je devine,*" he says, squinting into my eyes. "*Tu es thailandaise?*" Because I ignore him, he continues. "*Eurasienne?*" I shake my head. "*Japonaise. C'est ça.*" I roll my eyes dramatically at the bartender. "I give up."

Jan returns from the restroom and answers, "She's American from New Orleans."

The bartender smiles and asks us what we want. I shrug. "Mojitos," he decides.

The soda and mint mix easily with the rum; the liquor slips through me. Before I realize it, the man has ordered us another round, promising he'll be back. The place is packed. I look around to find Jan talking to a group of people, mainly a beautiful licorice-colored man with long dreadlocks. The music's loud now, so I don't mind sitting by myself, not having to talk to anyone. The air's filled with some repeated rhythm that puts one in a trance. But all I hear are Olivier's words: *So I can love someone else. Just a little bit.*

It's been two weeks since we've really talked. Olivier leaves messages, begs me to call him back, he's worried about me, but I won't call him. I need to move on, be strong, let him love someone else, just a little bit.

I overhear shreds and pieces of conversation, mostly young men talking about things I no longer care about. After a third mojito, though, I can join in on anything.

"Are you finished talking about cars?" I ask in my slurred French, addressing two men about my age, in their late twenties, standing next to me.

"As a matter of fact, we are." One of them I hadn't noticed earlier comes into focus. His eyes are like the sea, all wavy and lit from another source.

"I'm Kim," I say, swallowing the last drop of liquid sugar from my glass. I'm more than tipsy. My limbs feel separated from my body. The faces and voices are spinning, but there's something liberating about it all.

"I'm Valéry."

"That's a woman's name . . . in English," I tell him.

"Paul Valéry was not a woman." He smiles. "My friends call me Val. This is Thomas."

I stand up and sway until Val catches me by the wrist.

"Thibault?" I ask, squinting at him. "You know my brother?"

"Tho-mas." His friend smiles.

Val laughs, shaking his head.

"It's not funny. They're all gone. Everyone I've ever loved. Thibault, Poppy, Olivier, Flora, poof! Just disappeared."

Val introduces another friend of theirs, and after a few banal exchanges, I start making my way to the door, barely balancing myself along the bar counter.

Outside, it's cold and dark. My head is killing me, and I can't find my purse or my keys. I just want a cab to take me and drop me off at the end of the world. When I turn around, Val's there in a taxi with the back door open, gesturing for me to get in the backseat with him.

"I don't want to talk to you," I tell him, scooting to the opposite side. "I don't want to take care of you, and I definitely don't want to care *about* you, because I'll just leave or make you go away, or—"

"*Vers la rue Goncourt,*" I hear him tell the driver. He fastens my seat belt around my waist and stops to stare at me. His eyes, at first dark green, are now bluish with gold flecks.

"*Je suis désolée.*" I truly am sorry. I feel queasy.

"Look, I don't need taking care of," Val says calmly. "You, however—"

"Me neither. I don't need anybody," I say, staring out the window. The city is a blur, and I hate myself for wanting to be so self-sufficient.

Once in the apartment—Val's, I assume—he pours me a large glass of water and hands me a bathrobe. It's soft and over-size and smells good.

"I'll be in the other room." Val kisses me on the forehead and shuts the door gently behind him. The bed is warm. There are photos on every wall—black-and-white urbanscapes, a barber's chair, a lunch counter, a single promising shoot of golden jonquil. I need air. I want sleep, love. I want Olivier so much, it aches. My heart is beating fast, and my tongue is thick with rum. I open the window and trip back into bed, pulling the covers over my head, counting the beats of my heart until I'm deep in sleep.

IN THE MORNING, my head feels like a half-cracked coconut. I'm able to brush my teeth with a new toothbrush I find laid out on the counter, but the bristles against my gums make the pound-ing in my head even stronger. In the other room, Val has set up a tray with big bowls of coffee with cream and thick slices of bread with cold salted butter. He sits there with the win-dows wide open, the light illuminating him as he reads *Photo* magazine.

"*Bonjour.*"

"*Du café?*" Val's dressed in a white sweater and faded blue jeans and smiles at me, openly, gently.

"Aspirin," I beg.

He nods and points to two Doliprane and a glass of water on the tray before me. I must have made a fool of myself last night. I start to apologize but don't really want to and suddenly realize that I don't know what I'm doing here. I grab my coat.

"Thank you for everything, but I have to go."

"So soon? I thought we—"

"No, I'm sorry. I've got to go." I dress hurriedly. Before I leave, Val hands me my purse and keys.

"You left them on the bar last night."

He kisses me on the cheek as I thank him. He asks me to write down my phone number. I take the elevator down to the street. I'm in a neighborhood I'm not familiar with. September fills the air with the cries of schoolchildren and crisscrossed light, signs of fall. I forgot to call Laure to wish her happy birthday again this year. I stop to call my answering machine. Olivier has left three more messages. For an instant, I tell myself that I will finally call back, but I can't bear to talk to him, not just yet. Grignon. I have to speak with him, too, but he's away at some conference. As I walk down the boulevard, a cyclist swishes by, and then I remember the dream.

Grignon has had an accident, broken his leg, and he limps to my grandfather's house. I feed him a bowl of hot oatmeal and assure him that tomorrow he'll be fine for the Tour de France. Every time I try to spoon the oatmeal into his mouth, the crowd cheers. Olivier steps up to the home plate, playing to the spectators, but it's not his turn to bat. Grignon reminds me that I have the list of players, the order of things, and that I must read it carefully before calling the shots.

A FEW WEEKS later, Val and I plan to meet for dinner. Dinner turns into a weekend, and soon we are spending as much time together as possible, photographing the city, the urban landscapes of its outskirts. I realize that I am much more random and spontaneous in what I shoot. I want whimsy and chance. Val is more meticulous, much more painstakingly exact, than

I'll ever be. But I like this about him. Even in the kitchen, he trims all the vegetables to the same size, takes the exact temperature of meats and sauces. I throw in whatever I can find, tasting and rectifying as I go along. Val makes a simple but delicious *croque-monsieur*, with warm béchamel thick with cheese. He teaches me about Sancerre and other wines of his region.

His physical beauty is abundant—a strong swimmer's body, dark, curly hair, and deep blue green eyes—overwhelming sometimes. He is thoughtful and measured. And although he is a bit too careful at times with his emotions, I am attracted to him, but I will not fall for him.

Val's mother calls one day to talk. She wants to meet me ever since Val told her how important I am to him. "He doesn't say that often," she informs me. She wants us to come and stay in Blois, visit Tours. Before we hang up, she warns me that Val's fiercely independent, feels constrained in France, and is considering a job offer in French Guiana.

"I know he's sent résumés to all the French territories— New Guinea, Guadeloupe, Tahiti," I tell her. "He's waiting to hear back from someone in French Guiana. I know he really wants that job with the tourist commission. He's planning on going there anyway, I think."

"He's usually so reserved, so quiet," she answers.

Val is anything but quiet. We talk all night, as though time's running out. We listen to music, read passages from our favorite books to each other, spend happy moments in the kitchen. We roll out fresh pastry, taste Jack Daniel's, dream of places we want to visit in the world. We take turns critiquing photos.

I tell myself not to fall in love with him, but I am drawn to his fiercely independent spirit, his desire for a new start in a new country. And the sheer pleasure of his youthfulness. We are the same age, and for once, age matters. Although sometimes, because of my life with Olivier, I feel so much older. We also talk about the future, a month, a year from now, but none of it seems possible because I sense the same restlessness in Val that was inside of me.

He shows up one evening with an armful of long-stemmed sunflowers and a bottle of Sancerre blanc. "I've been offered the job in Cayenne."

I congratulate him. I'm actually happy for him until he tells me that he's leaving in less than a month. I'm surprised by my own sudden desire to beg him not to leave, something I would never have imagined ever telling anyone.

"I have something else for you," he says before I can answer. He presents me with a battered Patrick Cox-WillBe shoebox.

"Shoes? What's wrong with these?" I point to my new Stephane Kélian boots I bought at the sales.

"Open it. I went to Montreuil today to the flea market."

Inside are photos. Tinted browns and faded colors, odd-looking faces, children who look grave and wise beyond their years.

"Who are these people? You didn't take these," I say, handing the box back to him.

He pulls them out one by one and starts spreading them out on the kitchen table. "Aren't they beautiful?"

They are, in a strange way. Fragments of mismatched lives. An old man lying in bed, staring straight at the camera. Twins dressed in white, playing with a wheel and a stick. Portraits of dogs and women in simple frocks lounging by a lake. "They were all there together, and I thought they were interesting, sort of already their own family album."

Val looks for a notebook through the pile of mail sitting on my desk. He finds one under some unopened letters from Olivier, letters I can't bring myself to read yet. Val takes the notebook Louis gave me before my trip to Asia and flips through the photos of Laure and Madame Song and starts arranging the new faces in some creative chronological order. He starts pasting them in, writing invented names and dates for each. "This one here, what do you think?" He holds up a square five-by-five black-and-white. Five girls, various ages and sizes but the same face, the same cotton dress, each girl a little taller, lankier, wiser, more adventurous, than the previous.

"Val, let's go, we're going to be late. Jan wants you to meet Roberto and Eggle, her Italian friends who live in French Guiana. We're meeting them at Giuseppe's restaurant. Paolo's waiting for us."

When we arrive, Paolo smells of sweet tomato sauce and garlic as he hugs me warmly while kissing Val hello. Even though he thinks Val is handsome and sweet, he doesn't approve. "A bit too floating," Paolo told me once. "He is so talented. What could he possibly photograph in the jungle? Trees and leaves and roots and ants, pesky mosquitoes. No people. He is no Italiano. Without people, Kim, we are nothing."

He takes us to where Jan is seated at a table for six. "We're meeting Jan's friends, no? The Italians?"

"Yes, especially now that he's been offered the job, it will be nice for him to know someone in French Guiana."

"I'm sorry," Jan says, kissing us hello. "Roberto called right before I left to say that he and Eggle have to go back to Kourou immediately. His wife is a little hypochondriac," she explains to Val. "She always has something."

"I don't know how anyone can live in that part of the world," Paolo adds. "No Prosecco, no pasta, no cheese." I shoot him a look, to stop being so negative.

"She's an archaeologist, right?" Val asks, pulling out my chair for me before Paolo does.

"I'll give you their info before you leave," Jan tells him.

"Well, Kim will meet them, too, when she comes."

Jan and Paolo look at me, and I look at Val. This is the first I'm hearing of it. Paolo says, "You are not going to South America."

I shrug, not sure what to answer. Val smiles. "Of course she'll come, as soon as I can figure out where I'll be."

"Everybody's leaving." Paolo throws up his arms. "Gilles in Switzerland for an exhibit. Giuseppe in Italia—"

"They're coming back," I tell Paolo, convincing myself as well. "We're all coming back. Val's leaving in about three weeks, though. The French Guiana tourist industry has offered him a full-time position."

"Good, we still have time." Paolo calls over a waiter to bring us food, drink. Later, he pulls me aside. "At least he is more your age. But tell me, what is it that you see in him? Yes, he is *bello,* very *bello,* but he will break your heart."

"You think everyone will break my heart. It's too late. My heart's already broken," I say matter-of-factly. "I have nothing to lose and everything to gain. I'm not afraid."

Val winks at me from across the room. I am drawn to his sense of adventure and his own doubts of wanting to stay in his birth country of France. This is something familiar to me.

I tell Paolo about his mother, how Val took me to meet his family in the Loire Valley. They greeted me as though I were already part of the family. Amid châteaus and rivers, they told me stories of how Val, at the age of twelve, would be in the kitchen at 5:00 a.m., rolling and baking fresh croissants for breakfast. His mother kissed him on the top of the head and whispered to me how sad she was now about him leaving so soon. "Can't you do anything to stop him from going?" she asked.

Someone brings over plates of colorful antipasti, fried zucchini, and clams in tomato sauce to start. "*Mangia, mangia.* I have ordered you such a wonderful meal, tomorrow you will be crying to come back." Paolo takes my hand, looks at Val straight in the eyes. "Some of us, we know the *importance* of food and friends."

After dinner and a long walk back to Val's place, we get into bed and talk about when I will join him in French Guiana. "As soon as you can," he says hopefully. "But I don't really even know where I'm going to be living . . . and this job with the tourist board doesn't pay a whole lot . . . but it will give me my start."

I can hear the anxiety in his voice and tell him that it's okay, I won't join him until he says it's time to come. Then he says softly that he thinks he loves me. I'm not sure I've heard him correctly, but he goes on to whisper something about the timing not being right. Timing is everything in relationships, and if things were different, he says, maybe we could have had a future.

Val falls asleep closer to me than ever before. I am almost off the bed, my bare foot rubbing back and forth against the cold hard locks on his half-packed suitcase. I look over at his beautiful face. His eyelids move rapidly, darting back and forth, a sign of a dream at once familiar and long forgotten. His restlessness worries me. I have been here before.

XXV

HEARTS OF PALM

༄

The untold want, by life and land ne'er granted,
Now, Voyager, sail thou forth, to seek and find.

—WALT WHITMAN

*E*VER SINCE I RETURNED TO PARIS FROM MY GRANDFATHER'S funeral, my presence in this city feels more and more unfounded. Olivier and I have started calling each other regularly again, never really mentioning the violent incident that morning after my return from the States. He wants to know if I've read his letters. No, I tell him, not yet. I try to busy myself with work, but teaching English to young, cool French advertising execs is wholly unsatisfying, and now that Val is gone, there is a new emptiness; I miss what my life might have been with him.

He keeps asking me to come and visit him in French Guiana. It seems like the perfect place to run to—a former penal colony. I want to go because, more than anything, I want to know if Val is happy where he is, if he misses me at all, and most important, if he has found peace. If he is happy there, maybe I will be, too. I also want to know this new place, the taste of the rain in the forest, the shape of the houses in Cayenne, the depth of the shadows on the streets at night, the names of the trees outside his window.

But he has been able to call only a few times. Sometimes the phones don't work at all, and I sit and wait for him to call, telegram, or fax. A sign that I'm still with him. He does write long letters from places called Kourou, Surinam, Cayenne. He writes that he loves me but doesn't know if he can offer me a stable life. Slowly I start to pack boxes, give away things that matter to me—maps of certain cities, a few menus with notes, first editions signed by visiting poets, and a poster of Hopper's *Hotel Room* from a trip to Spain. Soon I will be leaving again, and it seems that this is one way I've learned to say good-bye.

Sometimes I want to be selfish and tell Val to come back, that I'm ready to be with him. But perhaps he is more lost than I am. I know that I must go to South America to see him one more time, lay to rest any notions of regret in not having pursued our relationship. So I buy a round-trip ticket, Air France direct Paris–Cayenne, and on my way to the bookstore, I stop at the Institut Pasteur for my yellow fever vaccination.

I look up French Guiana in the atlas. I want to be able to locate myself on the map: 52.18° W, 4.49° N. Humid. Tropical. So close to the equator, to the heart of the earth. *Guiana,* Native American meaning "Land of Many Waters." I've been reading up on the jungles and rivers of the Amazon, noting which creatures are able to outlive others. I'm fascinated by stories of people surviving for days in the darkness of unfamiliar territories, lost and hopeful, drinking and eating only what's on their path.

Olivier calls late one night, in a wine-induced state of nostalgia. He is driving along some road and tells me that we'll always be connected. "Like two sturdy mountains with peaks that never touch but rise together from the same earth. I'm not a poet," he says, "but that's the way it is."

"I don't want to be a mountain," I tell him.

"Then you're the moon that rises and sets behind the

mountain." In the background, I hear a woman's voice. "Are you there? Sorry, we almost swerved off the road."

"You'd better hang up. You don't want to be distracted."

"Ah, Keem—"

I hang up the phone before any more of Olivier's drunken words come between him and the woman in the passenger seat.

He calls again several nights later while Jan, Paolo, and Gilles, Brigitte, and Hervé are having a bon voyage dinner for me.

"Where are you?" I ask Olivier, sneaking a peek in the kitchen. Jan is torturing me by not letting me in.

"In Venice, on business."

I want to ask him if he's alone but bite my lip instead. "Is it foggy?"

Paolo hands me a glass of *frizzante* and a wedge of Parmigiano-Reggiano.

"Very. And cold. Just like you like Venice."

"Olivier, I'm going someplace . . . warm. Tropical."

"When are you coming back?"

"I don't know. I may not for a long time. I'm leaving in a few days."

"So soon?"

"Isn't this what you've always wanted? 'France is too small for both of us,' you've always said."

"You'll be back."

I wish I could be as sure as Olivier. Before I have time to imagine him accompanied by another woman, dining at Harry's Bar, I hang up the phone. Paolo passes around a huge platter of crostini and the thinnest miniature pizzas. I take a bite. The white and blue basil blossoms burst in my mouth.

"Paolo. *Grazie.*" He brings out a large round platter of

plump figs and paper-thin slices of San Daniele. "Where do you get these products?" I ask. The ham is sweet, creamy, and salty at the same time.

"You know I have my sources," he says, beaming, thrilled that I appreciate his resourcefulness. "You'll miss me when you're eating iguana belly and mosquito salad."

"Val says there's wonderful fish and game."

"It's savage, unruly . . . rural, and so unlike you, Keem," Paolo yells.

"It's not rural. It's jungle," I correct him.

We finish the crostini as Jan brings out her roast duck with dried pears and prunes. We finish with salad and a platter of my favorite cheeses, Roquefort, Rocamadour, Perail de Brebis, and a fruited Comté. Brigitte scoops out her favorite rum raisin ice cream into bowls for everyone.

Gathered on the floor, sharing food, I feel that we're a family, an accidental gathering of beings, nourishing one another. I unearth my camera from the top of one of the packed boxes and take one last photo of this family.

ON THE AIR France flight from Paris to Cayenne, as we lift into the sky, I hold my breath but remind myself that I'm not afraid. Bridges and tunnels no longer frighten me; I don't panic as I used to, even though I am still geographically divided. But I know that there's peace to be found, not in Val or the continent, but in some remote region of myself. I will no longer bury my sadness in the Jean-Pierres of the world or other random and inappropriate men. I want closure and a peaceful good-bye, not another disappearing act.

Sipping a glass of red wine, I slip off my sandals and finally open the letter, one of several Olivier sent weeks ago, the weight of which alone made me set it aside. The paper is predictably beautiful, thick and textured, a cream-colored heavy vellum. His handwriting is legible, though airy, rounded, and contained equally in the space. I reread the words several times before I'm able to understand what he really wants to tell me.

Olivier writes how sorry he is that he didn't know how to keep me, that he wasn't equipped with the instruments necessary in measuring the level of sadness that had grown inside me. He knows now that my sadness stemmed from my own self-doubt, the hole inside of me that he couldn't fill.

I also know that every day was a stone in the solid erection of our private Babel. His, an ancient construction of architecture, patriarchy, and love. Mine, a strange dialect of good-byes and unknowns. He insisted on making me believe that I had come into his life to complete his universe, without ever acknowledging my own.

He writes that he thought of me as an angel sent down to save his heart from shriveling up. I was barely twenty-two when we met, and lost in Stockholm. I didn't know what it was to be a woman, much less all the roles I played—lover, chatelaine, confidante, stepmother. I wasn't good at any of these roles because I was only half there. Twenty-three when I finally left one adopted country to live with Olivier in another. I tried so desperately not to fall in love with the world he kept promising was mine—an instant family of caretakers, children, friends, a grand old house in Provence, the travels. I wanted everything under the condition that I didn't have to admit it to myself, or to anyone, for that matter.

I fold the letter up and lean back into the cushioned airplane seat. I slide into a thin sleep scented with fig trees, quince, and apricot. I'm holding a wild peach up to the light as the juice runs down my arms like fresh blood. Images of Laure folded into my lap, Olivier watching from across the room, his eyes wide with fear and love and longing.

WHEN I GET off the plane, Val's waiting at the airport in Rémire-Montjoly, a huge smile across his tanned face. He offers me a wide red hibiscus. His whole body is tanned and lean with South American sun. I take off my white linen sweater—I'm already beginning to perspire. He takes my bags and hugs me close to him, touching my hair and face as if I might not really exist.

"Tu es là." He kisses me again, and as he waves to the immigration officers and guides me gently to a waiting cab, I am reminded of his tenderness, the beauty he possesses inside and out. He snaps a photo of me, my eyes shaded from the brightness of the light.

The small communal taxi van to the city of Cayenne is filled with workers, their bodies a rich coffee color gleaming with perspiration. *"Ça va, chérie?"* they ask me in a patois that's both rhythmic and hard to understand. I smile and nod, sincere when I respond, *Oui, ça va, ça va très bien.*

The roads on either side are dense with trees and flowers I don't know the names of, scents I've never smelled before. Early afternoon heat dances off the macadam.

Cayenne is such a strange city. A noncity, it seems. The houses are dilapidated and leaning, folding in on themselves, their colors faded and scraped from sun and tired palm branches. Fresh fish and halved iguana stink in the open-air markets. People smile, such different faces. Arawak Indians and Noir-Marron, a large Asian population. Cayenne, the spice of my New Orleans childhood, and humid just like the Crescent City, but here at the edge of the map, the sun is brighter, harsher on the eyes and skin. The streets are hot and mostly vacant. The stoops of the Creole cottages are filled with old black men and women, gazing at the passersby, the whirl of a fan in the background the only movement.

We spend the first night drinking and dancing at a Brazilian restaurant. Eating *feijoada*, spicy beans and pork, mistakenly swallowing hot peppers the size of tiny marbles, spicier than anything I've ever tasted. My mouth is burning, and I love it. We're drunk with heat and happy. Soon with jet lag and *ti'punch*, Val's body next to mine out on the hotel balcony, I am slowly adrift in my own South American dream.

"*Bientôt, je te présenterai Tarzan,*" Val whispers, rocking me back and forth in the hammock. "Tarzan will take us upriver with Jan's friends Roberto and Eggle and some others."

I'm floating but restless. Even though I fantasize for a moment that I could stay here, I'm worried about Val. Somehow, I know that we will be together only the length of a river. On the ride from the airport, he told me that he can no longer read the papers, what's happening in his own country—random police controls, political corruption, the ever-present military police. But I know that his criticism is superficial. It's his restlessness that goes much deeper and is so painfully familiar. He will stay in the jungle because something is keeping him from feeling at home in the world. I promised I wouldn't care about him, but I do. Somehow, though, I know I won't suffer for it as I have with others. Because of the distance, I am starting to care for him like a treasured friend, a fractured image of myself.

IN THE NINE months or so that I've known him, Val hasn't photographed me that often, which is fine with me, but since I've arrived, he won't stop. Photo of me in the forest, on the boat to the Salvation Islands as we approached Devil's Island—pointing to the shack where Dreyfus was held prisoner for four years. Photo of me drinking with the French Legionnaires on St. Joseph's Island, where no tourists are allowed. Standing along the potholed road from Sinnamary to Kourou, waiting for a van to take us up to the famous Chutes Voltaire.

Here I am leaning into the wind, standing tall among branches of the gigantic bamboo forest. The rain had just started, a thick, rich pour that I started to dance around in, while Val instantly began chopping leaves for shelter. When that didn't work, he ran to a gathering of canopied trees, shivering. He told me to hold the camera, to protect it, while he looked around for something. I sat down butterfly style with the rain running down my face and limbs and took photos of the leaves and roots. There were noises I hadn't paid attention to earlier, cackles and screeches, but I wasn't afraid, even in the heart of the jungle.

I wanted a photo of it all. Val started screaming at me to stop taking pictures, that the camera was unprotected. He gathered our belongings and headed back to the beginning of the trail, screaming that I was ruining his camera, his career, his future. I gathered some moss and leaves and tried to wrap the camera, but it was too late. I stayed a few steps behind him as we walked the trail back, tripping over roots and suddenly aware of the snakes.

The rain finally started to dissipate as we reached the road. My heart was pounding, and I had blisters on my feet, bare in running shoes. I bent over to rub my legs, which were gleaming with the tropical moisture. I wanted to say something to Val, but he wasn't paying any attention to me. He grabbed the camera away and started rubbing it, checking the apertures, wiping water from his eyes.

"This is all that I own," he insisted, shaking the camera high in the air away from me. "It's all I have to prove that I was ever anywhere." Then he turned away and started walking down the road. I wanted to run after him, shake him up, and tell him that I understood what he meant but that I no longer felt the same way.

JAN'S FRIENDS ROBERTO, a financial adviser for the French space program, and his wife, Eggle, an archaeologist, are both from the outskirts of the city of Milano. According to Roberto, he is the space program. I don't trust him when he greets me hello for the first time and whispers that he "enjoys many extracurricular activities with Asian women." Eggle overhears and nods and smiles in a knowing way. I want to say something to let them know that whatever it is they're insinuating, I'm not interested. But they have been kind to Val and have agreed to drive us to meet a man named Tarzan.

Roberto speeds through pitch-black roads while briefing us on Tarzan, whose real name is Alain. "He comes from the Paris suburbs. He left the continent twenty years ago to settle in the Amazon."

Apparently, like many of those who have settled here, he has lost or broken something vital to his heart. He leads three- and seven-day survival courses in the jungle, where he sets up camp in a makeshift *carbet* along the Mana River. He takes tourists past the ruins of crumbling open-air prisons and shows them how to hunt and fish. He teaches how to gather wood and leaves, check for ticks, and mix *ti'punch* for cocktails.

I make a note to ask him about the courses; I always want to learn more about survival, mostly how to break branches and leave the most visible marks along the path in order to find my way back.

When we arrive at Tarzan's house, a creative assemblage of mixed exotic wood sticks and lots of plants, he greets us with dinner. Homemade boar pâté, *machoiran,* a local fish, cooked with coconut juice and fresh coriander, fried potatoes, and lots of rum with lime. Val hardly eats. I am hungry, but I take a moment to smell the food, wait until we are all seated. I savor the first bites and then eat heartily, savagely.

After dinner, we sit outside in the last of the cool darkness and tell stories, hitting away the mosquitoes as fast as we can. Val ignores us most of the evening. He takes photos of all the objects in Tarzan's house—Galibi Indian baskets, stuffed caiman heads, and the large cathedral wood tables.

Finally, after too much rum, we hang our hammocks outside, behind the animal cages, hungry for sleep before our journey up the Mana River with Tarzan.

"Kim," Val whispers, "I'm sorry for yelling. But this is my survival. You can do it anywhere—"

"Shhh. I understand," I whisper back. "It's okay. Go to sleep now." I gently rock his hammock with my foot, humming a tune until he falls asleep. I don't sleep well. Instead I watch Val through the thin gauze netting, fast asleep, rocking back and forth with the camera nestled close to his chest.

WHEN THE PIROGUE can't go any farther up the Mana River, Tarzan climbs out first. Then we follow carefully in his deep footsteps, up the slope to the top of the riverbank. He gives the women a half hour to hang the hammocks while the men haul up the staples. Eggle clears away a spot for her clothes and towels, her makeup bag, and several bottles of mineral water. She undresses in front of everyone and slips on a bikini too small for her full figure.

"Do you want to change?" she asks me. "I have another bikini. I'm sure Roberto would like to see you in it."

I shake my head and go to help finish setting up camp, because here, along the banks of the Mana, the sun will set in one hour. There is also talk of mandatory vaccinations against yellow fever and of the feared *papillonite,* a dreadful itching brought on by the powder of the wings of certain butterflies specific to French Guiana. I climb into my hammock, wrapped in a thin layer of gauze mosquito netting to protect me. I start taking notes, scratching my skin raw. I've made the tiniest of holes in the net so I can breathe at night. I can see Val through the hole. He's measuring the light, unwrapping rolls of film. He wants to shoot the sky. With every sway of the hammock, he appears and then disappears, but I keep reminding myself that I am the one in motion. The others who have joined our group were sent by their governments or institutions or are here because there was no place else to go. I am the one here by choice, in between houses while searching for a new country or preparing to return to one more familiar.

Eggle has asked Tarzan to take us out tomorrow for a ride on the pirogue, guide us briefly through the woods, and take us to the swimming holes. Tarzan agrees and goes on to tell stories of the Brazilian prostitutes. I can hear his booming voice filtered through the gauze net.

Tarzan also explains that there are no clocks because time is everywhere. When the sun rises, we will rise, wash ourselves in the river. We will spend the days fishing, swimming in creeks stained with flakes of gold. We will follow him through the tangle of jungle, search out *palmier* trees, and then chop until we reach the edible heart.

Every other day, we'll take out the pirogue to gather fresh drinking water from the source. We'll smoke our food in large flat leaves and drink warm rum with sugarcane and limes.

Tarzan's helper, Jean, a ten-year-old Noir-Marron boy,

shakes my hammock gently. He pops his smooth black head under the white netting to inform me in French that it's time for dinner.

I emerge from the hammock, wrap myself in a silk pareo the color of bruised banana flowers. Jean's uncle is also present. He speaks only Taki-Taki—a mélange of Dutch, English, and Portuguese—but seems to understand more than he intimates. He stares at the fire, humming to the trees as he gently wraps wild *pac* meat in broad flat leaves to smoke for our dinner. He keeps an eye on us from a distance as we drink too much rum, ask predictable questions about the dangers of snakes and caiman. I walk over to him with my tennis shoes soaked from the river in one hand. He takes two sticks and plants them in the sand next to the fire. He places one shoe upside down on a stick and then the other. "Dry like this." He smiles.

"Thank you."

He then points to an array of mismatched jars he has set out to rub the meat—tiny round yellow peppers and bright orange pastes. I pick up one of the jars, and just then Eggle lets out a cackle as she imitates the Galibi Indian women who accompany her on her digs. Arms flailing and her heavy breasts swinging in the open for all of us to see. In the faltering light, she is grotesque, her attempt to be a native something or other unbearably painful.

Jean's uncle shakes his head, mumbles something in Taki-Taki, something that sounds like sorrow or 'morrow. I want to apologize but instead hand him the jar of paste, warm and glistening. He dips his pinky in it, licks it clean, and nods, smiles at me, waiting. I do the same, and immediately my nose begins to moisten, my palate is on fire. It is deliciously hot, but I still grab the rum to wash it down. He winks, then hands me a flat wooden utensil and gestures for me to do as he is doing. I do not want to offend him, so I rub the fiery paste into the meat, pour it lavishly into the *couac* grains. We even fry fresh pineapple rounds in a honey-thickened pepper sauce for dessert. When dinner is prepared and spread out among us, Jean's uncle sits off to the side, tending the fire.

After dinner, Jean's uncle comes to me, rocks the hammock gently. He hands me my dried tennis shoes. They're a bit deformed from the sticks and crack when I put them back on my feet, but I thank him. When the sun starts to set, I lie in the hammock, cover myself with the mosquito netting, and listen to the others tell stories.

Val has set up the tripod. Eggle wants a group photo, but Val prefers the chance details: rum-soaked anecdotes, bleeding mosquito bites, someone taking a leak in the woods, intricate spiderwebs, and rows of *poulet boucané* (flattened whole chickens smoked on sugarcane). I no longer understand this madness for fixity, the desire to stop time, the illusion that, with a camera, we're able to put the pieces back together, make something whole and durable.

WHILE FINISHING AN assignment in St. Laurent du Maroni, Val sends me on a bus to Cacao to visit the town. He has promised to join me shortly afterward, after his shoot. While bumping past villages and more jungle and water, I spot the natives earthing out their place, planting and harvesting, excavating ruins of demolished prisons. I watch them speed by as they bend their bodies to the shape of the river, their arms rippling with the heat of the water.

I think about what I've learned in this strange part of the world, about survival and how time has also taught me a lesson—things of the world come when they do, with or without my will.

I realize that I can't rush finding home. And I also know that I'm stronger, somehow, without Olivier. Though at times I miss him so much, it hurts. I feel for him in the middle of the night, like a missing limb. I miss my parents back in New Orleans, my mother and father before them. I think of my brother and sister, my grandfather's ashes somewhere in a garden in New Orleans, and my mother, who will love me from a safe distance, the one she needs. Flora, who wanted so much to be with the living, and what she taught me about life before dying. I miss the High Alps, the beautiful and solid house. Little Laure, who is becoming a woman with her own doubts and questions. I think of Jan and Thibault. Of the men I believed loved me and the ones I know who did. The sharing and giving, the divisions and sacrifices. They all seem part of another life.

It is here, in this former penal colony of punishment and tangled grace where everyone is doing time, that I am finally able to forgive myself for leaving Olivier, for leaving my family all these years. I'm also able to let go of the obsolete ghosts of my early childhood.

I think I may finally understand what it is I want—to return to the States and reacquaint myself with English, my family, and begin another journey, toward the discovery of myself. I want to be a woman with her own identity, her own story. I must start writing, not just playing with words, as Jean-Pierre—the self-proclaimed successful poet—has always made a point to remind me. I think of the days with Tarzan, and Grignon, who also taught me that I'm a survivor, that the marks and traces are what make us beautiful, and there is joy in knowing that I still have much to live and learn.

The bus lets us out at the entrance of the village. I find a pay phone and put a call through to Olivier.

"I'm in South America," I shout at him through the crossed

telephone wires, swatting at the fat black mosquitoes that dive into my skin.

"What are you doing all the way over there?"

"I told you I was going."

"I didn't think you'd really leave. Are you happy, Kim?"

I bite my lip. Olivier sounds happy. I nod and then shake my head. "You know better than to ask me that." He laughs a quiet, deep laughter, a very private joke about my haphazard pursuit of happiness. "That's not why I left." The words sound foreign and echo back into my ear. Soon there's too much static, and our voices fade in and out, overlap each other's thoughts. My skin is bleeding now where the fattest mosquito has decided to bite.

"Call me, call when you return. Or wherever you land."

"I'm losing you," I yell, over the static.

WHEN I FINALLY arrive in Cacao, Val isn't there waiting for me. I know he's working, but part of me was hoping that he'd be here. I know that he will stay in French Guiana.

I make my way through the village to the marketplace, where a few vendors are setting up fruits and homemade sweets of rice stuffed into leaves, huge bowls of soup with cilantro and hot peppers, fried garlic and shallot garnish. It is so hot here, and I'm suddenly disoriented with the noise and heat and lack of water. Where is Val? I wonder. Where is Olivier? What part of the globe am I on?

A slim, tall woman in a brown sundress is standing next to me at the fruit stand. "I'm Catherine. You look lost," she tells me in French.

"Pleased to meet you." I shake her hand, and she raises it again to shield her pale blue eyes from the sun, trying to beckon to a bunch of children running wild through the market.

"I'm waiting for someone," I explain in French.

"*Vous êtes . . . française?*"

I explain briefly that I'm not French, but my friend is, and we're here on our last stop before I make my way back to Cayenne, back to Paris.

"You look like my daughter, who actually looks like her father . . . he's Hmong. There—" She points and waves. "There's my little girl. It's lunchtime. Would you like to join us? Come, you must be hungry."

Catherine takes my hand and my backpack and leads me to the house near the market where she lives with her Hmong husband, their children, and his family. Catherine's daughter waves to me, and with her friends, they run along beside us up to the house.

I see or imagine a wrinkled-faced woman who peeks out behind the door.

"My mother-in-law," Catherine explains. She beckons to me. Her face fans out like a broad porcelain plate. The old woman's eyes are like silver rivers, glinting with the knowledge of all that has passed through her. In her presence, I feel as if I'm in a long-lost dream. Maybe it's the heat, the smells of this new city, the waiting for an imminent departure. She takes my hands in hers, and I feel linked.

The old woman smiles, then she and Catherine and the children start preparing the floor, sweeping and laying down straw mats and the low table for lunch. I want to help. I move toward them, wanting to touch them to make sure I haven't imagined this hospitality in such a foreign land. It seems I have seen them before, if only in my dreams.

When I walk, I feel the weight of sleeplessness knock in my joints. In a hammock, the body is always curved and never at ease. The only place to lie down flat is on the water itself. Lately, when I rock myself to sleep at night, I can feel the earth and all its waters move inside of me. Whole rivers flow through my bones. Asia pulses through my arteries. My mouth is the Gulf of Mexico. The Red Sea divides my heart. All the continents I've crossed, all the water in between.

The old woman hands me a heavy, ripe fruit I've never seen before, although its dark pink flesh and pungently sweet odor are familiar. She passes me an earthenware bowl filled with the red juice. It's warm and sweet on my tongue. Sit, she gestures.

The family is already seated, but I want to wait for Val. I look toward the village, across the water to the horizon. The light is still too rich for him to come now. There will always be another photo to take, another last image to capture. Val is like me in so many ways that it is both exciting and sad to be a witness to his search, his restless energy. But because I am aware that he is just at the beginning of his journey, one similar to my own, I know that my moving to French Guiana would only be running away again.

I take the old woman's hand, grasping it as she leads me to the table. Catherine's daughter sits between her mother and me. She's got large black eyes and smooth brown skin, but the same laughter as Laure, the same precocious way of looking at the world. The closer she scoots to me, the more I realize she doesn't look like Catherine at all.

"She's got her father's eyes and willpower," Catherine whispers as if she's read my mind. The child speaks sounds that could be Korean for all I know, but since I can't answer in her language, I hand her a bowl of rice, gesture with my chopsticks for her to eat. She smiles and hands me a porcelain spoon.

"Here, spoon for rice," the little girl says, giggling into her tiny hand. Then she looks proudly across at her grandmother, who nods and slurps her soup. Catherine looks at her daughter, goes to touch her hair, but the little girl leans toward me instead. She takes my left hand in hers, traces her tiny index finger along the lines and creases.

"Lots of marks," she says. "This your lifeline." She points to the center of my palm. "And this, your heart."

∽∾∾∽∾∾∽∾∾∽∾∾∽∾∾∽∾∾∽∾∾∽∾∾∽

MIDNIGHT PASTA THREE WAYS

*J*an and I often made bowls of pasta late at night after our ventures in the city. After my trip to French Guiana, I returned with a hot pepper paste that we would stir into almost everything, including these pasta dishes. We would eat, laughing at ourselves and no longer crying for the same reasons.

MIDNIGHT PASTA #1: SPAGHETTI WITH PANCETTA AND CREAM

*Y*ou can always rely on pasta, cream, and cured pork to make you feel better. Use only the freshest farm eggs available.

1 teaspoon extra-virgin olive oil
5 ounces pancetta, lardoons, or good-quality thick-cut bacon, diced
1 small yellow onion or 2 shallots, thinly sliced
Fresh-ground black pepper, to taste
Hot red pepper flakes (optional)
½ pound spaghetti
2 to 3 tablespoons crème fraîche or whipping cream
2 large egg yolks

1 cup freshly grated Parmigiano-Reggiano
Garnish: fresh-chopped parsley, basil, or mint

Heat olive oil in a large skillet on medium heat. Add pancetta and cook, about 6 minutes, until beginning to crisp but not burn. Add onion, black pepper, and hot red pepper flakes, if desired; stir, and cook about 2 minutes.

Cook spaghetti in salted boiling water just until al dente. Drain, reserving about ¼ cup pasta water. Add pasta to skillet with onions and pancetta. Whisk together crème fraîche, egg yolks, and ½ cup of Parmigiano-Reggiano. Toss into pasta and stir, adding some of reserved pasta water if too dry. Divide pasta into 2 warmed bowls. Serve immediately. Add another crack of pepper and remaining cheese, and garnish, if desired.

Midnight Pasta #2: Spaghetti with Zucchini, Mint, and Pine Nuts

*S*ometimes I add fresh or smoked salmon to this dish.

1 tablespoon extra-virgin olive oil
1 shallot, sliced
2 small firm zucchini, cut lengthwise and sliced
Salt and fresh-ground black pepper, to taste
1 teaspoon hot red pepper flakes
½ pound spaghetti
2 tablespoons fresh mint leaves or fresh dill sprigs
*½ cup freshly grated Parmigiano-Reggiano or Pecorino
    Romano*
⅓ cup toasted pine nuts

Heat olive oil in a large skillet on medium heat. Add shallot and cook, stirring occasionally, about 5 minutes. Add zucchini and cook about 5 minutes. Season with salt and pepper. Add red pepper flakes.

Cook spaghetti in salted boiling water just until al dente. Drain, reserving about ¼ cup pasta water. Add pasta to skillet with shallots and zucchini. Heat about 1 minute, adding some of reserved pasta water if too dry. Remove from heat, add mint, half of Parmigiano-Reggiano, and half of pine nuts. Toss to combine. Divide pasta into 2 warmed bowls. Serve immediately with remaining cheese and pine nuts.

MIDNIGHT PASTA #3: PENNE WITH POPPED TOMATOES, ANCHOVIES, AND ONIONS

> 1 to 2 tablespoons extra-virgin olive oil
> 1 pint ripe cherry or grape tomatoes
> Salt and fresh-ground black pepper, to taste
> Pinch of sugar (as needed)
> 1 small onion, thinly sliced
> 2 garlic cloves, smashed and chopped
> Hot red pepper flakes, to taste
> 4 to 5 anchovy filets
> Handful of black olives (such as Niçoise) or 1 teaspoon black
>   olive tapenade
> ½ pound penne
> Garnish: Parmigiano-Reggiano or Pecorino Romano

Heat olive oil in a large skillet on medium high to high heat. Add tomatoes and cook, tossing often, about 10 minutes. Cover and let cook about 3 minutes. Uncover, season with salt and pepper and a pinch of sugar. Add onion, toss, and cook about 2 minutes. Add garlic, red pepper flakes, anchovies, and olives. Lower heat.

Cook penne in salted boiling water just until al dente. Drain, reserving about ¼ cup pasta water. Add reserved pasta to skillet with tomatoes. Toss in pasta and heat about 1 minute, adding some of reserved pasta water if too dry. Toss to combine. Divide pasta into 2 warmed bowls. Serve immediately. Add another crack of pepper and garnish, if desired.

XXVI

HUNGRY AFTER ALL

❧

W HEN I RETURN FROM CAYENNE, ADJUSTING BACK TO CITY life is difficult. I feel overdressed and underwhelmed, and I wander the streets like a sleepwalker, hesitating through a thick, complicated dream. I pass the *sans abri,* the shelterless, one I recognize as the African man Laure and I used to bring food to on the corner of rue de Grenelle and boulevard Raspail. He nods and smiles as I walk by. He calls me *Louisiane.* I buy him a sandwich and a Limonade, then make my way up the boulevard and through our old Saint-Germain neighborhood, pressing my face to the darkened windows of Barthélemy, my favorite cheese shop, and break my vow not to call Olivier.

He's the one who calls first, though, two days after my return from South America.

"So you've landed," he says.

I nod yes, at a loss for words. "I miss you," I tell him shame-lessly. "I know I shouldn't say it, but there it is."

"You know, I would never admit it, but I do miss you. I won't allow myself to feel it. It's too late."

And we continue to talk like this, as we have for years now since our separation. The words are different, sometimes about how so much has happened that perhaps we are beyond the point of being able to reconstruct a life together, but we are always basically saying the same thing: that we loved each other, that I wasn't ready for all the love he had to give me, that his biggest regret was not knowing how to keep me. He calls to tell me that he understands why I had to leave but that we will love each other always. Then, before hanging up, he insists that he needs to get on with his life, forty-six, nearing fifty, and desperately avoiding being alone.

I want to tell him that leaving for me was an act of survival, and as I've learned, one can leave and still love. But as I had promised to be an independent woman, he has promised never to open his heart again, especially to me. When we say these things, it feels as though someone is punching me deep in the gut.

The next evening, the phone rings, and it's Olivier again.

"*Bonsoir, Kimette.*"

"*Bonsoir, Olive.*" Oh, leave.

"I hope I'm interrupting you." He thinks that since I left, I should be spending all my time writing.

"Are you calling to tell me I broke your heart or that you're getting married?"

"I'm never getting married again."

"I'm leaving, Olivier."

Silence.

"I'm leaving Paris. I know that's what you've wanted since our separation."

Silence.

"Stockholm is where we were the happiest," we say almost in unison.

"And Venice."

"And Baix, and Corsica . . ."

There is another long silence as we take in the absurdity of our words. We were happy everywhere, yet here we are nostalgic for each other, baffled by the fact that we are connected by just a tiny host of wires.

"Do you remember the poem?" Olivier asks.

Of course I do. A poem by Milosz translated into French I sent him after our very first meeting, about not wanting to know about the past, about the sweetness of ignoring the paths that lead to one another.

"Laisse-moi la douceur," Olivier recites, *"d'ignorer le chemin qui m'a mené jusqu'à toi. . . ."*

How could I have ever wanted to ignore the trail of what led him to me, ignore the importance of the past? I wait for Olivier to say good night and hang up first. I sit in the dark and doze off with the phone clutched close to my heart.

FOR WEEKS SINCE my return from French Guiana, I have lost my appetite, eating mostly small spoonfuls of yogurt late in the night, a few slices of salted tomatoes, and stale *pain au chocolat*. Sometimes I make myself eat a hot ham-and-Gruyère crêpe from an early morning street vendor near Saint-Michel. I crumple up the warm waxed paper tight in my fist and watch the tourists as they emerge from the RER station, looking both weary and lost as they try to juggle luggage, passports, and maps.

I know it is time for me to leave this part of the world, but it seems Olivier is everywhere. I still don't go past 81, rue Saint-Louis-en-l'Île, the first in now a long series of O & Co. stores. In almost every neighborhood, I walk past one of the many L'Occitane shops, take in the clean, sharp scent of fresh milk soap, bright lemon verbena.

On Delta Airlines international flights now, Olivier's face glides past on the screen to promote a new line of products.

Sometimes it is just the scent of rising bread flecked with olives and rosemary, the sharp memory of a meal we shared. It is these moments when I still hunger for him, for a reminder of why I left.

Although Olivier and I are still friends, we have not been able to see each other after all these years, just a chance meeting once in a café on the rue de Buci. *"C'est trop dangereux,"* he tells me over and over again. There is danger in opening up the old wounds, of exposing the raw heart.

"Je suis devenu humble." I taught him humility, he claims. *"Mais tu m'a quand même fait souffrir."* But I caused him to suffer.

No matter how intelligent a separation can be, there are still traces of the failed relationship—rejection, destruction of the ego, raging jealousy.

We don't talk much about the other people in our lives. He tells me, though, that he still thinks he and I should have had children, that I *need* to have a child in order to complete the circle, create the history I have been missing my whole life. He hints that he thinks he has finally met a woman he can love. Not the woman from Strasbourg, another, but she knows all about us. That we'll always be linked. *Et toi?* he questions hesitantly.

I don't tell him, but I'm still wondering what it will take to make me feel that home is with someone else. At least I'm not as restless as before, although I will never stop looking at maps, tracing another route, packing bags, ready to discover how other people feel at home in the world, taste what it is that grounds and comforts them. I want to one day again brave the South Korean winter in search of a familiar face. I want to go back to a riverside *ginguette* and squeeze fresh lemon over hot fried *éperlans*. There are so many flavors to try—street food late at night in Bangkok, jewel-colored moles in Puebla, all the varieties of rice dishes in the world.

For now, I have learned that home is in my heart—in all the places and people I have left behind. It's in the food that I cook and share with others, in the cities I will come to know, and in the offerings of street vendors around the world—from South Korea to Provence—in the markets I have yet to discover.

After I have made arrangements to start packing and ship my things back to the States, I fall into a deep, delicious sleep uninhabited by nightmares. I awake suddenly to the windows wide open, and a warm breeze blows through, the promise of a new season in the air. I rush to get dressed and run out into the city.

There is a feast of the senses as I walk through one of my favorite markets. This could be any street market in the world, filled with hungry people busy with the daily tasks of picking and choosing. *I want this, yes. I don't want that.*

I notice a dark-haired woman from behind, and just for a second, my blood races at the sight of *Omma.* I follow the woman from a safe distance, study her as she goes from vendor to vendor, balancing whole squash blossoms in her palm, pressing wheels of cheese to test for ripeness, tapping fruit, measuring and feeling the weight of it all before carefully making her choices.

For an instant, as she looks up and out into the crowd, I imagine she is still searching, even a quarter of a century later. I want to tell her that she made the right choice and that I'm still here in the marketplace, but no longer scrawny and scared. I am a woman, carrying my own full basket, freshly baked goods. But I lose her among the bustle as she disappears with an armful of flowers, leaving a trail of soft white petals behind.

I eye fresh apricots and golden plums, small spheres of melons, and shining spears of ivory asparagus. In turn, I weigh and test each for ripeness. This one, I nod, keeping one eye on the dwindling trail. *Un bon choix,* the farmer confirms. A good choice. It's ready for eating. He hands me a slice of melon, a taste of apricot; another holds out a piece of thick country bread. I let the fruit sweeten my tongue, take the bread in my hand. The crust is fragrant, warm. I break off a piece, a few crumbs scattering to the wind. The inside is soft and dense. I chew and swallow, suddenly aware how alive I am and how hungry, hungrier than I've ever been.

RECIPE INDEX